THE STRONGHOLD

PREFACE

It is well known that the Republican Party has struggled in recent presidential elections, losing four of the past six contests, and five of six in the national popular vote. The conventional wisdom is that the modern GOP suffers from two related problems: first, it has lurched too far to the right on key national issues; and second, its shrinking coalition of older, white, married, rural, and male voters is out of touch with the "rising American electorate" of female, nonwhite, unmarried, urban, and inner suburban voters. These problems are real, but as an explanation for the party's presidential woes they are incomplete.

Meanwhile, national Republicans have been very competitive in congressional elections. Two years after the party's presidential struggles began in 1992, Republicans captured the House and the Senate, ending a forty-year period of Democratic dominance. The GOP controlled both chambers for a dozen years and then, after losing control for two cycles, recaptured the House in 2010. Unlike the previous era of persistent divided Congresses—the first six years of the Reagan administration—when John Boehner and his fellow Republicans held the House in 2012, it marked the first time in the party's 160-year history that a Republican Speaker had ruled for more than one term without a companion majority in the Senate.

In this book, I argue that the Republican Party is a Congress-centered and specifically a House-heavy party because congressional Republicans made choices and staked out positions during the post-Reagan era that tended to benefit themselves at the expense of the party's presidential candidates. This shift created a feedback loop between the institution and ideology, in which the GOP's power became more concentrated in Congress as the party became more conservative, and the party became more conservative as it became more anchored to Capitol Hill. Because conservative Republicans in Congress have paid little electoral price for their policy positions and political choices, they quite rationally moved the party ever rightward. It's no coincidence that the party's ideological self-marginalization has coincided with its growing strength in Congress, and especially the House of Representatives. Until and unless the electoral incentives change, congressional Republicans will continue to lead the party toward presidential obsolescence.

Key figures in the so-called Republican establishment recognize the problems caused by the party's congressional wing. Led by chairman Reince Priebus, the Republican National Committee in early 2013 published a blueprint for the party's recovery. The *Growth and Opportunity Project* (known as the GOP report) specifically cited the liabilities of the party's "federal" wing—meaning its congressional delegations. The GOP report recommended that the party repair its image and refashion its message for the broader electorate by turning to its governors and other state officials for ideas and leadership.

But a full-scale national party recovery is complicated by the desire among conservative Republicans to double down on the strategy of maximizing the power Republicans derive from their dwindling older, white, male voter base. Indeed, at the very same moment the RNC's appointed commission was producing the *Growth and Opportunity Project*, some conservative organizations and Republican politicians were calling for more restrictive voter identification laws, the end of winner-take-all assignment of Electoral College votes by state, and even repeal of the Seventeenth Amendment, which a century ago empowered citizens to directly elect U.S. senators. These are not the actions of partisans who believe they can win Senate and presidential elections with new ideas designed to appeal to an expanding electorate; they're the acts of party leaders resigned to the grim prospect of winning by drawing ever more fervent support from an ever smaller base.

The GOP's transformation from a strong presidential party into a Congress-centered party began more than two decades ago, and the politician most responsible for it is Newt Gingrich. It is Gingrich, not the lionized Ronald Reagan, who should be remembered as the most significant Republican politician of the late twentieth century. As I shall argue, the Georgia Speaker understood that the institutional imperatives of modern conservatism made control of Capitol Hill important, even if that meant surrendering the White House.

The Republicans' stronghold in the U.S. Congress—their polarizing House caucus especially—has become a political and electoral liability. This book is the story of how and why the Republicans transformed from a strong presidential and weak congressional party to the opposite.

THE STRONGHOLD

1

THE PATH NOT TAKEN

The 2012 election results were tough medicine for Republicans to swallow. Many conservatives and Republicans believed that Barack Obama was a left-wing radical and a failed president. He headed into the campaign with a national unemployment rate above 7.5 percent, and no incumbent president had won reelection with an employment rate that high since Franklin Roosevelt. During Obama's first term, deficits and the national debt ballooned, and even if a lot of the spending was the result of Bush-era policies, many of the same conservatives and Republicans who had long remained silent about fiscal responsibility had suddenly discovered austerity in the hope that fiscal gloom would further damage Obama's reelection bid. To those on the right, the president was a "hopey-changey" public relations gimmick now exposed as a fraud. Convinced that most American voters shared these sentiments, conservative radio and television talk show hosts repeatedly compared Obama to Jimmy Carter. Now it was time for Obama to suffer in 2012 the same fate Carter did in 1980, when Ronald Reagan defeated him in a landslide.

In the year leading up to the election, national polls forecast a close race with a slight but hardly insurmountable Obama edge. It was entirely reasonable for those who thought the president should lose to predict that, in fact, he would lose. Their expectations were fueled by electoral signals emanating from conservative media outlets. Ignoring the rigorous and eventually spot-on predictions of an Obama win by *New York Times* psephologist Nate Silver, who called every one of the fifty state outcomes, many Republicans turned instead to the comforting analyses of UnSkewedPolls.com and its founder, Dean Chambers, who claimed that national and state polls were systematically biased in favor of Obama and that Mitt Romney would prevail.[1]

But as the actual results became clear on Election Night, Republican delusions ran aground on electoral reality. The most bizarre moment of the night—and for Democrats and liberals, the most satisfying—was the sight of Republican political guru Karl Rove, certain that his internal calculations showed a Romney victory, being humiliated on national television by Fox News Channel anchor Megyn Kelly.

Barack Obama had won reelection. His national popular vote margin was smaller than in 2008, and in all but three states his winning margin over Romney was smaller than it had been four years earlier against John McCain. The president also lost two states, Indiana and North Carolina, that he had won in 2008; otherwise the electoral maps were identical. But the win's the thing, Obama won, and there are no consolation prizes even for close runners-up. To many conservatives and Republicans, the 2012 presidential election results were a devastating rebuke and a dissonant signal that their view of the president, of his policies, and perhaps of the country itself differed significantly from that of a majority of Americans.

The usual postelection hand-wringing and recriminations commenced even before the electoral bunting had been packed away. Winners staked claims to the political capital they had supposedly earned now that the voters "had spoken"; losers licked their wounds, questioned what they had done wrong, shifted blame onto others, and began figuring out what corrections they needed to make before the next cycle. Two years earlier, the Democrats answered for their failures in the 2010 midterms. In what President Obama called a "shellacking," the Democrats forfeited control of the House of Representatives and lost net seats from their Senate majority. Now the partisan shoe was on the other foot: in the coming months, Republicans would begin the wrenching process of self-examination.

The pains of this ritual were especially sharp because the four months following the election brought little good news for national Republicans. Although President Obama did not emerge unscathed from the fiscal cliff or sequester showdowns with House Republicans in late 2012 and early 2013, by midwinter his approval numbers were rising as the GOP's numbers tanked. A mid-February Bloomberg poll showed the president with his highest approval ratings since September 2009; meanwhile, a Pew Research memo reported GOP approval at 33 percent—a twenty-year low—and further noted that Republicans had not been above 50 percent since the midpoint of George W. Bush's presidency.[2] The early months of Obama's second term offered conservatives and Republicans some hope: within the span of a few weeks the president and his administration were confronted by simultaneous scandals involving domestic spying by the National Security Administration and targeting by the Internal Revenue Service of certain political groups' tax-exempt status. And late 2013 brought the biggest policy embarrassment of the Obama era—the bungled rollout of the Affordable Care Act's state health insurance exchanges.

Nevertheless, the months immediately following the 2012 election were an unhappy time for Republicans and conservatives. The key question they needed to answer was this: Why is the party, especially in presidential and U.S. Senate races, losing what look like winnable elections? Republicans and conservatives produced two quite different sets of responses to this question.

In March 2013, Republican National Committee chairman Reince Priebus gave the party's official answer. In search of both diagnostic judgments and prognostic advice, the RNC had commissioned a postelection task force to examine the results. After poring over polling data and soliciting the opinions and advice of more than a thousand relevant individuals, in March 2013 the task force issued its findings in a glossy, graphics-rich document entitled *Growth and Opportunity Project* (known as the GOP report). The report's primary conclusion was that given the country's rapid demographic changes, the Republican Party would continue to lose elections, especially presidential contests, until and unless it found ways to expand its political appeal to a broader audience of American voters. The GOP report included recommendations for softening the party's off-putting image as a male-dominated, judgmental, and unsympathetic coalition of moral scolds; a plan to reengage and appeal to the growing Latino swing vote that is steadily trending toward the Democrats; and a call to reverse the strategic, tactical, and technological advantages the Democrats now enjoyed.

The GOP report was a mission statement and set of goals designed to return the party to power by broadening its appeal to the rapidly changing American electorate. We can call this public accounting, and related efforts, the *recovery path* to regaining political power.

At the very moment the RNC was conducting its self-flagellating critique, some Republican politicians and allied conservative groups were mounting a strikingly different restoration campaign. Less obvious and certainly less likely to be broadcast, this second path toward regaining power—or at least *retaining* current levels of power— proceeds from an entirely different strategic assumption, namely, that Republicans should find new and more creative ways to squeeze as much electoral and political power as possible from dwindling levels of public support.

Sean Trende of RealClearPolitics, for example, challenged the conventional wisdom that the GOP must broaden its appeal to nonwhite voters, arguing instead that the party could actually resuscitate itself by doubling down on its current, white-dominated electoral coalition. Trende noticed that while the overall turnout rate fell between 2008 and 2012, the nonwhite voter share actually increased, from 26 percent to 28 percent; typically, when turnouts drop the electorate becomes older, whiter, and more affluent. "The increased share of the minority vote as a percent of the total [2012] vote is not the result of a large increase in minorities in the numerator, it is a function of many fewer whites in the denominator," he wrote. Trende estimated that seven million white voters went missing in 2012, and that future Republican presidential nominees could win if they found ways to identify and mobilize them. Trende's arguments echo those of Karl Rove in 2000, when he suggested that missing white evangelicals cost Bush a national popular vote majority in that year's election.

During the 2013 fight over immigration law, mainstream pundits generally agreed that congressional Republicans needed to support a comprehensive reform package or else risk isolating Latino voters, thereby dooming the party to decades of minority status. Again, the presumption is that a full-blown recovery requires the party to reconstitute itself. Trende argues, however, that failure to broker an immigration deal may not be as electorally fatal for Republicans as many believe.[3] Other electoral analysts challenged Trende's assumptions and conclusions,[4] and even if Trende's disappearing white voter diagnosis is correct, there is a healthy debate as to whether his strategy of maximizing white voter turnout is in the Republican Party's best long-term interest. Just because it's possible to pull the electoral equivalent of an inside straight, that doesn't make it a smart bet. But it is tempting, perhaps even rational, to argue that the GOP doesn't need to overhaul its strategic assumptions about voter outreach.

How might a party act if it does not believe it needs a major, recovery-style overhaul? What type of legal, structural, or other rule changes might a party with shrinking voter appeal pursue in order to maintain or even augment its political-electoral power? One way is to augment the relative power of its voters at the expense of voters for the other party. It might push for reforms that suppress or limit voter participation, such as gutting key provisions of voting rights law if this law mainly benefits people likely to vote for the other party. If the party benefited from majorities in many small states with few Electoral College votes but was in the minority in large states, it might pressure the legislatures in those large states to replace their historical use of the winner-take-all-electors rule—the model used by forty-eight of the fifty American states—with either a proportional method of assigning electors or the House district–based elector assignment method used by Maine and Nebraska. If such a party perceived that it was at a disadvantage in Senate races because the other party's urban voters outnumbered its own rural voters in too many states, it might call for an end to the popular election of U.S. senators.

There's no need to cite these examples hypothetically, of course, because in recent years a number of Republican politicians, party strategists, conservative thinkers, and affiliated groups have advocated or pursued every one of these rule changes. While Reince Priebus and the Republican National Committee made a vivid and public display of their determination to follow the path of recovery, elements within the party and its affiliated conservative groups, including at times Priebus himself, were feverishly promoting a second and very different strategic response. If recovery entails attracting more people to vote Republican, this second response— let's call it the *retrenchment path*—is premised on maximizing the power of a fixed or shrinking share of Republican votes and voters.

Despite their unwillingness to address it directly in reports like *Growth and Opportunity Project*, some party establishment leaders realize there are limits to a recovery-only path to revival. Journalist Tom Edsall, one of the most astute chroniclers of political developments in the Republican Party and the conservative movement over the past three decades, noticed a glaring and likely intentional oversight in the GOP report. "There is," Edsall observed, "at least one crucial problem that the authors, all members of the establishment wing of the party, address only peripherally and with kid gloves: the extreme conservatism of the party's primary and caucus voters— the people who actually pick nominees. For over three decades, these voters have episodically shown an inclination to go off the deep end and nominate general election losers in House and Senate races—or, in the case of very conservative states and districts, general election winners who push the party in the House and Senate to become an instrument of obstruction."[5] Even if party elites aspire to a full-scale recovery, the party's rank-and-file supporters may hold distinctly different views about what ails the national Republican Party—and thus what, if anything, should be done to fix it.

Recovery and retrenchment are not mutually exclusive options. Parties can and should seek ways to expand their appeal to as many voters as possible, while also trying to extract as much governing power from the voters they already attract and the offices they already hold. Some electoral-minded choices are entirely rational no matter how electorally competitive a party is, or whether it controls the Congress, the White House, both, or neither. For example, trying to draw more favorable boundaries for U.S. House districts always makes sense for both parties, no matter how many House seats they hold; after all, the point of gerrymandering is to maximize the number of seats won per vote received—no matter how many votes that may be. Democrats can complain until they're blue in the face, so to speak, that greater state-level Republican influence over post-2010 redistricting helped Speaker John Boehner maintain his House majority in 2012—the first post-redistricting cycle of the new decade—even though Democratic House candidates nationally received 1.5 million more votes than did Republican House candidates. That's how gerrymandering works.

Retrenchment, on the other hand, is particularly attractive to the party struggling to expand its appeal to a changing electorate. The key question is whether the national Republican Party, as presently constituted, can effectively pursue a true recovery, or at least pursue recovery and retrenchment options simultaneously—and if not, then why not.

In this book, I argue that in the quarter century since Ronald Reagan left office, the Republican Party has become a Congress-centered party, and specifically a House-anchored party. One of the consequences of this transformation is that the GOP has been inclined toward retrenchment solutions that tend to favor the party's congressional wing, often at the expense of developing a fuller and more meaningful national recovery that would help its presidential candidates be more competitive. Why has this occurred, and why might it continue? Because, so far at least, the GOP has paid a small price—and in some cases even been rewarded—for policy and political choices it has made in support of its congressional caucuses. Until the incentives and disincentives change, congressional Republicans will continue to drag the party down a path toward presidential obsolescence.

Weak Tea and Strong Borders

Before I lay out my primary argument, let's digress briefly to examine the most significant political development following Barack Obama's 2008 election and one of the biggest domestic policy fights following his reelection in 2012—respectively, the rise of the tea party movement and the national push for comprehensive immigration reform. The tea party movement and immigration policy presented two important test cases of whether today's Republican Party is capable of a true strategy of recovery. In both cases, the GOP chose retrenchment.

The emergence of the tea party movement is the most transformative political development since Barack Obama's inauguration. Kindled by a handful of pioneering activists and sparked by a few seminal moments, most notably CNBC analyst Rick Santelli's famous February 2009 rant on the floor of the New York Stock Exchange, the tea party was a national political force by summer 2009. Tea party leaders helped organize local, state, and national protests against specific Obama policies, especially the stimulus package (the Recovery and Reinvestment Act) and later Obamacare (the Affordable Care Act). More generally, tea partiers object to the size, scope, and fiscal management of the national government, a stance that also implies strong disapproval of certain Bush-era policies, including the Troubled Assets Relief Program (TARP), passed by a Democratic Congress and signed into law by President George W. Bush.

Initially a loose confederation of several groups with hundreds of local chapters and a defiantly bottom-up, purportedly leaderless structure, the tea party movement presented itself as the self-appointed savior of American government and politics. Although many of its ideas and key activists were drawn from the existing conservative universe, the tea party's emergence gave the Republican Party a booster shot of political adrenaline that political professionals could never have delivered. With Republicans completely out of power in Washington for the first time since Bill Clinton's first two years in office, the tea partiers' critique of the Obama administration provided the kind of conflict-based narrative the national political media crave.

Tea partiers formed several organizations, including the Tea Party Patriots, Tea Party Express, Tea Party Nation, and the National Tea Party Federation. The movement's agenda is a volatile mix of calls for constitutional originalism and "judicial restraint," appeals for social and moral rectitude, and complaints about oppressive taxation, loose monetary policy, and an overgrown welfare state. Insofar as there is a unifying theme, it is the desire that the United States somehow return to its pre–New Deal political arrangements, if not its founding-era traditions. Journalists Matthew Cooper and Rebecca Kaplan catalogued many of the explicit components of the movement's turn-back-the-clock "legal brief," including stricter interpretations of the federal government's implied powers under the Constitution's commerce clause and "necessary and proper" clause; clarifying or even reversing the Fourteenth Amendment's birthright citizenship guarantee, the Sixteenth Amendment's income tax authority, and the Seventeenth Amendment's provision for popularly elected U.S. senators; eliminating certain cabinet departments, of which Commerce, Education, and Energy are the most commonly mentioned; and finally, enacting a balanced-budget amendment and empowering states, by a two-thirds majority, to repeal any law passed by Congress. In terms of specific Obama-era policies, most tea partiers oppose cap-and-trade regulation and reject the idea that climate change is caused by human activity (or is happening at all), and they want stronger borders and tougher amnesty standards for undocumented immigrants. But above all else, the tea party sprang to life from its opposition to Obamacare. For tea partiers, this government expansion represents a turn toward tyranny—hence the powerful symbolism of another Boston Harbor–style revolt against oppression.[6]

The tea party movement takes great pride in its leaderless and decentralized organization; it claims to be a truly grassroots, organic movement. Political analyst Jonathan Rauch compared its structure to a starfish—a decentralized organism with no head and no brain that can easily mutate and adapt. But such organizations, Rauch argued, also have liabilities. They are easier to mobilize in order to stop something than to build consensus on alternatives, and their members tend to be intransigents who "regard compromising as a sellout." Rauch warned that organic, grassroots groups can be easily overtaken and co-opted by impostors and opportunists.[7] And that's exactly what has happened. With the top-down funding and behind-the-scenes orchestration of industrialist brothers David and Charles Koch, some tea party activists were, if unwittingly, serving as foils for the corporate agendas of the Koch brothers and their allies, who channeled money into the movement via organizations like Americans for Prosperity.

Tea partiers are neither a random nor a representative subset of Republicans or even conservatives. They hold distinctly different and sometimes revanchist views toward racial minorities, about the role of government, and by extension about the current intersection point of both: the Obama administration. On the question of attitudes toward minorities and homosexuals, political scientist and pollster Chris Parker of the University of Washington found that white Americans who described themselves as "sympathetic" with the tea party were less likely to describe African Americans and Latinos as "honest," "trustworthy," and "hard-working." They also held less tolerant attitudes toward homosexuals.[8] A 2010 Pew Research survey showed that tea party identifiers expressed the highest rates of anger with the government of any demographic or partisan group. The share of tea partiers who expressed anger—43 percent in March 2010, 47 percent by September 2010—was more than double the national average.[9] Parker found that more than a third of all self-identified conservatives, regardless of race, believe President Obama is "destroying the country"—an unsurprising result, except that it turns out that only 6 percent of non–tea party conservatives hold this view, compared to 71 percent of tea party conservatives.[10] In a more expanded study of the tea party movement, *Change They Can't Believe In*, Parker and coauthor Matt Barreto conclude that tea partiers' core anxieties derive from a deep-seated belief that "the America they know, the country they love, [is] slipping away, threatened by the rapidly changing face of what they believe is the 'real' America: a heterosexual, Christian, middle-class, (mostly) male, white country," and that these changes are "subverting their way of life, everything they hold dear."[11]

While the tea party movement originated from political anger with a governing philosophy its adherents associate with Obama and the Democrats, there is also a certain disgust reserved for Republicans viewed as complicit with liberals and Democrats. It is not lost on tea partiers that some of the policies they criticize were enacted by Obama's predecessor. "Big-government conservative" George W. Bush and the Republican-controlled Congress passed the Medicare prescription drug benefit, the most costly expansion of health care in decades, plus a pricey, subsidy-filled farm bill. And of course, Bush's treasury secretary, Henry Paulson, engineered the $700 billion TARP bailout of Wall Street firms in late 2008. That tea partiers threatened Washington's so-called Republican establishment—be they members of Congress or Republican National Committee party leaders—only made the movement more attractive as a media storyline.

For establishment Republicans, the emergence of the tea party was both a blessing and a curse. The blessing was that a grassroots movement determined to take down the Obama administration mobilized itself almost overnight and captured the attention of the national media. The curse was that the tea party did not stop with Obama. Its followers were intent on removing other Democrats and apostate Republicans from office—and were prepared to do so, if necessary, independently of the party. They would recruit, nominate, and raise funds to support their own tea party–affiliated Republicans to run for Congress and state-level offices. And they would happily mount a primary challenge to any incumbent Republican who wasn't willing to embrace their agenda. In 2010, Republican electoral targets of obvious and immediate interest included Senator Arlen Specter of Pennsylvania, whose backing by President Bush during Specter's 2004 primary challenge from conservative Republican Pat Toomey had infuriated conservatives. Specter beat Toomey by fewer than eighteen thousand votes and went on to win his final Senate term. He then validated conservatives' suspicions by becoming a Democrat in the hope of being renominated in 2010. (He lost the Democratic primary, ending his political career.)

But the tea party wasn't only hunting for RINOs—Republicans in Name Only. In 2010 they fielded successful primary challengers against solidly conservative Republican incumbents like Alaska's Lisa Murkowski and Utah's Bob Bennett. The Republicans retained both seats—Mike Lee won in Utah and Murkowski became only the third person in U.S. history to be elected to the Senate by a write-in vote—but the party did not fare as well elsewhere. Ignoring state party leaders' preferred candidates, the tea party helped nominate losing Senate candidates Ken Buck in Colorado, Christine O'Donnell in Delaware, and Sharron Angle in Nevada. They drove Florida governor Charlie Crist from the Republican ranks into an independent Senate candidacy in Florida, helping Marco Rubio win there, and also nominated 2008 presidential candidate Ron Paul's son Rand in Kentucky, who won that seat. But those victories, along with the defeat of liberal lion Russ Feingold in Wisconsin by tea party–endorsed Ron Johnson, were offset by winnable seats lost to Democrats in Alaska, Colorado, Delaware, and, most painfully, Nevada, where none other than Democratic majority leader Harry Reid was in electoral jeopardy. Overall, five of the ten tea party Senate candidates won. Counting Republicans who replaced retiring Republican senators, those five winners were a sizable minority of the thirteen freshmen Republican senators elected to the 112th Congress.

Most electoral analysts agree that the defeats of these tea party–backed candidates, paired with losses in 2012 by similar candidates in winnable Senate races in Indiana and Missouri, almost certainly prevented Kentucky Republican Mitch McConnell from becoming majority leader. By 2012, even McConnell, whom almost nobody outside the tea party universe would accuse of being a RINO, faced intense pressure from this aggressive new movement. He felt compelled to hire Jesse Benton, a Rand Paul protégé, as his 2014 reelection campaign manager, and was so frightened about blowback from tea partiers that he didn't fire Benton even after the latter made disparaging public comments about his boss, who is theoretically the Senate's most powerful Republican. As *Salon*'s Brian Beutler observed, "It's an admission that McConnell would prefer to have his campaign managed by someone who admitted he doesn't believe in its mission rather than replace him with someone more loyal— because that would further antagonize conservative voters who don't trust him yet control his fate."[12] The tea party is purifying the Republican Party, but at the price of building governing majorities—at least in the Senate.

The 2010 House elections went much better for Republicans, who just four years after losing control of the chamber managed to flip it back by picking up sixty-three seats. And yet these results, so often described as validation for the tea party movement, were actually a mixed bag. The 109 tea party–endorsed House challengers boasted a win rate almost ten points better (27.5 percent) than non-tea party Republican challengers (17.9 percent). But congressional elections expert Gary Jacobson concludes that wave election factors— including Obama's declining approval ratings, an economy that had avoided disaster but was recovering slowly, higher enthusiasm among Republican voters, and high-quality Republican candidates strategically seeking election during such GOP-favorable conditions—were more important than tea party affiliation. Many of the districts flipped by Republicans featured moderate, "blue dog" Democratic incumbents who first won election in either 2006 or 2008 in Republican-leaning districts and would have been vulnerable anyway. Of the sixty-six races where Republicans beat or replaced retiring Democratic incumbents in 2010 (the Democrats flipped three seats in the other direction, for the net GOP gain of sixty-three), slightly more than half of the winners were tea partiers, giving

House Republican tea party candidates about the same fifty/fifty win rate as their Senate counterparts.[13]

The 2010 class of tea party House candidates had a significant effect on congressional politics even before the election. In July 2010, tea party favorite Michele Bachmann announced she was forming the House Tea Party Caucus, and became its chair. Some tea party–identified Republican incumbents, or Republican candidates running for Congress, refused to join, protesting that a formal structure within the House was antithetical to tea party principles or that they didn't want to create fissures within the House or Senate Republican caucuses. Still, more than five dozen House members and five senators chose to join Bachmann's caucus, immediately enlarging her national platform and almost certainly encouraging her 2012 presidential bid.

That same summer, Bachmann also announced her intention to challenge Texas colleague Jeb Hensarling, a close ally of Boehner's, for the position of House Republican Conference chair, the party's fourth-ranking position, in the 112th Congress. But after the November elections, when many top House Republicans, including Eric Cantor and Paul Ryan, announced that they were backing Hensarling, Bachmann withdrew her challenge. This would be the first of several missteps and defeats by Bachmann, including her uninspired presidential bid—later investigated for campaign finance violations—and the near loss of her House seat in 2012. By the next spring, her fortunes had plummeted: she announced she was resigning as chair of the Tea Party Caucus and would not seek reelection in 2014.[14] It didn't take long for the wolves to come after her. "Michele Bachmann was the chairman of the Congressional Tea Party Caucus and in that position did nothing," Karl Rove huffed on a Sunday morning show four days after Bachmann announced her retirement from the House.[15]

However much or little the tea party contributed to the Republicans' recapture of the House, there's no doubt that the 2010 results affected the ideological composition of the chamber. I will discuss the "House-ification" of the national Republican Party in detail farther on, but Theda Skocpol and Vanessa Williamson's analysis of the ideological shift in the House Republican caucus between the 111th Congress (prior to 2010) and the 112th Congress deserves mention here. In their book *The Tea Party and the Remaking of Republican Conservatism*, Skocpol and Williamson explain that an "amazing 77% of the newly arriving Republicans, including dozens of Tea Party-backed Republicans, are to the right of the typical Republican in the previous [i.e., 111th] Congress—and many are to the right of *almost all* continuing Republicans." The authors determined that the ideological shift between these two Congresses was larger "than any previous shift from one House to the next," including the shift brought by the famed 1994 Republican Revolution freshman class.[16] Congressional observers Thomas Mann and Norman Ornstein point to changes in the composition of the House's Republican Study Committee (RSC)—the chamber's right-wing caucus—during the past four decades to demonstrate the House's increasingly conservative tilt. When Paul Weyrich and his fellow activists formed the RSC in 1973, it included no more than 20 percent of the House Republican caucus; in the 112th Congress, fully 70 percent of House Republicans were members of the RSC.[17]

As Skocpol and Williams argue, while the extent of the tea party movement's contribution to the GOP's 2010 gains is not a settled question, it's almost beside the point. They provided a booster shot to a party struggling to regain its bearings. Whether or not it was actually the tea party that propelled Republicans back into power in the House (and nearly in the Senate) matters less than the belief—among tea partiers, the media, and Republican politicians—that the tea party was crucial. "While the conventional wisdom about the Tea Party as driver of the GOP victories sometimes gets carried away, we think the doubters underestimate the impact of combined Tea Party forces on the GOP momentum going into 2010," Skocpol and Williams write. "Most basically, grassroots Tea Party protests and local network-building helped the Republican Party escape the defeatism that pervaded party ranks after the massive defeats Republicans suffered in 2008 . . . [and] helped Republicans and conservatives to reset national agendas of debate."[18] This is a critical factor in the party's recovery-versus-retrenchment trade-off: the tea partiers are now a baked-in part of the Republican coalition. The GOP must deal with them regardless of how much credit the movement actually deserves for putting Boehner into the Speaker's chair in 2010 or keeping him there in 2012.

This was evident very early in Boehner's speakership when, in the summer of 2011, he was negotiating with President Obama on the budget and a potential debt ceiling default, which Boehner's caucus was using as leverage. Although the White House offered a package far more tilted toward spending cuts than tax increases, Boehner could not accept it because the Republican newcomers, despite their incessant focus on fiscal solvency, would not assent to any deal that included tax increases. Again, the intransigence of these new Republicans is a paradoxical by-product from the 2010 elections: because the Republicans recaptured the House by winning an overwhelming number of the swing districts in play, this new class of freshmen should have moved the new Republican majority toward the center, precisely because they *were* from swing districts. Instead, they moved the caucus further to the right. The situation confronting incoming Speaker Boehner thus differed from the one Nancy Pelosi faced when she became Speaker four years earlier. Newly elected Democrats in 2006 actually moved her caucus slightly to the center.

John Boehner is boxed in. Whether he owes his majority to the tea party movement or not is now literally an academic question. The stark political reality is that tea partiers believe they own him, or at least that he owes his position to them. They are not going to be cowed by his seniority, moved by his need to find bipartisan solutions, or frightened by warnings that the economy might take a nosedive—which is exactly what happened in August 2011 when the House held the debt ceiling hostage to its demands. New Republican members, whether tea party–aligned or not, aren't going to obey Boehner just because he holds the gavel or can flash his political scars from the Gingrich era. A full-blown party recovery is simply not high on their list of priorities—if it's on their agenda at all.

Calves Like Cantaloupes: The Battle over Immigration Reform

Among the essential components of the American myth is that the United States was founded by and has always been a nation of immigrants. Beneath the self-congratulation, however, is a deeper truth: our nation of immigrants hasn't always welcomed the next wave to arrive. The latest legislative effort to resolve this tension offers a good demonstration of the balance of power in the current Republican Party.

The current problem of undocumented residents and illegal border crossings dates to the 1986 immigration bill passed by Congress and signed into law by President Reagan which put a cap on the total number of legal immigrants into the United States. In the quarter century since, politicians from both parties and an array of think tanks and interest groups have called for a major overhaul of U.S. immigration law. Democrats and liberals have generally pushed for granting amnesty to the roughly twelve million undocumented residents now in the country, while Republicans and conservatives have pushed for stronger borders and higher deportation rates. Each party faces cross-pressures from within its respective coalition: the Democrats want to maintain strong support from the growing Latino population, but parts of the organized labor movement worry that American markets will be flooded with cheap labor. The Republicans have to balance the threat of white voter backlash against the fact that key sectors of corporate America want cheap labor.

During the 2008 campaign, Barack Obama promised he would push for comprehensive immigration reform in his first year in office. He broke this promise. In his defense, the country's dire economic situation demanded immediate attention to unemployment, skyrocketing health care costs, and financial regulation. The president also took early political beatings for his support of cap-and-trade and the stimulus package, and he felt he could not afford another major domestic fight. Whatever the economic case for immigration reform, it contains a very heavy dose of culture-war politics, including issues related to law and order, social welfare policy, and English-only statutes. So Obama avoided tackling the issue head-on and then, following the Democrats' 2010 electoral "shellacking," he had to turn his attention toward a reelection that was suddenly very much in doubt. Immigration reform would have to wait.

Obama won, and despite murmurs that Latinos felt betrayed by his broken promise to reform immigration, he managed to increase his national share of the Latino vote by roughly five points, to 72 percent. Before he took his second inaugural oath, Obama signaled that immigration would move to the top of his domestic agenda. Negotiations between the White House and Congress, and between the two parties on Capitol Hill, began in early 2013. Another Senate "gang" of moderates emerged as self-appointed bipartisan brokers, and this time there were eight of them: Democrats Michael

Bennet of Colorado, Dick Durbin of Illinois, Bob Menendez of New Jersey, and Chuck Schumer of New York; plus Republicans Jeff Flake of Arizona, Lindsey Graham of South Carolina, John McCain of Arizona, and Marco Rubio of Florida. Graham and McCain were familiar members of these bipartisan groups, as well as camera-hogging faces on the Sunday television shows. The other two Republicans, Flake and Rubio, were rookie senators from states with significant Latino populations. Rubio quickly became the object of intense scrutiny—most especially by the tea party movement that had anointed him in 2010 as a rising political star.

By summer, the Border Security, Economic Opportunity, and Immigration Modernization Act of 2013 the Gang of Eight drafted was moving steadily through committee hearings. The eight senators were pretty confident their legislation could attract a filibuster-proof floor majority of at least sixty votes, including enough Republicans to provide the imprimatur of bipartisanship. The bill's basic compromise was to pair stronger border security and immigration standards with amnesty for undocumented immigrants who aspired to citizenship.

A final hurdle was cleared when the Senate accepted an amendment by two other Republicans, Bob Corker of Tennessee and John Hoeven of North Dakota, to upgrade border security provisions. Because both Corker and Hoeven had certifiable conservative credentials and came from states with comparatively small Latino populations, pundits believed that their amendment might provide the political legitimacy necessary to persuade House Republicans to support the legislation.[19] On June 27, 2013, the final bill passed the Senate with sixty-eight votes. Every Democrat and fifteen Republicans voted aye. Thirty-two Republicans voted nay.[20]

Speaker Boehner and the Republican House majority were not interested in bipartisan solutions or bicameral cooperation. House

Republicans complained that the bill was weak on enforcement. Never mind that, with the recession, immigration rates had fallen and self-deportations had risen, or that estimated illegal border crossings were at a four-decade low.[21] Just as they had done with the stimulus package, the farm bill, and legislation designed to prevent people on the national terrorist watch list from buying firearms, House Republicans decided that their best course was to vote no in unison. Political analysts who understood the underlying ideological dynamics were not surprised.

Popular sentiment was aligned against the Republicans. A bipartisan majority of Americans wanted an immigration reform bill that paired enforcement upgrades with path-to-citizenship provisions. Polls also showed that Americans trusted President Obama more than congressional Republicans on the issue.[22] If put to a vote of the entire House, the bill would surely have passed. Yet Boehner made it perfectly clear that he would not support any immigration reform bill that didn't have majority-of-the-majority support of his House caucus—even if that House Republican majority had received fewer votes nationally than Democratic House candidates in 2012. The Speaker was thus defending the preferences of a majority of a popular vote minority—in effect, of an even *smaller* minority. Yet Oklahoma representative Tom Cole made it clear that House Republicans would not let these facts complicate their self-image as stalwart defenders of the national majority. "Why," he asked, "should a minority of the minority in the Senate influence a majority of the majority in the House? While most Senators aren't up for election next year, every member of the House will be on the ballot."

Representative Louie Gohmert of Texas and other Republican opponents to pathway-to-citizenship provisions insisted that, rather than pass their own bill and risk having the differences with the Senate's version worked out by a bicameral conference committee, they should simply pass no bill at all.[23] If this posturing didn't already send a negative signal, the House GOP's xenophobic fringe only made it worse. Referring to the so-called DREAM Act children—those illegally brought to the United States as children—Representative Steve King of Iowa declared, "For every one that's a valedictorian, there's another 100 out there that they weigh 130 pounds and they've got calves the size of cantaloupes because they're hauling 75 pounds of marijuana across the desert."

This intransigence frustrated Democrats as well as the Gang of Eight Republicans. The White House was furious. "It cannot be acceptable broadly and in the long term that immigration reform would be blocked because some minority of House Republicans is concerned about a primary challenge from the far right," grumbled White House press secretary Jay Carney. "That's not a good argument. It's not a good argument politically. It's certainly not a good argument economically."[24] What Carney's statement admits, however, is that bad political or economic arguments may be good electoral arguments for House Republicans, especially those who are more likely to see their careers ended by tea party–style primary challengers than by Democrats in general elections. As the *Wall Street Journal*'s Janet Hook pointed out, in the 112th Congress only one-sixth of House Republicans (38 out of 234) represented districts where Latinos made up at least 20 percent of the population.[25]

As we shall see in Chapter 2, national Republicans in 1990 shrewdly colluded with members of the Congressional Black Caucus to help pack nonwhite voters into majority-minority, Democratic-leaning House districts in order to create more Republican-leaning districts overall. But the result of these gerrymanders is that few House Republicans are compelled to interact more than fleetingly with nonwhite voters, and fewer still rely on their support to win renomination or reelection. So it really isn't surprising that House

Republicans care little about pathways to citizenship or a solution to the immigration problem, because they have little to gain from reaching an agreement. The vast majority of House Republicans worry very little about the party's declining performance among America's Latino population. At the ballot box, in their home districts, it isn't an issue.

No politician stood more squarely at the intersection of these two political developments—the rise of the tea party and the fall of immigration reform—than Senator Marco Rubio of Florida. He was a darling of the tea party movement in 2010 and, following Mitt Romney's loss in 2012, emerged as the great Latino hope for taking back the White House in 2016 and converting Latino voters to the Republican cause for a generation. Young, handsome, with a beautiful family and a compelling personal story, Rubio represents the largest swing state in presidential politics; in him, many Republicans saw—some still see—a one-man GOP revival.

But in the Republican cosmos, stars that yesterday shone brightly often fade quickly. In the two-plus years between his 2010 election and the 2013 immigration reform fight, Marco Rubio learned the consequences of tea party betrayal. As a Latino and a presidential aspirant, he knew he had to come out in favor of a comprehensive immigration policy that included some path to citizenship for undocumented immigrants with clean records—what conservatives call "amnesty" for "illegals." The legislation could include tougher border standards and increased funding for enforcement, but any hope Rubio might have of building a general election coalition to win the White House would have to include a citizenship component. Polls showed that Rubio or Jeb Bush—or even Paul Ryan— could capture at least 40 percent of the Latino vote if they backed a version of immigration reform with a path-to-citizenship provision.[26]

As a Gang of Eight senator tasked with constructing a filibuster-proof bipartisan majority behind immigration reform, Rubio put himself out front on the issue. By summer 2013, he was paying the price. Robert Rector of the conservative Heritage Foundation proclaimed that Rubio did "not read his own bill," specifically the provisions related to costs and enforcement. In a widely discussed essay in *National Review* in which they called for the bill to be killed, conservative commentators Rich Lowry and Bill Kristol specifically lambasted Rubio for claiming he didn't want to have to come back in a decade to pass another bill when, according to the Congressional Budget Office, the enforcement provisions conservatives found insufficient would require exactly that. Right-wing talking heads Ann Coulter and Glenn Beck were less diplomatic, dismissing Rubio as the "Dr. Kevorkian of the Republican Party" and a "piece of garbage," respectively. Attendees at an anti-immigration reform tea party rally held up signs calling him "Obama's idiot." Another proclaimed that "Rubio Lies, Americans Die."

Marco Rubio's journey from hero to apostate typifies the Republicans' dilemma. A talented, young, handsome conservative from the biggest swing state in the country who could draw Latino voters back to the GOP, Rubio might have been the Republicans' answer to Barack Obama: a politician with the star power to transform the party. He's no RINO, and may yet be the Republicans' 2016 presidential or vice presidential nominee. But for defying the tea party, Rubio will first need to do penance or see his—and perhaps his party's—presidential hopes dashed.

Beyond Rubio's political fate lies the larger point. With the rise of the tea party and with the vexing issue of immigration, the Republican Party faced a choice between the recovery and retrenchment paths, and each time chose retrenchment. Why? Don't rational political parties make choices that best further their electoral goals? Usually, but not always. When a party sets its course down a particular path, it often closes off options or preempts alternatives that seem patently beneficial in the abstract but are conditionally less preferable than doing the opposite, or doing nothing at all. That is the nature of path dependency: it alters the cost-benefit analysis of future decisions. The Republican Party's rising congressional fortunes have led the party quite rationally down a path that has made retrenchment more attractive and recovery less so.

Turning Right, Turning Toward Capitol Hill

Inside the Beltway, the conventional wisdom about what went wrong with the Republican Party can be simply stated: it lurched to the right. This "rightward lurch" explanation has gained a deep foothold within the national punditry, so deep that variations on the theme are too numerous to recount. The basic version goes something like this: The Republicans became too closely wedded to socially conservative attitudes and groups on issues such as gay marriage, contraception and abortion, and immigration; they became too beholden to corporate America and the financial industry, at the expense of defending American workers and middle-class voters; and the party stopped listening to anyone but the party's electoral base of aging white men, a cohort that is shrinking as a share of the U.S. population. As Republicans retreated further into their self-marginalizing ideological and demographic confines, Americans steadily lost faith in the party. It now seems stuck in time and out of touch with the transformations occurring across the country. "Half a century ago, Ronald Reagan, the man whose relentless optimism inspired me to enter politics, famously said that he didn't leave the Democratic Party; the party left him," said former Republican governor Charlie

Crist of Florida at the 2012 Democratic National Convention. "I can certainly relate. I didn't leave the Republican Party; it left me. Then again, as my friend Jeb Bush recently noted, Reagan himself would have been too moderate and too reasonable for today's GOP."

As a party defector, Crist is not unbiased. But his is hardly an isolated voice of disaffection. Although the list of quotes from party loyalists, political consultants, conservative columnists, and non-partisan analysts declaring that the Republican Party has become a radicalized rump coalition is too long to cite here, conservative columnist Michael Gerson provided a concise summary of the mood among so-called establishment Republicans. Gerson acknowledged that the party's "reversal of electoral fortunes" had many causes, including changing demographics, the GOP's lost advantage on foreign policy, and the subpar quality of its presidential candidates. "A full Republican appreciation of these disturbing fundamentals," Gerson wrote, "was delayed by the 2010 midterms, in which an unreconstructed anti-government message seemed to be riding a wave. Just two years later came that wave's withdrawing roar. The Republican nominee, Mitt Romney, lost by 5 million votes to a beatable incumbent presiding over an anemic economy. At the national level, Republicans have a winning message for a nation that no longer exists."[27] Romney's abandonment of his earlier, moderate positions fits the pattern of the party's growing conservatism and confirms a long-standing pattern of ideological hostage taking of its presidential candidates by the party's congressional wing.

As chronicled, respectively, by Rick Perlstein and Geoffrey Kabaservice in their superb books *Before the Storm* and *Rule and Ruin*, the rising power of conservatives within the party can be traced back to the Goldwater movement of the early 1960s (if not further).[28] In the ensuing half century, a party that once featured a strong contingent of moderates, including Romney's own father and many centrist governors and members of Congress, has become a strident coalition led mostly by conservative ideologues. By the start of the twenty-first century, the two most reputable centrist Republican groups, the Republican Main Street Partnership and the Republican Leadership Council, were for all practical purposes defunct.[29] The House Republican caucus today is more conservative than at any time in more than a century. In the past three decades, the House Democratic caucus has become twice as liberal, but the House Republican caucus has become *six times* more conservative.[30] The party's rightward shift is real.

But the "rightward lurch" explanation is incomplete. The ideological self-marginalization of the national GOP occurred at the same time the party grew in strength in Congress and particularly in the House of Representatives. This is not a coincidence. Nor is congressionalization a mere symptom or consequence of the party's shift to the right. As I will argue in this book, the congressionalization of the Republican Party has contributed to its rightward shift and, by extension, its declining presidential performance. As social science types might say, the relationship between the party's conservatism and its congressionalization is *recursive*—a feedback loop in which the GOP's power became more concentrated in Congress as the party became more conservative, and the party became more conservative as it became more concentrated on Capitol Hill.

This recursive relationship makes the party increasingly unable to execute a "first path" recovery. Congressional Republicans have too much to gain from the second path of retrenchment, and too much to lose by not following that path. Everywhere they look they see confirming evidence: in their tea party–led recapture of the House in 2010 just two cycles after losing it; in their retention of this majority in 2012 despite, as a party, drawing a million and a half fewer votes nationally than Democratic House candidates; in the belief among staunch conservatives that John McCain and Mitt Romney failed to win the presidency because they were too moderate; in the belief that using budget or debt ceiling deadlines to hold the government hostage reflects the priorities of the broader public, not just the opinions of congressional primary voters in safe Republican House districts and red states.

This book examines national Republican politics in the quarter century since President Ronald Reagan left office in 1989. The central argument is easily stated: the congressional wing of the Republican Party has eclipsed its presidential wing, and its rise has come at the expense of the party's presidential fortunes. Corollary to this overall argument is the further, more specific claim: the GOP has become not just a congressional party but one centered on the House. It derives its energy, ideas, and strength—and many of its political problems—from its House caucus. This pattern of increasingly House-centered Republican politics created a self-feeding loop in which the party became more conservative as it became more Congress-centered, and more Congress-centered as it became more conservative. As a result, the party is now defined by its path-dependent preference for retrenchment rather than recovery as a strategy for restoring its fortunes. If it cannot break this vicious cycle, the GOP will continue to struggle in presidential elections even as—and precisely because—it remains competitive in congressional elections.

Some party elites recognize this institutional problem. In the Republican National Committee's post-2012 GOP report, after a brief introduction and snappy "by the numbers" set of visuals, the first paragraph of the first section states: "The GOP today is a tale of two parties. One of them, the gubernatorial wing, is growing and successful. The other, the federal wing, is increasingly marginalizing itself, and unless changes are made, it will be increasingly difficult for Republicans to win another presidential election in the near future."[31]

That's exactly right. The Republican Party's federal wing is indeed in trouble, and its problems emanate from Capitol Hill—especially the (fittingly) southern side of the Capitol ruled by Speaker John Boehner and the House Republican Conference. The GOP's transformation into a Congress-centered party, and the problems this has caused, cannot be laid at Boehner's feet. The change began more than two decades ago, and the person who set it in motion was Republican speaker Newt Gingrich. There is a case to be made (and I will make it here) that Gingrich, not Ronald Reagan, should be remembered as the most significant Republican politician of the past half century. If we want to understand what has happened to the modern party, we must begin with the years leading up to Gingrich's 1994 Republican Revolution to gain a sense of just how revolutionary it really was.

2

CREATIVE DESTRUCTION

In January 1988, Ronald Reagan and George H. W. Bush were moving in opposite directions and at distinctly different paces. As the seventy-seven-year-old Reagan began the final year of his presidency, his closest allies and harshest critics wondered whether the years had finally caught up with him. He had already had a few shaky public moments during his second term. Though she didn't report it at the time, CBS White House correspondent Lesley Stahl later recounted that during her 1986 exit interview with Reagan, the president's eyes were "milky" and he offered a weak handshake.[1] Six years later, the Reagan family announced what some insiders had long known: the former president was suffering from Alzheimer's disease. By then, the Berlin Wall had fallen and the Soviet Union had collapsed, validating many of Reagan's late-term foreign policy choices.

In February 2011, Reagan's son Ron published a book to commemorate the hundredth anniversary of his father's birth. In it, he implies that signs of Alzheimer's were evident while Reagan was still president, perhaps as early as his father's wobbly performance during the first 1984 presidential debate against Walter Mondale. Reagan's stepson Michael has challenged this account.[2]

Although Ron Reagan doesn't think anyone working in the White House at that time was fully aware of how far the president's health had declined, he believes that had his father's early-onset Alzheimer's been diagnosed at the time, Reagan would have resigned the presidency. In that case, George H. W. Bush would have been running in 1988 as the incumbent president rather than the incumbent vice president. As it was, Bush was struggling to emerge from Reagan's shadow and looking for ways to distance himself from some of Reagan's second-term problems, especially the Iran-Contra scandal. With his eyes fixed on the Oval Office, Bush traveled the country, spending as much time in Iowa and New Hampshire as possible. The vice president—especially because he *was* vice president—recognized that he had to establish a unique identity for himself by exhibiting the independence Americans demand of their presidents. Getting out of Washington wasn't a bad idea.

Bush had lost the 1980 Republican nomination to Reagan. To claim the nomination this time, he had only to get *past* Reagan, not, as he had failed to do in 1980, go through him. But before he could begin disentangling himself from Reagan, the vice president first had to separate himself from a nettlesome field of Republican challengers determined to assume Reagan's mantle for themselves. Many conservatives were suspicious of the vice president; the whiff of ideological centrism he carried had doomed his 1980 presidential bid. Although Bush now enjoyed many institutional advantages he had lacked eight years earlier, he also faced new obstacles, many of which were not immediately—some would say never—obvious to him or his political advisers.

The Republican Party was changing in ways that were not particularly amenable to a Bush presidential candidacy or presidency. Conservatives within the party, such as rising star Jack Kemp, had begun to build a new legion of supporters on and off Capitol Hill. The Republicans Party's remarkable string of seven presidential victories in ten cycles was about to end. The story of how that happened—and what the coming changes meant for the GOP—starts with the end of George Herbert Walker Bush's long political career.

A Pat on Bush's Back

The 1988 Iowa presidential caucuses, as always, were the first important test of presidential candidates. The two major-party winners that night were regional favorites: Senator Bob Dole, Republican of Kansas, and Missouri Democratic representative Dick Gephardt. The shocking news was the big loser—Vice President Bush, who finished third with 19 percent, not only behind Dole's 37 percent but also in back of televangelist Pat Robertson's 25 percent. From his war-hero exploits in World War II to eight years as vice president, Bush had spent almost his entire adult life in public service. But Robertson—the president of the Christian Broadcast Network (CBN), son of former Virginia senator Willis Robertson, and a first-time presidential candidate with no governing experience—bested Bush in the same state where just eight years earlier Bush had beaten his current boss, Ronald Reagan.

For the Bush campaign, Robertson's second-place finish was not a complete surprise. Doug Wead, a top family adviser who would later develop the phrase "compassionate conservative" for George W. Bush, had warned the vice president he might face serious resistance from evangelicals. Robertson himself sent very clear signals of his intent to make the transition from pulpits to politics. Since the 1984 election, his CBN had been funneling millions of dollars into the Freedom Council, an organization Robertson formed as a non-profit, nonpartisan citizen mobilization group with himself as its first president. He later installed Paul Weyrich's protégé Dick Minard to run the organization and ceased hosting *The 700 Club*, the CBN program that at its zenith gave him a national audience of nearly thirty million. When a 1986 Internal Revenue Service investigation threatened the Freedom Council's tax-exempt status, Robertson promptly disbanded it, freeing Minard to lead the newly formed Draft Robertson for President Committee. Robertson then declared that he would run for president if three million Americans signed a petition calling for him to do so. He formed a fund-raising organization, the 88 Club, with a stated goal of raising more than a quarter of a billion dollars through one-time $88 contributions from three million supporters.[3]

These religious divestments and organizational investments paid early dividends when Robertson won the votes of a majority of delegates to the 1986 Michigan Republican state party convention. That victory created tension between Robertson's supporters and Bush's backers in Michigan—a state, like Iowa, where Bush defeated Reagan in 1980. Although Wead had given Bush a reading list of key evangelical tracts so that the vice president could better converse with Christian religious leaders, these homework assignments were far too little, far too late.[4] In 1987 Robertson built on his Michigan win with a victory over Dole and Kemp in the 1987 Iowa straw poll. The reverend was surging.

Robertson's constituency was largely made up of evangelicals, charismatics, and other social conservatives who for decades had avoided electoral politics because they viewed it as an improper public expression of private faith. Those reservations began to fade in the mid-1970s, after former Georgia governor Jimmy Carter proved that open expressions of Christian faith could bring rewards at the ballot box. As evangelicals gradually abandoned Carter during his star-crossed lone term, their influence within the GOP grew from a fringe faction to a formidable fraction. Although some of the Christian groups mobilized during this period, such as Bread for the World, were nonideological or even liberal, most were formed to defend the traditional family, oppose abortion and homosexuality, and in general promote Christian conservative values through citizen mobilization and policy influence in Washington and the state capitals. The Supreme Court decision in *Roe v. Wade,* recognizing a constitutional right to abortion throughout the country, was the major issue around which the Christian right crystallized; but in an era of rising divorce rates, rising crime, rising out-of-wedlock births, growing recognition of homosexuality, and a general post-1960s sense of hedonism, abortion was hardly the only issue. Christian conservatives felt they had to save the America they had grown up in. James Dobson's Focus on the Family, Donald Wildmon's American Family Association, and Beverly LaHaye's Concerned Women for America were all created between 1977 and 1979, and although each advanced different causes, their missions overlapped. The capstone organization was the Moral Majority, founded in 1979 by televangelist Jerry Falwell. The Moral Majority fizzled out within ten years, but during the 1980s Falwell chaperoned the courtship and eventual marriage of the Christian Right and the Republican Party. Robertson's presidential campaign was thus not an isolated case of a religious conservative suddenly leaping into national politics out of nowhere. He represented a rising tide of political activism on the religious right. Especially within the Republican Party, the traditional barriers between church and state in politics were coming down.[5]

Although Robertson's stunning second-place finish, ahead of Bush, was the story on Iowa caucus night, there was another Republican casualty as well: Jack Kemp. Kemp was confident and telegenic, a political natural and rising media star. A disciple of supply-side economist Jude Wanniski, he is generally credited with convincing President Reagan of the merits of supply-side economics. It was an achievement that Kemp managed to attract national attention: he represented an obscure district outside Buffalo, New York, and in the mid-1980s the Republicans had been in the minority in the House for three straight decades.[6] He was a darling of the party's business wing, but to have any chance of winning the nomination he also needed to attract sufficient support from social conservatives. History frowned upon his White House ambitions: the last House incumbent to win the presidency had been James Garfield, more than a century earlier. Because Robertson and Kemp were both trying to play the role of party insurgent, the reverend's campaign effectively prevented any Republican from unifying social conservatives in order to execute a successful assault against Bush from the vice president's weakened right flank. Without the backing of evangelicals and other social conservatives, Kemp was ultimately a second-tier candidate.

Although Kemp was unlikely to win the 1988 nomination even if Robertson had not entered the race, had Kemp been the GOP's 1988 presidential or even vice presidential candidate, some of the conflicts that later emerged between the Bush White House and the House Republican caucus might have been averted. For Bob

Dole, 1988 was not the year to run as a Republican moderate—unless, like Bush, one had the institutional advantages of the vice presidency, including the implicit blessing of Ronald Reagan. Even if Dole had been interested in running as Bush's sidekick, Bush could never have chosen him: the Republican primary electorate clearly demanded a running mate who was satisfactory to social conservatives.

Newt Gingrich, rightly remembered as the Republican who had the vision and electoral plan to finally break the Democrats' stranglehold on the House, had an extra political gene that Kemp, who considered himself an autodidactic policy wonk and economic intellectual, possibly lacked. But Kemp did figure out how to move the national policy debate using only the fulcrum afforded to him as a House minority member—a notable and famous member, to be sure, but a minority backbencher whose authority derived almost solely from his ability to assert it. Kemp's political career taught the coming generation of congressional Republicans that they could exercise power even if they never managed to cast a majority vote.

Robertson's performance in the Iowa caucuses delivered an equally important lesson: a candidate who mobilized evangelical churchgoers could compete in low-turnout, high-intensity races. Amazingly, three-fifths of Robertson's supporters were participating in the caucuses for the first time.[7] Twenty years would pass before another candidate, Barack Obama, would mobilize first-time Iowa caucus-goers the way Robertson did in 1988. Although he didn't have the organization or legitimacy to steal the nomination from an incumbent vice president with deep roots in the Republican establishment, his candidacy changed the nomination calculus for all subsequent Republican presidential primaries. The awakening of religious conservatives would soon be felt in congressional primaries too.

In his speech to the assembled delegates at the Republican National Convention in New Orleans that August, Robertson spoke of America as a tale of two cities—one liberal, degraded, and doomed, the other conservative, righteous, and prosperous. After contrasting the best of (Republican) times wrought by the Reagan-Bush era with the worst of (Democratic) times that preceded it, and before doing his partisan duty and endorsing Bush, Robertson endorsed a higher power than the forty-third vice president of the United States. "There is another word," he bellowed, "that the Democrats did not mention once in their platform and not once in the acceptance speech of their candidate. It is a 'G' word: The name of God. Ladies and gentlemen, our president, Ronald Reagan, was not ashamed to ask the assembled delegates at our convention in Detroit to bow their heads in silent prayer to God. As Americans, we are not ashamed to pledge allegiance to a flag that is a symbol of one nation under God."[8]

With a big assist, four years later, from Bill Clinton and his feminist, lightning-rod wife, this stance would eventually expand into an interparty culture war. But first, happy religious warriors rose to prominence by directing their ire at fellow Republicans whom they deemed insufficiently doctrinaire. Such self-correcting and sometimes self-destructing behavior was not new to the GOP. But just as the Democrats' own litmus-test politics during the preceding quarter century had ripped apart the New Deal coalition, the rise of Pat Robertson and similar figures in the 1980s and 1990s set in motion a similar pattern for Republicans.

Insofar as his nomination for president constituted victory, George H. W. Bush was the big winner of 1988. What the future president didn't realize—not yet, at least—was that he had won his party's nomination but lost the war for the party's future.

Young Boy's Network

The day after Robertson's address, the new Republican nominee named his running mate: forty-one-year-old senator James Danforth Quayle. Few Americans outside the Washington Beltway or his home state of Indiana had ever heard of him. During the campaign and throughout his tenure as America's forty-fourth vice president, Quayle would come to be regarded as a national dunce—a punch line and a political punching bag who, after his four-year term ended, mostly disappeared from public view and made only a halfhearted, monthlong bid for the 2000 Republican nomination. Far lesser lights than Quayle still get slotted ahead of the former vice president for important speaking roles at Republican conventions, and many within GOP circles appear happy to let him fade quietly into history. Yet his political story foreshadowed important aspects of partisan and cultural politics during the next two decades.

Quayle was elected to the Senate in 1980, a breakthrough year for Senate Republicans. Running in Indiana against the presumably unbeatable incumbent Birch Bayh, he became one of twelve freshman members of that history-making Republican Senate class. The party captured three open seats and defeated nine incumbent Democrats to give the GOP its first majority since a brief two-year period at the start of the Eisenhower administration. In addition to Bayh, the notable Democrats whose careers were ended that year included former presidential nominee George McGovern of South Dakota, Idaho's Frank Church, Wisconsin's Gaylord Nelson, and Herman Talmadge of Georgia.

Republicans and conservatives had a mixed reaction—insofar as they had a reaction—to Quayle's selection by Bush in August 1998. Many didn't think much of Quayle simply because they hadn't thought about him at all. He was inoffensive but not especially inspiring. His main biographical complication was his Vietnam War–era service, in particular the suspicion that his family had pulled strings to secure him a billet in the National Guard. The major political knock against him was that he was an intellectual and legislative lightweight. But far worse than any liabilities he brought to the ticket was that he didn't seem to bring any assets. *New York Times* political reporter Tom Wicker summed up the conventional wisdom: "Senator Quayle brings the Republican ticket no state it might not have won otherwise. He makes possible no particular strategy—mollifying conservatives, appealing to the Midwest—that Mr. Bush could not have served with another, perhaps better selection. He assures the support of no dissident faction, and it's unlikely that he can close Mr. Bush's personal gender gap."[9]

In the weeks leading up to the convention, most vice presidential speculation had centered on two familiar names: Dole, the stalwart senator from the dying Rockefeller wing of the party who had been Gerald Ford's running mate in 1976; and Kemp, the public face of the renegade House Republicans. Seeking to establish an independent identity for himself, Bush decided to tap somebody less conventional. Not everyone in his camp was pleased. Word leaked out that James Baker, Bush's longtime friend and closest political confidant, considered Quayle a bad choice. The consensus in terms of Quayle's upsides was that the young senator offered a fresh, even handsome face—a peek into the party's future. But Kemp also met that standard. Ed Gillespie, then a young staffer working for a still relatively unknown Texas congressman named Dick Armey, remembers being surprised by Bush's pick. If he and many of his fellow young Hill staffers had a preference, it was Kemp. "For the Dick Armey types of the world, Jack Kemp was the person we most looked up to," Gillespie recalls.[10]

Quayle's youthful looks and obscurity prior to his selection were also potentially problematic on gender grounds. In 1980, for the first time in a presidential election, women voters outnumbered men. By 1984, women cast six million more votes, and in 1986 they outnumbered men at the polls for the first time in a midterm cycle.[11] Accordingly, in the 1980s both parties began to pay greater attention to female voters. After 1984 Democratic nominee Walter Mondale broke the gender glass ceiling with his vice presidential choice of Representative Geraldine Ferraro of New York, there was some expectation that Republicans in 1988 might respond in kind. The GOP had legitimate good reasons to worry about women voters: Reagan's approval ratings, which held mostly steady among men during his second term, had fallen from 60 percent to 43 percent among women during the three years leading up to the 1988 convention.[12]

Although there were few female governors or women in Congress of either party at the time, the Republican bench wasn't particularly thin—or not any thinner than the Democratic bench. If Bush could make any claim of a short supply of female candidates, his selection of a young, virtually unknown senator with a pretty boy image and a thin legislative record only undermined it. In effect, Quayle's presence suggested a lower threshold of achievement or competency for men to be chosen for the national ticket. By late August, polls showed Democratic presidential nominee Michael Dukakis leading Bush by double digits, a lead driven by his solid support among women. More daunting was the fact that fully 28 percent of Republican women—versus just 5 percent of Republican men—cited Quayle as cause for them to consider voting Democratic. "After the Quayle selection, women Republican leaders privately fumed not only at the choice, but at the suggestion that women would ignore Quayle's views and vote for him because he is physically attractive," wrote one political scribe at the time. "[They] fear that the anti-abortion Indiana senator who shares the religious right's view of family issues will alienate the numbers of women needed to win the fall election for Republicans."[13] Ultimately, Quayle did not derail the GOP ticket. Bush even carried women nationwide, if barely—just 51 percent to 49 percent. As of this writing, he is the most recent Republican presidential nominee to do so.

Both major parties had yet again nominated all-male tickets, but gender changes were accelerating in Congress in ways that were problematic for the Republicans. Just twenty-six women served in the 100th Congress of 1987–1988. The twenty-four female House members were almost evenly split between the parties, with thirteen Democrats and eleven Republicans. Each party boasted one female senator: Kansas Republican Nancy Landon Kassebaum and Maryland Democrat Barbara Mikulski. In the preceding 99th Congress, the parties actually achieved perfect parity with thirteen female members each—and the gender tiebreaker arguably went to the Republicans, who boasted two senators (Kassebaum plus Florida's Paula Hawkins) to go along with eleven GOP women in the House, versus thirteen Democratic women on the House side.[14]

By today's standards—in which Democrats in the 113th Congress account for 80 percent of the Senate's twenty female members and more than three-quarters of the seventy-eight women in the House[15]—the gender parity of the late 1980s seems like a relic from some distant political past. Since then, Democratic women have outgained their Republican counterparts in almost every congressional election. In the current, 113th Congress, the Democrats' House delegation from California alone has almost as many women (18) as female House Republicans from all fifty states combined (19).

Even if Bush in 1988 had chosen the person several critics at the time said was the "correct" Indiana Republican senator—the widely esteemed Dick Lugar—it probably would not have affected the underlying gender dynamics in Congress. The Republicans were paying some attention to gender politics, but not nearly as much as they should have been. Gender issues did not have much detrimental effect on Republican electoral fortunes—at least not yet, and definitely not at the congressional level. But that was about to change.

Conservative Opportunities and Opportunism

George Bush and Dan Quayle coasted to an easy victory over Michael Dukakis and his running mate, Senator Lloyd Bentsen of Texas. The Bush-Quayle ticket carried forty states and dominated every region of the country, giving the GOP its third consecutive presidential landslide. After taking the oath of office in January 1989, the new president called for a "kinder, gentler" nation. Down Pennsylvania Avenue, however, the Democratic hegemony persisted and the prospects for a kinder, gentler bipartisanship were slim and growing slimmer. The Senate Democrats had a new leader, Maine's George Mitchell, who had replaced the aging Robert Byrd. On the House side, Speaker Jim Wright of Texas was still in control—but briefly. Four months later he would be forced to resign the speakership. The path that led to Wright's fall began earlier in the decade, and the politician who almost single-handedly carved that path was upstart congressman Newt Gingrich of Georgia.

Immediately upon his arrival in Washington in 1979, Gingrich surprised his colleagues by declaring that he intended to lead the Republicans to a congressional majority and become House Speaker. During the mid-1980s, Gingrich distinguished himself as a potent, promising figure both within the conservative movement and in the House minority on Capitol Hill. He attracted the attention of conservative stalwarts like Heritage Foundation cofounders Ed Feulner and Paul Weyrich, and direct mail fund-raiser and publisher Richard Viguerie, who in May 1982 featured an interview with Gingrich on the cover of his magazine, *Conservative Digest*. In that piece, Gingrich called for the "proliferation" of conservative interest groups so that movement conservatives could expand beyond the core institutions like the National Conservative Political Action Committee. "The article revealed a politician who knew where he was going and seemed utterly confident he would get there," writes political historian Lee Edwards.[16]

In January 1983, Gingrich, who was already leading some of the brown bag strategy lunches Feulner and Weyrich hosted each week at Heritage, took a big step forward with his "conservative opportunity society" speech. In it, he outlined seven policy-oriented principles for a conservative ascendancy.[17] His language about opportunity notwithstanding, Gingrich's real political strength was tactical and opportunistic thinking. As a rookie congressman, he led the drive to expel Michigan Democrat Charles Diggs. Following the disappointing 1982 election, he took the advice of former president Richard Nixon, who told Gingrich he needed to create a platform for himself. So Gingrich teamed with fellow House members, including Mississippi's Trent Lott, Pennsylvania's Robert Walker, and Minnesota's Vin Weber, to form the Conservative Opportunity Society, a group of conservative legislators who met weekly to develop strategy. The speech further raised his national profile.

Themes like "opportunity society" were transmitted throughout the conservative policy community by new organizations designed to foster cooperation, coordination, and shared messaging among Washington's conservative policy advocates. Weyrich's regular luncheons were a draw among conservative intellectuals, writers, foundation heads, and think tank types. Later, Grover Norquist added his weekly Wednesday meetings for trade association and organizational activists. Staffers for House Republicans convened once or twice a month in the Longworth House Office Building to strategize and share information, and Senate Republican staffers did the same on the opposite side of Capitol Hill. Although these groups sometimes coordinated with national party officials, most of this organic activity occurred outside and beyond the realm of the Republican National Committee or even the House and Senate campaign committees. What political observer Thomas Edsall later called the "interlocking alliance" and "new conservative labyrinth" of conservative and Republican power was starting to emerge, and all the components were there: elected officials, staffers, activists, and thinkers.[18] And the impetus came from congressional Republicans like the young Newt Gingrich.

The term *opportunity society* quickly took hold. In early 1984, as he began to position himself for reelection, President Reagan used the term in his State of the Union address. He also made the notion the centerpiece of his keynote speech on March 2, 1984, to the assembled delegates at the Conservative Political Action Committee's annual conference in Washington. "An opportunity society awaits us. We need only believe in ourselves and give men and women of faith, courage, and vision the freedom to build it," the president said. "Let others run down America and seek to punish success. Let them call you greedy for not wanting government to take more and more of your earnings. Let them defend their tombstone society of wage and price guidelines, mandatory quotas, tax increases, planned shortages, and shared sacrifices."[19] Consider what a coup this was for a three-term congressman from the Atlanta suburbs: Gingrich had reframed the national political debate, and words from his pen were now being mouthed by the political god whom millions of conservatives worshipped.

Robert Walker later suggested to Gingrich that the fledgling government television channel C-SPAN, which began broadcasting in 1979, could be used to embarrass the Democratic majority. So in May 1984, Gingrich took to the floor of the empty House, and with cameras running, lambasted Democrats for their support of the

Sandinista government in Nicaragua. The issue and Gingrich's critique mattered less than the reaction it prompted: Speaker of the House Tip O'Neill lashed out at Gingrich in personal terms on the floor and was later rebuked for breaking House rules of decorum. Then, in 1986, when former Delaware governor Pete du Pont decided he needed to disentangle himself from GOPAC, the political action committee he had created, so that he could run for president, he picked Gingrich to run the organization.

Jim Wright took the Speaker's gavel after O'Neill retired in 1987. Wright was an old-school southern Democrat but also a less formidable opponent than O'Neill, with whom Reagan had maintained a cordial working relationship. Gingrich successfully targeted Wright for enriching himself with a shady book deal (much as Gingrich himself would later do). Behind every Democratic stumble and blunder, it seemed, the irascible congressman from Georgia was lurking, ready to pounce.

In ten years, the unknown backbencher had inserted himself directly into the national policy discussion, forced the most powerful figure on Capitol Hill to back down, forged his own political working group, and taken over a key electoral organization. "He came not necessarily as a bomb thrower, but as a dreamer," said former House colleague Guy Vander Jagt. "He was the only member, other than myself, that really believed that it was possible to build a Republican majority."[20] Vander Jagt, who died in 2007, probably overstated the matter—others also believed a GOP majority was achievable—but not by much. Idea man, dreamer, bomb thrower—by whatever label, Gingrich was a different political animal and a different kind of Republican. He preached opportunity but practiced opportunism, and changed the way Republicans talked and acted. Although Gingrich promoted ideas and talked governance, his early successes were almost uniformly about politics, not policy. He proved that winning in Washington did not necessarily require better ideas or solutions. Smarter strategies and tougher tactics were just as effective.

Bush's Hedges

George H. W. Bush was never comfortable on the campaign trail— not when he twice ran successfully for the House, nor when he twice ran unsuccessfully for the Senate. Not when he failed to win the 1980 Republican presidential nomination, nor even when he did win it eight years later. In many respects, Bush gained the presidency in 1988 despite himself, or at least by overcoming his political instincts, which campaign manager Lee Atwater, media consultant Roger Ailes, and other advisers worked assiduously to polish or conceal. Bush's awkwardness was particularly evident when he tried to play cultural politics, such as professing his love for pork rinds or expressing his devotion to defending the Pledge of Allegiance.

But campaigns are campaigns, and if a blue-blooded former Yale Skull and Bonesman had to reinvent himself to win the nation's highest office, so be it. Bush probably figured that once the votes were tallied he could return to the more dignified realm of the Oval Office and put the tawdry, superficial business of campaigning behind him. He learned otherwise. Not six months into his term, a national controversy erupted when the Supreme Court ruled in *Texas v. Johnson* that burning the American flag was a constitutionally protected expression of free speech.[21]

As a culture war skirmish, the flag-burning case could not have been better scripted for Bush. In 1984, under the political supervision of "boy genius" political consultant Karl Rove, Texas was rapidly transforming from a Democratic stronghold to a cornerstone of the new Republican South—a place less associated with Lyndon

Johnson or Lloyd Bentsen, and more and more identified with the likes of Phil Gramm, Tom DeLay, and Dick Armey. That summer the Republicans held their national convention in Dallas at the Reunion Arena. During the convention, a protester named Gregory Lee Johnson doused an American flag in kerosene in front of Dallas City Hall and set it on fire. He was arrested and charged with violating a state law that prohibits the desecration of sacred objects. A member of a marginal group called the Revolutionary Communist Youth Brigade, Johnson even had liberal legal icon William Kunstler on his Supreme Court defense team. He was the perfect political foil.

Such was Bush's luck that the case outlasted Reagan's entire second term and the opening six months of his own. And then there was the startling nature of the majority coalition itself: none other than Antonin Scalia surprised and angered conservatives by siding with the Court's four liberals in the 5–4 majority opinion penned by Justice William Brennan. The next day, during a luncheon speech in New York, President Bush was his usual prudent self. "I understand the legal basis for the decision," he said, "and I respect the Supreme Court, and as president of the United States, I will see that the law of the land is fully supported. But I have to give you my personal, emotional response: Flag burning is wrong—dead wrong—and the flag of the United States is very, very special."[22] This expression of personal disgust was echoed not only by almost all national Republicans but by the vast majority of Democrats. According to a *Newsweek* poll taken shortly after the ruling, about two-thirds of Americans disagreed with the Court.[23]

The president's response was reasonable in every sense: personally opposed, yet respectful of the Court's decision to protect even the most offensive forms of political speech. Yet conservatives, especially in Congress, immediately demanded something more forceful. On cue, one day and a luncheon meeting with Atwater later, Bush's prudence gave way to a call for a constitutional amendment to prohibit flag burning. Congress had overwhelmingly approved chamber resolutions condemning the Court, but it would be much more difficult to get two-thirds majorities in both Democratic-controlled chambers to send a constitutional amendment to the states for ratification. Within days of the ruling, Rich Galen, president of the American Campaign Academy, a Republican electoral training organization, said he would urge Republican candidates he advised to pummel any congressional Democrat who failed to publicly criticize the Court's ruling. "I would attack him," Galen said, "for being in favor of letting people who've never lifted a finger to help the country being able to sneer at it and burn the flag."[24]

Bush's legitimacy in this episode came under attack in a way that the patriotism of Ronald Reagan—that sunny optimist and fierce anticommunist—rarely did. There were a few cultural war skirmishes during Reagan's presidency. Reagan's World War II service record paled against that of his successor; an astigmatism prevented Reagan from serving in combat, so the government assigned him to public relations duties in Culver City, California, with the almost comically named First Motion Picture Unit. The Gipper didn't pick fights over the flag because he didn't have to. And yet here was Bush—who might easily have used his family's connections to avoid harm during World War II, but who became a decorated fighter pilot instead—having to make a grand show of waving the flag he had defended in actual, life-threatening combat.

To what benefit was this posturing by Bush and his White House? Not much. Almost every Democrat in Congress voted for resolutions condemning the Supreme Court's ruling, providing Bush and conservatives little political windfall. What the episode instead taught the president is that these moments were as much about validating the convictions of Republican politicians as they were opportunities to delegitimize their critics. President Bush gained little by making these symbolically powerful but empty gestures, but he had plenty to lose had he failed to make them. Conservatives, especially in Congress, were beginning to establish new party litmus tests, new marks for Republican politicians to toe—including their own presidents.

Bush also reversed himself on the hot-button controversy over affirmative action and the meaning of racial quotas in hiring practices. Again, this fight was initiated by events late in Reagan's term that came to a head after Bush took office. On the fourth day of Bush's presidency, the Supreme Court ruled in *Richmond v. Croson* that Richmond's minority business enterprise program—a preference system that awarded 30 percent of all city contracts to minority-owned firms—violated the Constitution's equal protection clause. That June, in *Wards Cove v. Atonio*, the Court ruled against another affirmative action plaintiff on a slightly different point of employment law.[25] By summer, the political fight over affirmative action had shifted to Congress, where Senator Ted Kennedy and fellow congressional Democrats were drafting new legislation to clarify and expand affirmative action law with the intent of counteracting key parts of *Richmond*, *Wards Cove*, and four other Court rulings that had raised the bar for affirmative action plaintiffs to prove discrimination. The political question was whether the president would support or veto such legislation.

Bush seemed to be of two minds on the issue, publicly advocating racial fairness but opposing any law establishing what he incessantly referred to as "quotas." That term became a cultural buzzword that divided liberals from conservatives. That summer, congressional Democrats passed and sent to Bush's desk a new bill to clarify the rights of petitioners to bring discrimination suits against employers. Whether he signed or vetoed it, Bush had to justify his decision. If he signed it, angry conservatives might cause problems in the upcoming midterm election and maybe for Bush's own reelection (or even renomination) prospects in 1992. Congressional Republicans would be furious. On the other hand, he had run an ad in the 1988 campaign that many Democrats viewed as race baiting. If he vetoed the bill, the White House would need to provide a strong rationale. During the bill's markup, Democrats worked to accommodate the president's objections, and independent experts assured the president that the bill established no quota systems for hiring. But the White House understood the word's potency.

On October 22, 1990, Bush vetoed the bill on the grounds that it established hiring quotas for employers. The Senate fell one vote short of the two-thirds majority needed to override the veto. A year later, the Democratic Congress passed another clarifying bill that again made it easier for plaintiffs to bring discrimination cases against employers. But the legislation also made quite clear that a statistical discrepancy between the racial composition of an employer's workforce and that of the surrounding community did not by itself constitute prima facie evidence of discrimination. On November 21, 1991, the president signed the new version into law. "I say again today that I support affirmative action," Bush announced. "Nothing in this bill overturns the government's affirmative action programs."

The political significance of these reversals is that Bush was learning on the job to check his prudential tendency to find common ground on controversial issues. In the flag-burning case, he made a swift reversal to avoid a conservative backlash. In the affirmative action fights, he staked out a conservative position from which he could later backtrack after claiming to have extracted concessions from Democrats. In the end, no real policy change was achieved in either instance: burning the flag remained constitutionally protected, and racial hiring quotas that never existed in the first place were not created. A lot of the political maneuvering was for show: for most of his public life, that's how politics worked.

What had changed were the audiences of interest. To some degree, Bush can be forgiven for bargaining only with the Democrats and viewing negotiation within his own party's congressional ranks as meaningless symbolism. Bush served two terms in the U.S. House during the Democrats' forty-year reign. He was ideologically sympatico with Republican House minority leader Robert Michel and other moderates who had dutifully carried the minority party banner for decades. There was little reason to believe that the bluster emanating from new corners of the Republican congressional minority—including Republicans elected in what was, at least for purposes of political window dressing, Bush's adopted home state of Texas—was more than a passing political fancy.

Bush came to understand—if a bit too late—that he must heed the demands of congressional Republicans, even if they were only the minority. A corollary to this revelation would become evident during his son's presidency, when the younger Bush, rather than pushing back publicly against his fellow Republicans at the point of legislative passage, simply issued signing statements to clarify where he differed with portions of bills passed by GOP majorities on Capitol Hill. But the elder Bush either declined to use such tactics or didn't realize he needed to bother. Either way, he blundered headlong into intraparty fights in which he quite reasonably may have presumed he would prevail. He was, after all, the president, and also the leader of his party. Soon he would be neither.

Race to Redistrict

Race became an integral part of the Republican power equation in the battle between the two parties to gain an electoral edge in the redistricting that would follow the census of 1990. At first blush, the Democrats seemed to have all the advantages. Although many states were under divided government, of the ninety-nine U.S. House seats in states controlled entirely by one party or the other, all but five were in states the Democrats controlled. The day after the 1990 midterm elections—in which Democrats picked up a net of eight House seats, expanding their majority to 267–168—former Democratic congressman Tony Coehlo of California, perhaps still smarting from having to resign his own seat under a cloud of investigation, boasted that Republicans had failed to "make the necessary inroads they needed in order to accomplish what they wanted to do. Without some major traumatic event, the Democrats will continue to control the House for the decade of the 90s as a result of yesterday's election."[26] To hear Coehlo and others tell it, Democrat Tom Foley of Washington would wield the Speaker's gavel forever.

But appearances were deceiving for two reasons. First, the vast majority of House seats—more than three hundred—were in states with divided partisan control. Second, the political climate had changed dramatically since the 1980 round of redistricting, especially on the issue of drawing more majority-minority districts to elect black and Latino members of Congress. In areas with large, concentrated minority populations, Republicans now had a strategic interest in colluding with minority politicians to create more such districts. As redistricting scholar David Lublin succinctly explains, "Republicans, avowed opponents of every other affirmative action policy and many other programs favored by African Americans, formed an alliance with blacks and Latinos to push for the creation of new majority-minority districts . . . because they hoped that packing black voters in a few districts would result in the election of more Republicans from the remaining districts."[27]

This shift represented a significant policy reversal for Republicans. In 1982, during the debates and eventual vote to extend provisions of the 1965 Voting Rights Act, the party had opposed creating more majority-minority districts. But in 1986 the Supreme Court issued a unanimous ruling in *Thornburg v. Gingles* that established clear standards for detecting and rectifying racial discrimination in legislative district-drawing. With that, the force of law now aligned perfectly with Republicans' newly realized strategic objectives.[28] Technological advances during the 1980s also yielded far better computer mapping software, giving the process new technical sophistication and thus greater opportunities for manipulation by both parties.

Combined with a dash of shrewd political maneuvering by the National Republican Campaign Committee, these changes persuaded Republicans in 1990 to pirouette 180 degrees on the issue of race-based gerrymandering. "Now, [Republicans] are encouraging minority groups to demand the redrawing of as many districts as possible," the *New York Times* reported that summer. "As an enticement, the Republicans are offering minority activists bargain-basement prices on the software and data bases necessary to compete in the redistricting game." Though minority groups and advocates were suspicious of this sudden generosity, the temptations were too strong. "The Republicans had an atrocious record on voting rights under the Reagan Administration and so there is a bit of discomfort among most minority organizations about the Republican initiative," Frank Parker, director of the voting rights project of the Lawyers' Committee for Civil Rights, said at the time. "[But] if they think they can benefit by helping us create minority districts because the adjoining districts will be whiter, well, then maybe our interests overlap."[29]

Indeed they did. Although the minority population nationally grew from 16.8 percent to 19.7 percent between the 1980 census and that of 1990,[30] the number of majority-minority districts doubled, from twenty-seven following the 1980 redistricting to fifty-six after the 1990 redistricting. This change was undoubtedly accelerated by race-based mapmaking.[31] In 1992 more freshmen African Americans were elected to the U.S. House of Representatives than in any election cycle prior to that—or any cycle since. The structural advantages created during the 1990 round of redistricting did not yield sufficient dividends for the GOP to capture the House in 1992. But the 1992 cycle was a key moment in the Republicans' quest to build House majorities. Its unintended consequence was to marginalize the party with racial minorities and thereby make the GOP less competitive in presidential elections.

Taxing Promises

If George H. W. Bush were ever put on trial for the charge of failing to foresee the coming upheaval in congressional elections during the 1990s, his first piece of exculpatory evidence would be the 1988 and 1990 U.S. Senate elections. To put it mildly, the results were underwhelming: the Democrats gained one net seat in each cycle. In 1988 a few notable seats changed partisan hands: future Republican Senate majority leader Trent Lott won the Mississippi seat vacated by the retirement, after forty-one years, of legendary southern Democrat John C. Stennis; moderate, pro-business Democrat Joe Lieberman defeated Connecticut liberal Republican Lowell P. Weicker, who had become a target of William F. Buckley and other conservatives; and Republican Conrad Burns—who would go on to become the longest-serving Republican senator in Montana history before his career was ended by the Jack Abramoff scandal—unseated Democrat John Melcher. The 1990 election was even more of a snooze. Only a single seat switched parties: college professor and liberal Democrat Paul Wellstone used a clever television ad campaign and a shoestring budget to defeat Minnesota Republican Rudy Boschwitz.

Lott was one of several Republicans who replaced retiring conservative southern Democrats; Weicker's defeat signaled the decline of New England Republicans; and Wellstone's win foreshadowed the vocal, liberal response to the Democratic Leadership Council's efforts to push the Democratic Party to the center. But the most instructive Senate contest during these two cycles may have been one in which the incumbent survived—barely. The 1990 New Jersey Senate contest between Bill Bradley and Christine Todd Whitman foretold the power of tax issues in the partisan fight to control Congress, much as Ronald Reagan's 1980 campaign changed the way taxes were used as a political issue in presidential politics.

A decade before his failed attempt to wrest the 2000 Democratic nomination from Vice President Al Gore, Bill Bradley was at the zenith of his political career: a serious national figure with a solid pedigree and star power. Elected to the Senate in 1978 at age thirty-five, the former professional basketball star and Princeton-educated Rhodes scholar quickly established a national reputation as a cerebral celebrity with all the hallmarks of a future president. He easily coasted to reelection despite the Reagan-led national Republican tidal wave of 1984, winning a second term with 65 percent of the vote. His image as the brainy jock served him well during the 1986 tax reform debates, in which he played a leading role on Capitol Hill and during White House negotiations. Heading into the 1990 elections—a presidential midterm cycle with a Republican incumbent in the Oval Office—Bradley was considered so unbeatable that New Jersey Republicans struggled to find a suitable contender to mount a serious challenge.

Christine Todd Whitman, the president of the New Jersey Board of Public Utilities, was a reluctant Senate candidate. Her husband and children didn't want her to run. Though she would have taken the job, she was more interested in executive politics and admits she ran in part to raise her statewide profile for a 1993 run for governor. But she was unconvinced of Bradley's invulnerability. So she entered and won the Republican primary and, once nominated, refused to play the role of sacrificial lamb. "It was really a nightmare for all the old boys here in New Jersey, because they didn't do anything for me," Whitman recalls. "Nobody helped me much because they thought it was such a losing cause." Nor did she get much help from Washington. The Republican Senatorial Campaign Committee initially pledged $300,000 toward the race, but in the end put the money into what it judged to be more competitive races. "They could say they ran a woman again"—following Mary V. Mochary's 1984 challenge of Bradley—"and show how open-minded the Republicans were. That was part of it: Let a woman run for this kind of thing because she probably can't win it."[32]

But the under-resourced Whitman mounted a creative attack on Bradley for something he had nothing to do with: the new state tax plan advocated by Democratic governor Jim Florio. Whitman hammered away at Bradley, who refused to pay the attacks much mind. After all, he was a U.S. senator. How was he to blame for state tax policy? Whitman recalls her utter amazement at how much traction Bradley allowed her to gain on the issue: "I just kept expecting any day for him to say, 'Look, I don't agree with raising taxes and I think it's too bad we have to do it, but the governor is facing extraordinary times.' He would have taken the issue away from me in a nanosecond. But he never did."[33]

Until the campaign's last days, Bradley's advertisements focused on reinforcing his public image. The ads proved to be ill-conceived and self-destructive. Instead of burnishing Bradley's jock-turned-wonk identity, the media campaign accentuated the weaknesses in his biography. One ad showed him shooting a basketball; in his final ad, his feet are casually propped up on his Senate desk. Even some supporters found the ads condescending and insulting. "He had his ads in the tank already, he had them set," Whitman said. "The very last ad, I'll never forget it. It had him sitting behind his desk in Washington opining on I can't remember what. And then he puts his feet up on his desk and he has sneakers on. In this state, where people had taxes on toilet paper, they were just furious about it."[34]

Despite significant voter anxiety about a variety of domestic and international issues, Bradley's messaging conveyed detachment, even arrogance. He was taking his reelection, and his constituents, for granted.[35] Finally, with Election Day fast approaching and internal campaign polls showing a tightening race, the Bradley team woke up and went on the attack. This last-minute effort was just enough: Bradley held off the surging Whitman by 55,190 votes out of nearly two million cast—a margin of 3 percent.[36] A previously unknown candidate had successfully nationalized a state tax dispute in a U.S. Senate contest and used the issue to rattle one of the most prominent Democratic politicians in the country, during a cycle that favored the Democrats. "I got the message," Bradley said in a postelection press conference.

Did he? And did his fellow Democrats? Bradley certainly hurt himself with a poor campaign strategy and foolish TV ads. But Whitman's relentless antitax theme revealed a soft underbelly that a platoon of Republican candidates would soon exploit. "Clearly [our] ads didn't address the issue. I'm not stupid. I'm not going to say the television was on target," admitted a rattled Michael Kaye, Bradley's media adviser, during a postelection press conference. "Did I sense the Florio thing was a problem? Yes. Do I think we are dealing with it? No. I think we weren't answering it worth a damn."[37]

Congressional Republicans had learned an important lesson, one that organizations like Americans for Tax Reform would soon

turn into a powerful, even paralyzing, demand: running on a platform of absolute opposition to any new taxes made for very smart
politics. It was a lesson President Bush was also about learn, the hard
way.

Of Will and Wallet

Bradley's electoral scare should have been warning enough for the
Bush White House as it headed into budget talks with congressional Democrats in early 1991. But the White House, and particularly Office of Management and Budget director Dick Darman,
were paying no more attention to the dangers of tax policy than
Bradley's advisers had. Over Darman's objections, the president had
made his famous "read my lips—no new taxes" promise during his
acceptance speech in New Orleans.[38] In his inaugural address—one
that, coming amid the slow collapse of communism in Eastern Eu-
rope, today seems oddly tilted toward domestic and economic
policies—the new president called for a "kinder, gentler" nation that
would address such domestic problems as poverty and homelessness.
He admitted that money couldn't cure all of these ills and, even if it
could, the Treasury was stretched too thin. "We have a deficit to
bring down," the president proclaimed. "We have more will than
wallet, but will is what we need."

From the beginning of Bush's presidency, Darman argued that
the key to reelection would be Bush's ability to create a record of
"successful governance." An Elliot Richardson protégé, Darman
believed, as did Bush, that voters rewarded prudence and doing the
right thing. He was conservative in a traditional policy sense but not
an ideological conservative. Policies, decisions, and deals should be
judged on their merits, he believed, not their political utility. Of
similar mind was Bush's first Treasury secretary, Nicholas Brady,

who had taken over at Treasury in late 1988, while Reagan was still in office. Brady had concluded from studying "Black Monday," the one-day, 23 percent stock market crash in October 1987, that Wall Street's worries about deficit reduction had been a contributing factor. The administration's thinking was also influenced by the bipartisan National Economic Commission (NEC), created by Congress in 1987 and tasked with providing recommendations for bringing down the national debt. The NEC members, including some Republicans, felt frustrated, even betrayed, by Bush's "read my lips" line at the New Orleans convention. When presidential speechwriters tried to insert the pledge language into President Bush's speeches in 1989 and 1990, Darman struck the lines so as to create political space for Bush to adopt some of the NEC's recommendations and move the country toward a more fiscally responsible budget. Yet Darman also occasionally caved to political pressure, inserting into Bush's 1990 State of the Union address a promise to "balance the budget without new taxes."

The 1990 budget battle was at once a fiscal argument about deficits in the wake of the 1987 stock market crash and the savings and loan bailouts of the late 1980s, a macroeconomic argument about the stimulating effects of lower tax rates, and a political argument about working in a bipartisan fashion with the Democratic Congress. Beneath the surface, this battle devolved into a fight between the Bush White House and congressional Republicans, especially the House Republican Conference. In the end, Bush did what he, his top economic advisers, and many Beltway minds thought was, for lack of a better word, the prudent thing to do: he broke the promise he made in his 1988 convention speech and raised taxes.

The fallout from that single decision is impossible to quantify and difficult to summarize, but it was a watershed moment for fin de siècle American politics, the conservative movement, and con-

gressional Republicans. The *Washington Post*'s veteran political reporter David Broder put it this way:

> Bush broke his tax promise because he faced the govern-
> mental reality that deficits would spin further out of control
> unless tax hikes were combined with spending curbs. He
> believes that stemming the deficit hemorrhage is not only
> good government but good politics; that it will produce a
> healthier economy in 1992, his re-election year and the year
> the Republicans have their best chance to regain control of
> the Senate and improve their strength in the House.
>
> But he could not persuade the House Republicans, who
> have been in the permanent minority so long now, 36 years
> and counting, that they have lost the political discipline of
> thinking about governmental responsibility. And that is the
> ultimate irony: Until the House Republicans can be given a
> share of governing responsibility, they will continue to raise
> hell with presidents of both parties. But as long as they act
> irresponsibly, as they've done again, they will probably not
> be given that power.[39]

Politically, the budget deal dropped like an atom bomb. Fiscal conservatives and many congressional Republicans—especially on the
House side—were outraged. The broken tax pledge irritated old
wounds and opened new ones within the GOP caucus. Among conservatives, it confirmed their worst fears about Bush. "If George Bush
had pardoned Willie Horton, or burned Old Glory on the lawn of the
White House, it would hardly have rivaled the flip-flop he has committed on taxes," the Heritage Foundation's Daniel J. Mitchell wrote.[40]

The tax pledge struggle between Bush the candidate and Bush the
president became a national political fight between the president

and Congress. Several congressional Republicans seized the moment to burnish their own credentials. The cantankerous four-term Texas representative Dick Armey, who had never drawn much attention outside Capitol Hill, generated national headlines by insisting on collecting signed pledges from Republicans for "no new taxes." On November 26, 1991, he took a dramatic step forward by attacking his own party's president on the *New York Times* op-ed page:

> President Bush is dangerously out of touch with the American public. Instead of listening to the elected people in his party most in touch with the average voter—House Republicans—he remains cloistered with aides who avoid action and favor blaming others for the nation's economic, and their boss's consequent political, woes.
>
> House Republicans are increasingly frustrated with the White House's wait-and-see attitude on the economy. . . . Unfortunately, our calls for quick action are rebuked by unelected officials like Richard Darman, the budget director, and John Sununu, the chief of staff, who advocate waiting for a more politically opportune moment to push for an economic growth package.
>
> These are the same people who, when the House Republicans passed my "no new taxes" resolution during last year's budget summit, urged the President to accept a package that called for new taxes and to try to push it past us anyway.[41]

The next day the *Washington Post* reported a rising intraparty revolt against the president: whispers that Pat Buchanan would soon announce his intent to challenge Bush for the 1992 Republican nomination, and a letter signed by four dozen House Republicans calling on Bush to appoint Jack Kemp as a special White House domestic policy adviser.[42] Much of the conservative anger about the tax deal was directed at the two Bush advisers Armey named in his *Times* op-ed, Darman and Sununu. OMB director Darman in particular endured withering verbal assaults; among other critiques, he was called the "Neville Chamberlain of the Republican Party." Conservative members of Congress were delighted by Armey's attacks. Ed Gillespie, who still worked for Armey at the time, remembers the *Times* piece as a rallying event for young, impatient staffers like him who were tired of being in the minority and equally tired of watching a president from their own party cater to the Democrats.[43]

In the end, the president's fiscal responsibility went unrewarded. Even though he too would eventually raise marginal income tax rates, Governor Bill Clinton of Arkansas relentlessly bludgeoned Bush in the 1992 presidential campaign about the broken tax pledge. Years later, Dick Cheney would articulate the political truth of that moment when he stated that "deficits don't matter." As for Broder's prediction about the fate of House Republicans, the eminent pundit who understood both parties from the center outward was as wrong as Darman, Brady, Sununu, and the president himself: House Republicans were not punished in either 1992 or 1994 for their ambivalence about rising deficits and the expanding national debt.

And where was the House's rising Republican star, Newt Gingrich, during this intraparty fight? According to Bush biographer Tim Naftali, the White House not only failed to anticipate the congressional revolt that followed their budget deal, it also took for granted that the revolutionaries would smile gamely and participate in the optics. But Gingrich, though he had privately agreed to the deal, refused to have his picture taken with the president and congressional leaders at the ceremonial bill signing in the Rose Garden—a boycott he hadn't announced to the GOP leadership and which "came as a shock" to Bush. "Gingrich's central insight," writes Naftali, "was that Reaganite tactics, which have proved so successful at the presidential level, should be applied to Congress."[44]

Bush, of course, had practiced his own divisive political tactics during his 1988 presidential run. But he probably never imagined that a politician from his own party would use such tactics against *him*, or subsume the needs and image of a Republican White House to the agenda of the party's minority leadership in Congress. He was the last Republican president to serve during the dying, New Deal Democratic era of congressional dominance, and had ample reason to expect that the status quo on Capitol Hill would continue. By the time he saw the electoral and political wave about to sweep through Congress—if he saw it at all—it was cresting above his head and about to crash over him.

Bombing over Baghdad

Like millions of their fellow Americans, on the night of January 16, 1991, President George H. W. Bush, Secretary of Defense Dick Cheney, National Security Council adviser Brent Scowcroft, Scowcroft's deputy and future secretary of defense Robert Gates, and White House Middle East adviser Richard Haass sat glued to their television sets watching as bombs dropped on Baghdad during the unforgettable opening moments of the Gulf War. Shortly after the bombing campaign began, a stunning four of every five American televisions were tuned to President Bush's live announcement that military operations were under way.[45] "Five months ago, Saddam Hussein started this cruel war against Kuwait," the president said from behind the desk of the Oval Office. "Tonight, the battle has been joined." Those memorable opening scenes and Bush's ten-minute speech brought to a head five months of economic sanctions, coalition building, international maneuvering, and domestic public rallying by the Bush administration to make the case for U.S. intervention in Kuwait to repel an Iraqi invasion. For the first time since Vietnam, the United States was at war.

The international negotiations prior to the war, the execution of the military strategy during it, and the exit strategy reflected a new use-of-force doctrine that quickly came to be associated with its namesake, Chairman of the Joint Chiefs of Staff Colin Powell. The eight-pronged Powell Doctrine permitted the use of force only when American security interests were at stake; sufficient and overwhelming force could be marshaled in order to limit casualties; there was broad international support for taking military action; the risks and costs were fully analyzed; and there was a clearly stated military objective and exit strategy once that objective was met. In less than a minute during his televised speech, Bush managed to summarize these principles and affirm that the United States and the twenty-eight allied nations with forces in the region tried to avoid war and chose force only as a last and necessary resort. Once begun, he said, the fight would be swift, overwhelming, properly resourced, and limited to its stated purposes. "Prior to ordering our troops into battle," Bush explained, "I instructed our military commanders to take every necessary step to prevail as quickly as possible, and with the greatest degree of protection possible for American and Allied servicemen and women. I've told the American people before that this will not be another Vietnam."

He delivered on those promises. The war was over in six weeks. A total of 148 Americans died, and when friendly-fire deaths are subtracted from the total, fewer U.S. soldiers died in combat than in noncombat accidents.[46] In a memoir coauthored with Scowcroft, published five years after his presidency ended, Bush relished recounting the dire warnings of Democratic senators Barbara Boxer and Ted Kennedy, who predicted thousands of American casualties. At one point in the Senate debate over military authorization, Kennedy bellowed that it was not too late to save the president from himself. But by early 1991, all but two Senate Republicans were on board. Because congressional Democrats were divided (as they would be again in 2002) over whether to go to war in Iraq, Bush had sufficient congressional backing to pass a United Nations–sanctioned use-of-force resolution in both chambers on January 12. He had built a formidable coalition abroad and, thanks in part to divided Democrats, a workable coalition in Washington.

If making a five-month case for war and prosecuting that war in just six weeks seemed too easy, in many respects it was. That ease became a key element in the electoral conundrum that soon faced the Bush White House: the short, efficient Gulf War was a military success wrapped inside a political failure.

For starters, the first war of the modern media age, broadcast in CNN-led twenty-four-hour news cycles, had a reductive and ephemeral quality. The initial popular fervor and rise in Bush's public approval came so quickly precisely because, anchored as it was to video game–like imagery of Scud missile attacks, that support was wide but not deep. As Stephen Graubard explains in *Mr. Bush's War*, Operation Desert Storm was "represented as a clean war," and thus easy, uncomplicated, and antiseptic. "The mass media story was still the war," writes Graubard. "But the war now refused to cooperate. The news had taken on a certain sameness day after day, and there were few new arresting pictures . . . and there was, inevitably, some movement away from the television screen."[47] The Bush reelection team learned that a quick, clean media war could lose viewers, and thus voters, almost as quickly as it attracted them. In electoral terms, the Gulf War was a curio, an object Americans picked up and briefly marveled at, and then set down and forgot.

Compounding the ephemeral nature of America's first fully televised war, argues Graubard, was the fact that its resolution offered a powerful reminder of declining Soviet influence. Although conservatives still credit Reagan, not Bush, with vanquishing the "Evil Empire," the task of transitioning the Soviets to a world in which it was no longer America's co-superpower fell, like many other residual political fights, into Bush's lap. He and Secretary of State James Baker were perhaps the ideal American political tandem to manage this transition. But they were less prepared for the partisan-electoral fallout from the end of the Cold War. The removal of the Soviet threat reduced the Republicans' natural advantage on foreign policy and military matters by redirecting public attention inward, toward those kitchen-table concerns an assertive young Arkansas governor spoke about incessantly.

The success of Operation Desert Storm had a longer-term consequence for Republican politics. It set the extraordinarily high standard by which the second President Bush's Iraq War would inevitably be judged. The Powell Doctrine worked during the Gulf War because the proudly prudent president adhered to its every principle. Indeed, liberal critics would later mock then–vice president Cheney and his role in the second President Bush's Iraq War— which flouted almost every principle of the Powell Doctrine—for the famous reply he gave as defense secretary in 1992 when he was asked to defend the first Bush administration's decision not to overtake Baghdad or dispose of Saddam Hussein. "For the 146 Americans who were killed in action and for their families," Cheney said at the time, "it wasn't a cheap war. And the question in my mind is, how many additional American casualties is Saddam worth? And the answer is, not that damned many. So, I think we got it right, both when we decided to expel him from Kuwait, but also when the President made the decision that we'd achieved our objectives and we were not going to go get bogged down in the problems of trying to take over and govern Iraq."[48]

For decades, the Republican Party had steadily built a branding advantage over the Democrats on foreign policy and defense. For the elder Bush, the lesson of America's first war in Iraq was that in a post–Cold War world, that reputational investment might yield smaller returns. But one Republican congressman was already anticipating the Gulf War's limited electoral value. In his biography of Newt Gingrich, *The Gentleman from Georgia*, Mel Steely argues that Gingrich was ahead of many fellow Republicans in recognizing that the party had to start offering more of a domestic agenda. As we'll see in Chapter 4, neoconservative foreign policy ideas and the Project for a New American Century arose later in the decade partly in reaction to Gingrich's domestic focus. But in the early 1990s, writes Steely, Gingrich's attention to domestic issues "was indeed reading the mood of the country correctly. . . . While Newt supported Bush and his masterful efforts to build an alliance to stop Iraq's aggression he also understood that the American people were fed up with big spending, unsafe streets, an education system that was a disaster and political and economic systems that seemed to care little about the great American middle class. The president and many other politicians failed to read this shift and paid the consequences in the 1992 and 1994 elections."[49] Gingrich had his eye on the congressional majorities he intended to build, regardless of what that meant for the Republican Party's post–Cold War foreign policy portfolio.

The Turtle Conservative

On December 10, 1991, ten weeks before the 1992 New Hampshire primary, former Nixon spokesperson and conservative agitator Pat Buchanan made it official: he would challenge his own party's incumbent for the 1992 Republican presidential nomination. In front of a small but energized audience on the steps of the state legislative office building in Concord, Buchanan sounded themes familiar to anyone who had listened to him on CNN's *Crossfire*. He scoffed at the notion of a "New World Order" and called for a renewed and vigilant American nationalism, built on the twin foundations of post–Cold War isolation and domestic market protection. He railed against the decline of traditional social values and demanded curbs on government power to tax the citizenry and regulate American industry. Midway through the speech, he asked and answered the question the media and the public make every candidate address:

> Why am I running? Because we Republicans can no longer say it is all the liberals' fault. It was not some liberal Democrat who declared, "Read my lips! No new taxes!," then broke his word to cut a back room budget deal with the big spenders. It was not Edward Kennedy who railed against a quota bill, then embraced its twin. It was not Congress alone who set off on the greatest social spending spree in 60 years, running up the largest deficits in modern history. No, that was done by men in whom we placed our confidence and our trust, and who turned their backs, and walked away from us.[50]

After the speech, Buchanan admitted that his candidacy was a long shot. He said he hoped his impact might be like that of antiwar senator Eugene McCarthy's challenge of incumbent Lyndon Johnson in the 1968 Democratic primary.[51] Despite running against an incumbent buffered by all the advantages the White House afforded, Buchanan had reason to be somewhat optimistic about his chances—or at least his potential to have an impact. "I couldn't get 2 percent of the vote against Ronald Reagan," Mr. Buchanan told George Will during an appearance on ABC's *This Week with David Brinkley* the day before he announced his candidacy. "If I can do well in New Hampshire and in the country, there is only one reason: Because George Bush walked away from the conservative base of his own party, because he promised not to raise taxes and raised them, because he said he wouldn't sign a quota bill and then signed it."[52]

Pat Buchanan never served in Congress; in fact, he had never been elected to any office. But his message and rhetoric strongly echoed the intraparty complaints emanating from Congress: the party is too soft, too accommodating, too centrist. His entry into the 1992 presidential campaign was just one of the dangerous portents for Bush that would come to a head that summer at the Republican National Convention in Houston. Although the threats at the presidential level had come from the outside, the behavior of the congressional Republicans during Bush's presidency gradually revealed a party that was beginning to devour itself. They were disappointed that their supply-side hero, Jack Kemp, was passed over for the vice presidency; they were puzzled by the selection of David Souter, a judge with a thin record and questionable conservative bona fides, to fill a key Supreme Court vacancy; and they were infuriated by Bush's apostasy on tax rates.

As bookends to Bush's presidency, the insurgent campaigns of Pat Robertson in 1988 and Pat Buchanan in 1992 sent unambiguous signals that, for conservatives, the transition from Ronald Reagan to George H. W. Bush was something to be resisted. At first, the newly elected President Bush found ways to assuage his conservative doubters, and the Gulf War provided a useful if temporary distraction to conservatives' growing wariness about the president's movement credentials. Bush's wartime popularity was only briefly able to paper over coalitional problems beneath the surface. Congressional Republicans stood with Bush on a lot of major issues—the Gulf War, judicial appointments—but intraparty grumblings on taxes and social issues, and tensions between the Oval Office and Capitol Hill, were often all too public.

With liberals tearing themselves apart and so-called Reagan Democrats still in ample supply, the Republican Party—or at least its presidential wing—enjoyed a moment of self-congratulatory confidence as the post-Reagan era began. But the conservative movement and its relationship with the Republican Party had already entered a combustible and fractious period. Conservatives' dissatisfaction with the Republican president would soon cause them to institution-shop. In the past, such dissatisfaction—with Dwight Eisenhower's centrism or Richard Nixon's self-destructiveness—redirected conservative energies toward state battles and, of course, the Congress.

Between mid-1990 and late 1991, Republicans began to realize that their twelve-year Reagan-Bush presidential coalition was a shambles. George H. W. Bush's approval ratings had fallen back to earth from their post–Gulf War highs. Politically and electorally, Bush was mortally wounded. The party's internal dynamics were shifting rapidly under his feet, and Lee Atwater—the shepherd he relied on to navigate the treacherous thickets of conservative movement politics—was no longer around to help. Despite demonstrating a far more aggressive use of military force than Ronald Reagan ever had, Bush proved incapable of managing his party's increasingly heterogeneous coalition. And he compounded his policy problems with tactical errors and a major policy blunder on taxes.

What neither Bush nor anyone else could know at the time was that he represented the end of a period of dominance for the GOP's presidential wing. Between 1952 and 1988, the party had lost just three of ten presidential elections. But Bush's one-term presidency saw the beginning of the creative destruction that eventually led the GOP to shift its energies toward its nascent, emboldened congressional wing. The 1992 election would provide powerful confirmation that the Republican Party was poised to reconstitute itself. A new generation of Republicans—especially the younger members of the House caucus—was already applying to congressional politics the same partisan strategies and tactics that Republicans had successfully deployed in presidential politics. As the GOP lost its twelve-year grasp on the White House, congressional Republicans believed that they now controlled the future of the party. And they were right.

3

REINVENTION

The dissolution of bonds between the Republican Party's conservative and moderate wings during George H. W. Bush's first three years in office was followed by a period of rapid reinvention. The time from Bush's final year in the White House through the first two years of Republican rule on Capitol Hill was among the most volatile and formative periods for postwar conservatism and for the party. Having helped turn out a Republican president, conservatives directed their attention to spearheading a GOP renaissance at the sub-presidential level. The party brought the southern strategy to fruition, swinging the region firmly into the GOP column. In 1994 Republicans captured both chambers of Congress for the first time in forty years and elected legions of new statewide and state legislative officials. This was the most important moment in Republican politics since the start of the New Deal. The four-year period from 1992 to 1995 saw a critical swing in the balance of power between the GOP's presidential and congressional wings.

The Reagan-Bush years—the longest continuous span of Republican presidential control since William Howard Taft left the White House in 1913—were about to end, but so too was the six-decade Democratic hegemony on Capitol Hill. Both developments fundamentally changed the political calculus for national Republicans. With the notable exception of their endorsement of the presidential line-item veto while Bill Clinton was in the Oval Office, Republicans began to use partisanship to augment their power over the institutions they controlled. This meant trying to devolve power to state governors and to Congress, and to limit the powers of the White House controlled by a man who, despite conservatives' efforts to stop him, would become the first Democrat since Franklin Roosevelt to be elected president twice. The congressionalization of the national Republican Party, coupled with a heightened focus by conservatives on using legislative power to push back against Great Society initiatives and thwart a Democratic president, altered the party's strategic and tactical options. The Democrats made complementary adjustments as they learned to lead from the Oval Office rather than Capitol Hill.

These changes in national party politics were partially obscured by the decade's tech-based economic boom and by the distractions of the Clinton impeachment. Beneath these diversions, however, the four years beginning in 1992 were an important pivot for the Republicans. Newt Gingrich replaced Reagan and Bush as the face of the national party, a development that created a complex set of problems and opportunities, and taught his colleagues new ways to fight and win. He and his allies built the Capitol Hill majorities that had eluded the party for four decades. And with those successes came not only power but responsibility.

Houston, We Are the Problem

By every account, the 1992 Republican National Convention in Houston was a disaster for President Bush. Almost everything that could go wrong did. All of Bush's political weaknesses were evident. His Gulf War approval bounce, which the year before reached seemingly unassailable levels, had evaporated. Rather than being hailed as a foreign policy victor, he came to Houston with an economic recession around his neck. His party was tearing itself apart, angry at everyone and everything—the Democrats, American popular culture, even its own president. Pundits would later ascribe the dysfunction in Houston to the absence of the late Lee Atwater, but even if the master political consultant had never died of brain cancer in 1991, his miracle-working would not likely have saved Bush. There were no riots or baton-wielding police, but Houston 1992 was the Republicans' Chicago 1968.

The president's problems actually began a week before Republican delegates descended upon Houston. Housing Secretary Jack Kemp, Newt Gingrich, and Republican congressman Vin Weber cowrote a memo urging the president to either reverse himself on taxes or promise a new set of tax cuts. The president had admitted to the media that breaking his no-new-taxes promise was a mistake, and the Democrats' 1992 presidential nominee, young Arkansas governor Bill Clinton, was taking every opportunity to berate Bush for his reversal. "Don't read my lips, read my plan," Clinton chirped incessantly, referring both to Bush's pledge and to the Clinton-Gore campaign's detailed economic program.

House Republicans demanded more than apologies: they wanted a policy reversal. Kemp predicted to the media that Bush would make a "dramatic announcement" during his acceptance speech.[1] Sure enough, Bush gave Kemp and his cohorts exactly what they expected:

Now let me say this: When it comes to taxes, I've learned the hard way. There's an old saying, "Good judgment comes from experience, and experience comes from bad judgment." Two years ago, I made a bad call on the Democrats' tax increase. I underestimated Congress' addiction to taxes. With my back against the wall, I agreed to a hard bargain: One tax increase, one time, in return for the toughest spending limits ever.

Well, it was a mistake to go along with the Democrats' tax increase, and I admit it.

Bush faced few good choices. Had he not renounced his tax reversal, there might have been a mutiny. But renouncing made him look weak and apologetic. He came across as just another politician who made promises he didn't keep.

The lowest moment of the convention was Pat Buchanan's speech. Although Buchanan never expected to win the nomination and never really threatened Bush's renomination, the Bush campaign was forced to accommodate him with time on national television. The president's advisers could only hope Buchanan's address wasn't as bad as they feared.

It was spectacularly worse. Buchanan railed against "radical feminism," abortion, "discrimination against religious schools," and homosexuality. His thinly veiled antifeminism helped seal Bush's fate among women, who voted majority Democratic that November and have done so in every presidential election since. "Elect me, and you will get two for the price of one, Mr. Clinton says of his lawyer-spouse. And what does Hillary believe? Well, Hillary believes that 12-year-olds should have a right to sue their parents, and Hillary has compared marriage and the family as institutions to slavery and life on an Indian reservation."[2] Despite superficial praise for Bush and sharp attacks on the Clinton-Gore ticket's "masquerade" convention in New York the previous month, Buchanan managed to immolate himself politically and incinerate the Bush campaign in the process.

For the Bush campaign, giving over the platform and microphone to agitated conservatives was an ideological deal with the devil brokered in a last-ditch effort to save Bush's presidency. There were, of course, the lingering suspicions about his conservative convictions. Reagan's long shadow and the imprimatur his legacy bestowed on his vice president initially allayed these doubts. Also, Michael Dukakis had run a weak campaign in 1988, being repeatedly outmaneuvered by Bush's more savvy team. If not for Dukakis's fecklessness, the fraying of Reagan's winning coalition might have been more evident then. By 1992, however, the reckoning was overdue.

Paleoconservatives viewed these intraparty tensions differently. To them, the new conservative vanguard was a virus without an antidote. "The [convention] was even more off-putting than the San Francisco Democratic convention of 1984—the one that celebrated liberal pressure groups and led to the Reagan landslide," remarked *New York Times* columnist Bill Safire, another former Nixon speechwriter. "Instead of asserting a congenial diversity, we touted a lock-step unity, during which the party displayed the basest of its base."[3] The notion that the Republicans were the party that caved to the pressure of its base—that the GOP had been captured by its identity groups—was a reversal of partisan fortunes. Just when the

Democrats under Clinton and the nascent, centrist Democratic Leadership Council had begun to rein in the very identity groups—feminists, minorities, homosexuals, union members, the poor, the handicapped—that Republicans had for years hung around Democratic necks, the GOP was suddenly paralyzed by its own identity group problems.

These groups did not suddenly emerge in the four years after Reagan left office. But they had either become more demanding or Bush was less capable than Reagan of satisfying their demands—most likely, both were true. Amid this political unrest, Bush's promise to propose across-the-board tax cuts simply didn't cut it. Many conservatives no longer believed Bush's promises. Whether liberals or moderates believed him was almost beside the point: many voters had come to see tax cuts as an insufficient answer to the nation's economic recession.

The president was taking fire from both sides. Buchanan had managed to mobilize the left's sundry liberal identity groups behind Clinton, yet Bush could not countermobilize the conservative identity groups upon whom Republicans relied. By summer's end his situation looked grim. Only one in four voters thought he had a plan to save the country from what turned out to be a rather shallow recession. But his ideas didn't really matter, because only one in seven voters viewed him as capable of delivering the type of change that 95 percent of Americans believed was necessary. The president already trailed Clinton among women; now he trailed among men as well.[4] He had clawed back a little bit from the huge margins Clinton built nationally during the Democrats' midsummer convention in Madison Square Garden. But Bush's convention polling bump was more molehill than mountain, and his small gains quickly evaporated. A week after the convention, his approval numbers were right where they had been a month earlier.

If the Bush campaign was not sufficiently battered by the convention's metaphorical storms, it was soon hit with a real one. Hurricane Andrew reached the coast of southern Florida on Monday, August 24, four days after Bush's acceptance speech. Florida wasn't yet a swing state; Bush had won it by twenty-two points in 1988. But the administration's slow response to the natural disaster couldn't have come at a worse moment for a president trying to reverse his image as a hesitant and diffident leader. He eventually held on to win Florida, but his huge victory over Dukakis four years earlier shrank to a piddling two points over Bill Clinton. Results in the other swing states were less kind to Bush. His presidency was finished.

A Republican House Divided, Part One

Although 1994 is rightly remembered as the signature year for a new generation of Republicans on Capitol Hill, the 1992 election was a crucial antecedent. Two important intraparty fights took place that year, one before the November general election and one after. Both foreshadowed the 1994 revolution, and both involved fights *among* House Republicans. The first was a primary battle deep in the center of the Republican heartland.

Oklahoma's Mickey Edwards was the kind of politician with whom Americans across the ideological spectrum could readily identify. A centrist who resisted the political tug of the young Republican upstarts elected in the late 1970s and 1980s, by 1992 Edwards was in his seventh term and had risen to the fourth-highest position in the Republican House minority. As one of the most powerful politicians on Capitol Hill, he was presumably one of the most electorally safe members of Congress. His fall was a signature moment in the clash between old guard Republicans and the ascendant new wave.

Edwards's sense of comfort contributed to his demise. The revelation that he was one of the worst offenders in the House banking scandal was particularly devastating. In a little more than three years, Edwards wrote 386 overdraft checks totaling $54,000. The grumbling in his heavily Republican district was not limited to Democrats. Several local Republicans called for Edwards to resign or at least retire at the end of his term. State and national party officials rushed to support him. The Oklahoma state party chair publicly announced his support for Edwards, and the National Republican Campaign Committee—led by executive director Tom Cole, who would later win the state's adjacent House seat and eventually chair the NRCC—pledged financial support. Edwards apologized and said he was "embarrassed and should be embarrassed" by his behavior.[5] But neither these apologies nor efforts by party insiders to solidify his position quieted his detractors.

Five challengers filed to run against Edwards in the 1992 Republican primary, including Ernest "James" Istook, who attacked him on procedural and ethical grounds. Istook hammered Edwards about the House banking scandal and also for abusing the congressional franking privilege, which allows members to send promotional mailings to constituents at taxpayers' expense. A key moment in the primary came during a televised exchange between the two men on the issue of pork-barrel projects. "It's not pork if you're bringing jobs that will be created anyway and you have them in Oklahoma rather than West Virginia," said Edwards. To which Istook, without missing a beat, replied, "A pig is a pig no matter whose pigpen it happens to be in."[6] In a political shock felt across Washington, Edwards finished third in the Republican primary. Istook finished second, won the runoff to capture the nomination, and that November won Edwards's seat to take his place alongside the young revolutionaries ready to change Washington politics by changing the politics within their own ranks. On primary night a weepy Edwards spoke about the end of his quarter century in Republican politics. "It's been good, and it's been great," he said.[7]

Newt Gingrich tried to claim that Democrats had somehow set Edwards up, but it was hard for him to rush to the defense of Republicans implicated in the House banking and post office scandals when he had led the charge earlier in the year to force the House leadership to release the names of the members who had abused their House banking privileges. Gingrich calculated that by virtue of their greater numbers and majority-party responsibility for overseeing how the House was run, Democrats would suffer disproportionately from the scandal's fallout. The 1992 elections proved him right. Republicans like Edwards became necessary collateral damage—especially in his case, since the GOP held his seat anyway. "Unlike the nonconfrontational Republicans who have led the minority party in the House," the *New York Times* reported, "Mr. Gingrich says the best way to save Congress is to destroy its reputation by any means necessary. That is what the bank scandal is mostly about for Mr. Gingrich, and why his is seemingly unconcerned that Republicans will be embarrassed by the disclosure that they, too, overdrew their accounts."[8]

This new generation of congressional Republicans was clearly banking on the idea that to defeat the Democrats they had to utilize procedural methods and raise ethical complaints rather than offer policy critiques. This was a smart strategy, partly because so many of the programs that Democrats had enacted during the New Deal and expanded during the Great Society polled rather well. In purely fiscal terms, spending on the unpopular items—pork-barrel projects, bounced checks from overdrawn accounts during the House banking scandal—was a pittance compared to entitlement programs. The task was to make political mountains out of pork-barreling molehills.

Everyone got in on the act—even former President Reagan, who never served a day in Congress. In the middle of his otherwise optimism-laden speech at the Houston convention, Reagan waded momentarily into Capitol Hill politics:

> A lot of liberal Democrats are saying it's time for a change and they're right. The only trouble is they're pointing to the wrong end of Pennsylvania Avenue. What we should change is a Democratic Congress that wastes precious time on partisan matters of absolutely no relevance to the needs of the average American. So to all the entrenched interests along the Potomac—the gavel-wielding chairman, the bloated staff, the taxers and takers and congressional rule makers—we have a simple slogan for November 1992: Clean House!
>
> For you see, my fellow Republicans, we are the change. For 50 of the last 60 years the Democrats have controlled the Senate. And they've had the House of Representatives for 56 of the last 60 years. It's time to clean house. Clean out the privileges and perks. Clean out the arrogance and the big egos. Clean out the scandals, the corner-cutting, and the foot-dragging. What kind of job do you think they've done during all those years they've been running the Congress?

Policy was almost totally absent from Reagan's complaint. His critique wasn't about what congressional Democrats had passed or blocked, his party's policy triumphs or the opposition's failures. His indictment focused on procedural norms, bloated staffs, and "privileges and perks." This was Reagan's last convention speech in a long string that dated back to the thundering call to arms he issued at the San Francisco Cow Palace in 1964. That the Great Communicator took time to digress from his valedictory address to dip his toe, however briefly, into the cesspool of congressional politics was a clear signal that congressional Republicans believed they had a real chance to finally dethrone the Democrats.

A few nights later, Bush likewise did something very unusual in a presidential nomination acceptance speech. He too paused to talk about the upcoming congressional races, voters' frustrations with many incumbent legislators, and the arrival in Washington in January of what was expected to be a huge class of newcomers. "But Americans want to know," Bush asked, "where's proof that we will have better days in the Washington? I'll give you 150 reasons. That's how many members of Congress are expected to leave Washington this year. Some are tainted by scandal; the voters have bounced them the way they bounced their own checks." The president then promised to meet with every one of the newcomers "before they get attacked by the PAC's, overwhelmed by their staffs, and cornered by some camera crew."

A procedural, anti-institutional pitch is not the sexiest electoral argument. But in 1992 it proved to be a salient and potent message. Unfortunately for Bush, such appeals did him little good. But they did work for the House Republicans, who had a surprisingly strong cycle despite losing at the top of the ballot.

To almost nobody's surprise, Gingrich was reelected as Bob Michel's top deputy in the House minority leadership. Unlike his deposed colleague Mickey Edwards, Gingrich intuitively understood the new political realities on Capitol Hill and, specifically, how to capitalize on public animosities. The C-SPAN camera episode on the House floor, continual agitation about the House check-kiting scandal, and the aggressive attacks on the Democratic leadership were all part of his grand design to gain control by fomenting citizen anger and then channeling that anger at the Democrats. Believing Republicans could capture Congress only by first tearing it down, Gingrich and his cohorts ratcheted up public fury about how politicians behaved in office and toward Congress itself.

As for the fallout from the Edwards-Istook battle, when minority leader Michel announced he would retire after nineteen terms in the House, Istook promised major changes at the top of the GOP hierarchy: "The new leadership will be both sharp and blunt, which is what the public is looking for. You are going to see lines of distinction more clearly drawn between us and the Democrats in Congress."[9] Perhaps still embittered by his loss, Edwards later warned that the new Speaker's rhetoric and methods would ultimately fail. "Sometimes, I think his strategies are counterproductive," said Edwards in 1994, just months before Gingrich and the GOP captured Congress. "It has managed to destroy public confidence in government institutions. It has been detrimental and it hasn't meant more Republicans getting elected."[10] The political realities on Capitol Hill were changing too quickly for the Oklahoman, who had come of political age during a congressional era that suddenly seemed like a distant relic.

Although Edwards's parting shots would later be validated during the Gingrich-led 1995 government shutdown, during the 1990, 1992, and 1994 elections Gingrich proved that individual candidates and even an entire party could win by using guerrilla-style tactics to undermine public support for government. He debunked the Beltway conventional wisdom that voters will assign a party the responsibility of majority power only if it acts responsibly while in opposition.

Whether Edwards was correct about the change in tenor and targets, or was merely lashing out, he could not have been more wrong about the effectiveness of the House Republicans' tactical posture in 1992. Two decades earlier, political scientist Richard Fenno wrote about the common rhetorical strategy adopted by many of the members of Congress who had given him exclusive access to follow them on their campaigns. Challengers and even incumbents could successfully run "for Congress by running against Congress," converting constituent anger against specific members of Congress or the institution generally into wins in their districts. Under Gingrich the GOP would nationalize these animosities. He recognized that in order to create a new Republican majority in his image he first had to destroy the very institution he aspired to rule.[11]

Reflections and Recriminations

On the final day of the 1992 campaign, in a last-ditch attempt to save his presidency, Bush made appearances in six swing states. At one point between stops, the president and his closest family members, including his eldest son, crowded into Air Force One's presidential cabin along with the Oak Ridge Boys to join in signing the gospel standard "Amazing Grace." During a campaign rally later that day at Louisville's Standiford Field, the beleaguered president emotionally recounted those moments. "I wish you could have heard these guys singing those beautiful gospel songs. It made us—not a dry eye in the house," said Bush with his famously garbled syntax.[12]

Last-minute appeals for heavenly dispensation were not enough. The next day, the Democratic ticket of Bill Clinton and Al Gore won 43 percent of the national popular vote, carried thirty-three states, and amassed 370 electoral votes. Independent candidate Ross Perot drew 19 percent nationally and, perhaps most embarrassing for Bush, finished ahead of the incumbent president in Bush's summertime home state of Maine. On his path to the White House, this son of a U.S. senator, Yale baseball star, and World War II hero fighter pilot had steadily climbed the Washington political ladder, from Congress to the Republican National Committee chairmanship, from head of the Central Intelligence Agency to ambassador to China. But on Election Night 1992, Bush suffered the indignity of becoming just the ninth president to be turned out of office by the American electorate. His political career was at a sudden, painful end. "It's been good and strong, and I think we've really contributed something to the country," he said upon returning to Houston the day after the election. "And maybe history will record it that way."[13]

The political autopsies quickly poured forth. Many analysts blamed the defeat on a short but not insignificant recession that, although abating by autumn 1992, had not yet reversed sufficiently to allow Bush a late-stage comeback. Others said he underestimated Clinton's unique talents and state-of-the-art campaign, a mistake compounded by the loss of Republican political guru Lee Atwater, who in 1991 died tragically at age forty from cancer—just three years after masterminding Bush's dramatic but controversial 1988 comeback against Dukakis. Conservatives said Bush's apostasy on taxes and other issues left him without a base of support. Columnist Charles Krauthammer offered a charitable and not entirely unreasonable view: George H. W. Bush was a victim of his own successes. "Bush's was not a failed presidency, but a completed one," he wrote in the days following Bush's defeat. "History called upon him to do two things: to close out the Cold War and thwart the ambitions of a reckless tyrant in the Persian Gulf. . . . Bush was born—and trained—for these two jobs. But only these two. By the end of four years, there was nothing left for him to do."[14] Most conservatives, however, tended to view Bush as a weak-tea version of Ronald Reagan, his presidency a continuation of Reagan's mistakes without his predecessor's resplendent triumphs. To devout Reagan Republicans, the explanation for Bush's loss was quite simple. "The country elected Bush to continue Reaganism," said GOP House member Vin Weber of Minnesota. "He lost because so many people around him felt they had to discredit Reagan's policies."[15] The disintegration of the GOP's Reagan-built presidential coalition was evident in the 1992 election results. In fact, Reagan's selection of Bush as his running mate in 1980 and his support of Bush's presidential candidacy eight years later helped put Bush in a position to destroy the very coalition Reagan assembled.

There were legitimate reasons for Bush to conduct himself differently from his predecessor. Having come from the Rockefeller wing of the party, he was genuinely less conservative than Reagan. Republicans surely recognized that the two politicians represented different traditions within the party. And every new president—especially the first incumbent vice president to win the office in more than a century and a half—needs to put his personal stamp on the office. To mimic Reagan in every detail would have undermined Bush's presidential authority.

That said, it is unfair to blame Bush for all the intraparty problems that emerged on his watch. The political climate had already begun to change while Reagan was in office, and the storms of conservative change were destined to gather no matter who was president. The challenges issued from the isolationist Buchanan wing; the nascent conservative legal movement embodied by the Federalist Society; the resurgence of Pat Robertson and a newly politicized evangelism; the disaffected grassroots conservatives increasingly tuning in to vocal radio hosts like Rush Limbaugh—any or all of these groups might have been slowed or tempered by a third Reagan term, were he permitted (and mentally able) to serve. Reagan's 1984 reelection and Michael Dukakis's bungled 1988 campaign kept a coalition together that began to fight more openly after Reagan was gone.

For movement conservatives who had come of age during the twelve-year Republican White House reign, Bush's coda to the Reagan presidency was unacceptable on many levels. Their ideological objections to Bush were partly personal: he was a Republican literally born to a family, an era, a region, and a partisan tradition distinctly different from the Goldwater-Reagan model. It was in many ways the tradition the Goldwater-Reagan model was created to fight. Other Republicans with eastern or mainline Protestant backgrounds had converted to the new strain of modern conservatism, but Bush either did not see the light or didn't want to. "Bush never understood the coalition," said Americans for Tax Reform founder Grover Norquist, with palpable disdain. "And he never respected it, either."[16]

In the wake of his father's electoral defeat, George W. Bush was also idle. This was not a new experience for him. W's adult life contained nearly as many personal failures as his father's had successes. After serial stumbles in the oil business and a star-crossed bid for a U.S. House seat, the younger Bush seemed to find his niche as president of baseball's Texas Rangers. His father tapped him to be one of seven top campaign advisers for the 1992 election, serving as an enforcer and watchdog—a role he took very seriously. The president's eldest son was learning the family business. But by the early 1990s, the political star of his younger brother Jeb seemed to be burning more brightly.

While W was also stung by "Poppy's" loss, he did not ascribe the defeat to biased media or the economic recession. He pointed to a more convenient target: Buchanan and other fringe elements within the Republican Party. The son was furious that reactionaries had mounted an intraparty primary challenge that sapped valuable resources from his father, delegitimized the president among the GOP's base voters, and weakened him against Perot and Clinton in the general election. "George W. became the keenest student of [his father's] defeat," writes Jacob Weisberg in *The Bush Tragedy*. "He saw that his father had been undermined from both sides: failing to bond with evangelicals, while being seen as pandering to them."[17] The younger Bush would never forgive these factions for what they did to his father, and he would not forget. He would soon embark on his own political career, partly to vindicate his father and partly to distinguish himself from him.

A Republican House Divided, Part Two

The 1992 elections were not a complete disaster for the GOP. Republicans lost the White House and one net Senate seat, but they gained ten seats in the House. This split result only validated the strategic choices made by Gingrich's nascent cadre of congressional insurgents. If their messaging and tactics worked during an otherwise bad Republican cycle, it was easier to side with rebels like Vin Weber over tired old voices like Mickey Edwards.

With Newt Gingrich number two behind Michel, the second key fight for the GOP's congressional future was between Gingrich ally Dick Armey and Jerry Lewis to be chair of the House Republican Conference. If the Istook-Edwards episode was a key fight among Republicans for the right to seek a House seat, the Armey-Lewis fight in December 1992 was an equally important postelection struggle for power within the House Republican leadership—and in the long term, for the future of congressional Republicans. On the undercard was another generational battle with significant long-term implications: pit bull Tom DeLay of Texas versus Ohioan Bill Gradison for the job of conference secretary.

The Armey-Lewis fight was a perfect proxy for the GOP's internal conflicts. Lewis, the incumbent, was a seven-term veteran and Republican Main Street Partnership moderate from California, a state that not only birthed the political careers of Richard Nixon and Ronald Reagan but once formed the electoral backbone of national Republican politics. In 1990 Lewis told House Republicans they needed to stand behind President Bush's call for a tax increase. Armey, the firebrand representative from the Dallas suburbs, had served four terms and was still rising up the Republican ladder. Winning a leadership position would be another big step. He had already made a name for himself with his public opposition to the Bush tax deal that Lewis supported. The Texan's chief reason to believe he could beat Lewis was that he already had: despite Lewis's objections, the House Republican Conference had sided with Armey in 1990, voting 62–32 to oppose Bush's tax plan.

Although House leadership votes are conducted by secret ballot, the results were immediately leaked to the press: Armey won narrowly, 88–84. Istook explained the result by saying Republicans felt they needed "an aggressive tack to highlight the differences between Republicans and Democrats on taxes, spending and overregulation." Ed Gillespie estimates that Armey's eighty-eight-vote total included at least thirty and probably closer to thirty-five of the forty-seven Republican rookies elected the month before. If true, it is no surprise that Armey's winning coalition skewed not only younger but more southern. "I see confrontation as a tool," Armey chirped after his victory.[18] He would use that tool often.

Ratifying the changes under way, DeLay also beat Gradison. DeLay was a bit of a loose cannon, and Gingrich and Armey were suspicious of him. Three years earlier, DeLay had run the failed campaign of Representative Edward Madigan of Illinois against Gingrich for the minority whip post. DeLay was odd man out among the three southerners serving alongside Bob Michel. (The trio's rise also signaled the growing power of the GOP's southern delegations in Congress.) But even if DeLay did not form an ironclad troika with Gingrich and Armey, his victory over Gradison provided yet another win for the young Republicans over the old guard. Michel, the totemic figure of the old guard, came under intense pressure from within his caucus to get with the new program or get out of the way. That pressure, once restricted to bomb throwing from a few backbenchers, now came from those sitting next to him at the leadership table—and who wanted him gone. Michel's days as minority leader were numbered.

Even though his star and those of many of his confederates were rising, Gingrich was demure in the immediate aftermath of the 1992 election. Perhaps he felt chastened by his own electoral scare that year: a 980-vote recount victory in the Republican primary over a former state legislator whom Gingrich outspent nearly ten to one. His behind-the-scenes activities heading the Conservative Opportunity Society and GOPAC notwithstanding, Gingrich signaled a willingness to cooperate with the new Democratic president. "My impression is there will be a serious effort to reach out" to the White House, Gingrich told *USA Today* a few weeks after the election. "The country wants a period of working together and my advice to freshmen is: 'We are here as Americans. Being a Republican is subordinate.'"[19] Whether Gingrich really meant this at the time only he will ever know. His actions in the next few years would contrast starkly with his magnanimous bipartisanship in the afterglow of the elections.

Even for two-term presidents leaving office under force of the Twenty-Second Amendment, the annual White House Christmas party can be wistfully nostalgic. For President Bush, the holiday party four weeks before he yielded the Oval Office to Bill Clinton was a chance for his critics to gloat. Fresh off his intracaucus victory over Jerry Lewis to become the third-ranking member of the House Republicans' minority leadership, Dick Armey was in attendance that night, as was his nemesis, Dick Darman. Since the 1991 tax cut deal, the OMB director had endured repeated attacks from Armey and other conservatives. Now Armey found himself moving up in Republican circles at the very moment Darman and other Bush advisers were packing up their offices. Perhaps slightly intoxicated from holiday cheer and heady vindication, Armey sidled up to Darman at the party and spiked his punch. "Bill Clinton and I finally have something in common," said Armey. "We both owe our jobs to you."[20]

Rookies Rule (or Maybe They Don't)

To understand why those two intraparty fights mattered so much to the future of the Republican House, it is important to pause momentarily to recognize how tectonic the 1992 shift was for the Republicans—even in a year when they failed to flip either chamber of Congress. With so much attention paid to the Democrats' winning the White House after three landslide losses, not to mention a presidential election featuring the strongest showing by a third-party candidate since 1912, the congressional results were overlooked. But this huge class of newcomers would set the political tone on Capitol Hill for the next two decades.

The two parties elected a combined 110 House freshmen in 1992, including 63 Democrats—the party's highest figure in nine cycles. The high number of freshmen was, of course, partly because the 1992 election immediately followed reapportionment and redistricting. That process continued a late-century pattern of reapportioning House districts from aging Rust Belt states to growing

Sun Belt states. These demographic shifts put old incumbents at risk and created new, open seats that elected legislative rookies by default. The 1992 results also confirmed the wisdom of the GOP's decision to broker the deal with the Congressional Black Caucus to draw an unprecedented number of new majority-minority districts that packed Democratic voters into fewer districts, improving Republican competitiveness elsewhere.

Nevertheless, not since the 118-member freshman class of 1948 had the two parties combined to elect so many rookies. For Republicans to have netted House seats against the tide of a victorious first-term president of the opposing party was no small feat. The fifty-two-member Republican House freshman class of 1980, which benefited from Ronald Reagan's coattails, was bigger than the 1992 class of newcomers, and 1992's cohort would be bested two years later in the 1994 Republican midterm landslide. But not since the fateful 1966 election—the cycle immediately following Barry Goldwater's pathbreaking presidential bid, when fifty-nine new Republicans won—had a GOP House freshman class as large as that of 1992 been elected without the aid of a victorious Republican president's coattails.[21] And with just 176 total Republicans in the incoming 103rd Congress, the 47-member rookie Republican class constituted more than *one-fourth* of the party's House seats. They arrived in Washington determined to shake things up.

Republican calls for congressional reform during the campaign, as noted earlier, were motivated to some degree by pure partisanship. The reasonable expectation was that if the public and the media turned against Congress, the Democrats as the majority party would suffer disproportionately. In the summer of 1992, two junior House Republican incumbents—thirty-two-year-old freshman Jim Nussle of Iowa and thirty-nine-year-old sophomore Christopher Cox from California's Orange County—each delivered one half of a two-part lecture hosted by the Heritage Foundation on the topic "Why Congress Doesn't Work."[22] The lectures provide a useful window into the thinking of the new generation of congressional Republicans.

Cox gave the first, more diagnostic lecture. He complained about the explosion in congressional staff. He decried the passage of giant appropriations bills at the eleventh hour, often with few if any members bothering to read the bills' particulars. "Whether or not this President is going to go toe to toe with the Congress," Cox concluded, "the American people are ready. They have had it. Ross Perot did not materialize out of nowhere." Nussle followed with a series of prescriptions for reform, including term limits, ending the franking privilege, reforming the budget process, and creating a merit pay system that benchmarked members' pay to their ability to pass balanced budgets. Two weeks earlier, in a meeting with White House chief of staff John Sununu and counsel C. Boyden Gray, Nussle had suggested that the president consider vetoing the annual legislative appropriations bill to send a signal to Congress that Republicans were serious about fiscal issues.

Although Cox and Nussle did not spare congressional Republicans, their companion lectures were more critical of Democrats, if only because so many of the problems they identified were by-products of the Democrats' long, hegemonic rule over both chambers. If these Republican critiques sound like nakedly partisan politics, keep in mind that political scientists by this time had also noted Congress's steady transformation into a sclerotic, self-preserving institution whose members deployed various tools to maintain power, including the franking system, the strategic use of incumbent- and party-protection gerrymandering, and the proliferation of casework and pork barreling to appease constituents. Rising reelection rates were proof that the high turnover levels witnessed in the first two decades after World War II had given way to a "permanent Congress."[23] In the second half of the twentieth century, members of Congress had become masters of incumbent protection, which also meant the perpetuation of Democratic majorities. Even if Republicans had self-interested reasons to depict Congress as a failed institution, their criticisms were hardly without merit.

Now that they had won office, the Republican rookies immediately called for structural reform. They demanded that Democrats and Republicans alike honor many of the promises they had made to voters during the election, including a balanced-budget amendment, twelve-year term limits for members of Congress, and a presidential line-item veto. "I firmly believe, to get substantive issues through [Congress], you have to concentrate on reforming the process first," said Ohio freshman Republican Deborah Pryce. "We want to start at square one."[24] But as a minority party with little power to set public policy, the smarter play for Republicans was to focus on structural and procedural reforms—and to harry the Democrats at every available opportunity.

Meanwhile, the Democrats, enjoying unified control of the federal government for the first time in twelve years and foreseeing no end to their majorities, were more interested in enacting progressive policy changes. The balanced-budget amendment, term limits, the line-item veto, and budget performance–based merit pay were quickly relegated to fantasy status. So Republican freshmen scaled back their agenda to the set of rules over which they *did* have control: Republican caucus protocols and minority leadership positions. Once again, however, the new arrivals quickly ran headlong into institutional resistance. The editorial board of the *Washington Times* wrote:

When the 47 freshmen Republican members arrived in town and met in conference to elect their leadership in December, more than a few of them were surprised that no one was challenging Robert Michel of Illinois as minority leader. Mr. Michel was House point man in President Bush's efforts to reach an accommodation with Democrats in Congress. Some veterans of the House suggested publicly, and many suggested privately, that this was more than merely a tactic of Mr. Michel's—that he was accommodationist to the bone in the go-along-to-get-along style of Republicans whose fondest wish is to lick the spatula once the majority party is done making the batter for its cake.[25]

If the rookies couldn't unseat Michel and install their own minority leader (presumably Gingrich), they weren't about to settle for a Michel-style "accommodationist" elsewhere among the legislative leadership. They would continue to agitate for reform.

The 1992 class also featured record numbers of female and non-white members—the latter, again, having benefited substantially from the 1990 majority-minority gerrymanders. Congressional challengers ran as fresh-faced mavericks, and many benefited directly from the damage caused to incumbents by the House banking scandal. But these new rebels were not exactly apolitical novices or outsider yahoos. Three-quarters of the 110 House newbies and all but 2 of the 11 new senators had political backgrounds, and almost half of the new House members had served in their state legislatures. (As I will discuss later, the tea party newcomers who won their seats in 2010 included far more political amateurs.) "These folks ran campaigns against Washington, corruption, insiderism and perks precisely because as politicians they understood the feelings of their electorates," noted the *Washington Post* in an op-ed published on the eve of Clinton's inauguration. "But for the same reason, they also ran on the sensibly basic issues the electorate was most worried about, notably the economy and health care. That's also why you've been hearing less talk from them since the election about symbols and more about 'ending gridlock' and getting things done."[26]

To signal their seriousness and bipartisan solidarity, 110 freshmen from both parties initially planned to do something that seems almost inconceivable today: meet in Omaha, Nebraska, for a preinaugural retreat to discuss ways to work across the aisle to reform the House. They called for the formation of a temporary bipartisan panel—later known as the Hamilton-Gradison Commission—that would be tasked with issuing recommendations for reforms to congressional procedure. But at the last minute the Democratic freshmen suddenly backed out of the Omaha summit. When the Republicans heard the news, most of them also canceled their plans. In the end, just fourteen rookie Republicans showed up. The 1994 election, the seating of the Republican-controlled 104th Congress, and the government shutdown of 1995 are typically cited as the seminal events that led to America's current era of polarized, partisan politics. But the inability of newly elected and uncompromised politicians to meet to achieve a bipartisan consensus about how to move the country forward, or at least improve the operations of Congress, was a powerful signal that the Clinton era would be no less contentious than the Reagan-Bush years—and might even be more divisive.

Jim Istook, the revolutionary within the revolution who beat Mickey Edwards in that titanic Oklahoma House Republican primary, was one of the fourteen Republicans who dutifully trudged to Omaha. If any member of the 1992 freshman class typified the new face of partisan and political reform, it was Istook. There he was in Omaha, weeks before he would be sworn in or cast his first vote. Yet the idealistic Istook already seemed deflated. "I believe most—if not all—of us campaigned against Congress. It was us against them," he said. "Now, we find we're about to be one of them."[27]

Getting Healthy on Hillarycare

The president's critics on both sides of the aisle were troubled by his decision to let his wife manage the administration's sweeping health care reform. Although she would receive significant assistance from Ira Magaziner and other presidential aides, Hillary Clinton served as the political face of the effort. She held countless meetings as chair of the Task Force on National Health Care Reform, eventually doing what only two First Ladies had done before her: testify before congressional committees on Capitol Hill, three in the House and two in the Senate. At stake were her reputation and her husband's top domestic priority.

Bill Clinton had campaigned vigorously on the issue, staking his election and national brand on a promise to deliver a reform that had eluded many presidents before him. With Hillary Clinton assigned to devise the administration's plan and shepherd it through Congress, health care reform promised to be a political war of the first order. Whether it was impolite, ungentlemanly, or even sexist to capitalize politically on the fact that a controversial First Lady was leading the task force, the Republican opposition and its allies in the insurance industry could not be blamed for the operational and political missteps made repeatedly by Clinton and the White House. The health care fight was also a key early test of the GOP's not-going-along strategy; it set an important precedent for the party's congressional behavior for years to come. If the Democrats were going to tee up political opportunities, congressional Republicans had to prove they could knock them out of the park.

Gingrich had long been anticipating and even itching for a major policy fight. In *The System*, their definitive book about the Clinton health care episode, *Washington Post* reporters Haynes Johnson and David Broder report that Gingrich anticipated the issue's arrival well before Clinton even declared his candidacy:

In Spring of 1991, more than a year before the Democrats nominated Clinton, Gingrich was discussing long-term political strategy with a friend as they strolled around the Washington monument at about six o'clock one morning. In a moment that he recalled vividly, Gingrich seized by the conviction that the "next great offensive of the Left," as he put it, would be "socializing health care," because the Left, as he put it, was "gradually losing power on all other fronts, and they [had] to have an increase in the resources they controlled. We had to position ourselves in the fight before they got there or they might win."[28]

Gingrich's political calculations made perfect sense given the political conditions: the Democrats really *did* look like a doomed and directionless party. In 1991 conservative Republicans on Capitol Hill still adhered to the canonical belief that government growth necessarily favored the Democrats, and partisan resistance for resistance's sake really did offer the promise of electoral and political rewards for the GOP. By the end of the decade, these conditions would change. But in the early 1990s, Gingrich was wise to put his trust in them. Two years later, when a Democrat entered the Oval Office, it was time to attack.

To Gingrich, stopping Clinton's health care reform meant refusing to cooperate. Any Republican compromise, he knew, would reward the White House uniformly, leaving scraps of praise at best for minority Republicans. Although conservative political adviser Bill Kristol is often credited with stressing the importance of depriving Clinton of a health care reform victory, as a practical matter blocking the reform fell to congressional Republicans, not conservative strategists. Nor did Gingrich really need instruction from Kristol: he understood the asymmetrical realities of the new, highly polarized partisan era he was helping to create. The new rules on Capitol Hill dictated that a minority party that goes along with a policy decision is unlikely to receive any credit when it succeeds; but if the policies eventually go wrong or become unpopular, the minority will share the blame. The winning strategy for the minority party in the post-Reagan era was simple: do not cooperate, do not compromise, do not seek bipartisan solutions—ever, on anything. Years later, Democratic presidential aspirants John Kerry and Hillary Clinton would pay the price for ignoring this lesson when they cast their votes for the Iraq War resolution in October 2002; congressional Republicans led by John Boehner in 2009 and 2010 benefited significantly from remembering this lesson by resisting every bipartisan overture made by Barack Obama and congressional Democrats on the stimulus, health care reform, cap-and-trade, the debt ceiling crisis, the so-called supercommittee negotiations, and other matters.

A final point: lest one think one think that Gingrich and his cabal of revolutionaries-in-waiting had no actual power in 1993 and early 1994 to thwart Clinton on health care, that is true only in the strictest sense. Even without sufficient Republican votes to block "Hillarycare" in the House, Gingrich and his allies sounded rhetorical alarms about the bill's costs, risks, size, and threats to Americans' freedom of choice. Moreover, they had vital votes in the Senate, where the Republicans, though also in the minority, still had tough and strategically placed senators who acted as legislative bulwarks. "There would be no compromise—at beginning or end—with Gingrich and his forces. And he was not alone," write Johnson and Broder. Because former Gingrich House colleagues, including Trent Lott, Texas's Phil Gramm, and Indiana's Dan Coats, "shared his determination to sink the Clinton plan and replace the Democrats in power," their resistance "would erode the support" that Rhode Island's liberal

Republican John Chafee had been building for a bipartisan health care compromise that could pass the Senate.[29]

Gingrichites were not running the Senate—at least not yet. But in 1993 and 1994 they were sufficient in strength in the Senate to run Clinton's plan aground, which is exactly what Gingrich needed in order to position himself to seize the speakership. Oppose, block, obfuscate, delay, criticize, and stall: these were the tactical exigencies of the post–Bob Michel generation of congressional Republicans. Michel was technically still in charge in the House, but not for long.

Don't Be Like Michel

By the autumn of 1993, Bob Michel had seen enough. He had served thirty-seven years in the House, the final seven as minority leader. An infantryman in World War II, Michel was wounded in battle and had won two Bronze Stars and the Purple Heart. After he returned from the war, he got a degree from Peoria's Bradley University, went to work for local congressman Harold Velde, and then won the seat when Velde vacated it. Thirty-seven years later, saying he was sick of members "trashing" the House, on October 3, 1993, the seventy-year-old Michel tearfully announced he would retire from Congress. At a time when many conservative Republicans still nursed grudges toward former president Bush, Michel provided a telling explanation for why it was time to go. "Had George Bush won reelection, I would have felt obliged to see his Administration through," he said.

Michel's announcement generated a flood of speculation. House Republicans would now almost certainly be led by Newt Gingrich, but the political maneuvering for other leadership roles began right away. "The music starts now and in the next few weeks we'll see

Gingrich, [Henry] Hyde, Armey and others circling the chairs," quipped one House Republican aide.[30] Most political commentators praised Gingrich's vision and verve, and conservatives who had grown weary of Michel's accommodating approach relished the prospect of an aggressive new generation of Republicans. "For Clinton, it's going to mean more aggressive opposition, certainly after 1994, and probably now," Heritage Foundation congressional expert David Mason predicted.[31] American Conservative Union president David Keene offered polite tributes to Michel but was buoyed by the prospect of a more assertive generation of Republicans gaining power in the House. "The post-Michel era is the post-Reagan era, and it means the Reagan babies are taking over the Republican Party," chirped Representative Dana Rohrabacher of Orange County, California.[32] To conservatives, the tools necessary to reverse the Democratic majorities had been locked away in a closet by a go-along-to-get-along generation who seemed content to remain a permanent minority. No figure embodied the old guard more than Michel. Now—finally—his career was ending.

The guardians of Beltway virtue bemoaned what they anticipated would be a precipitous decline in bipartisan civility under the Gingrich-led revolutionaries. Gingrich was the man who infamously turned the House cameras on the chamber to reveal hundreds of empty seats, who had embarrassed Tip O'Neill into a public apology, and who took down O'Neill's successor, Jim Wright, over a book deal scandal Gingrich himself would later duplicate. The *Washington Post* editorial page conveyed the prevailing sentiment:

Many in Mr. Gingrich's party think these are just the traits needed to help the Republicans escape their status as a seemingly permanent minority in the House. But Mr. Gingrich— or whoever actually gets the job—could profit from contemplating the virtues of Mr. Michel and some of his like-minded predecessors. The cut-and-thrust of ideas sharply stated and contrasts sharply drawn needs to be tempered by a civility that can even sometimes be of use to those who display it and which makes it possible to get some of the nation's business done in the House.[33]

But Newt Gingrich had his own problems. He would soon discover that some of his fellow Republicans already had their daggers out for him.

Gingrich's replacement of Michel was a tectonic moment in congressional politics. The cooperation between centrist Republicans and Democrats that prevailed for most of the postwar period came to an end. An entire generation of moderate Republicans from the Northeast and Midwest, along with their moderate Democratic counterparts from the southern and western states, had retired, died, or been replaced. According to scholars who track such matters, the share of party-line or near-party-line votes was already rising and would rise further in the next two decades.[34] The comfortable era of spirited disagreement followed by consensus yielded to an era of polarization. More than any other politician within the Washington power elite, Gingrich personified this shift.

The 1992 election and, to a lesser extent, the 1990 cycle had combined to yield a new cohort of Republican agitators who arrived on Capitol Hill primed for revolt. Many of the congressional Republicans elected in those two cycles realized that they had two sequential battles to fight. The second was to be waged outwardly against the entrenched Democratic majorities and the institutional inertia that had kept the Republicans in the minority in both chambers for most of the postwar era. But first, they had to fight an intramural battle against the Republican elders—a war waged by a new generation of assertive, mostly younger Republicans who came of age in the 1960s or later. Robert Michel's was the most prized scalp of that war.

Clinton's inauguration meant that for the first time in a dozen years, the Republicans controlled neither chamber of Congress nor the White House. Powerlessness can be frustrating, but also liberating. A party can experiment with new ideas and give voice and power to new leaders. The minority is free of responsibility and compelled to redouble its efforts to regain power. From the first moments of the Clinton administration, rather than negotiating with the Democratic majority as Michel and his Republican predecessors had done, Newt Gingrich, Dick Armey, and their allies chose to resist. Sometimes their resistance and political firebombing backfired. But more often than not they succeeded in forcing Clinton to address Republican critiques—a distinct departure from the silent treatment Republicans received during the four decades when the GOP minority was stewarded by a more accommodating set of leaders.

Though not as divisive or ugly as the interparty battle, the fight within the party had important consequences for how Republicans would conduct political warfare. Those who gained prominence within the party during this period did so by being resisters rather than innovators, and by learning how to fight with the weapons available to them. As the party in exile, the GOP learned how to generate headlines, cause problems for the Democrats, and create new political opportunities. Sometimes the out-party's tactical approach meant gumming up the legislative works on Capitol Hill or embarrassing the Democratic majority with procedural and public relations gimmicks. Other times it meant setting Republican sights on political opponents of convenience, like target-rich appointee Lani Guinier, or on Hillary and Bill Clinton directly. Other than on NAFTA and other exceptional cases, Gingrich and his House kinsmen consistently chose to resist rather than negotiate. They rejected the political and partisan norms that had governed Congress for decades because they believed there was a political payoff from creating stark contrasts and fighting for the sake of fighting. Their faith in these principles was about to be rewarded in ways most of them had only dreamt about.

Revolution, 1994

For Republicans, the 1994 midterms could not have been sweeter. The GOP picked up a net of fifty-two House and ten Senate seats to capture both chambers of Congress. Tom Foley became the first sitting Speaker to lose an election since the Civil War. Longtime Ways and Means chairman and Chicago machine fixture Dan Rostenkowski, the second most powerful Democrat in the House, lost to a challenger who wasn't even alive when Rostenkowski first won his House seat. The Republicans' forty years in the wilderness were over. Flipping the Senate was almost as sweet a victory, given just six years of Republican rule during those same four decades. There were many winners on that fateful Tuesday, but the night indisputably belonged to one man: Newt Gingrich.

The brilliance of Gingrich's coup was his strategic realization that he could nationalize the House races, complemented by the tactical wisdom he displayed in finding, training, and supporting a slate of candidates who would run as a united front on the same message. The Contract with America provided the policy backbone, and crafting it was an important part of the strategy: it offered an affirmative alternative more compelling than merely saying "We're not the Democrats." It conveyed seriousness—a plan, complete with a checklist, against which voters could later hold the GOP accountable.

Within months of taking office, the Republicans would deliver on nine of the contract's ten provisions. (Only term limits failed, narrowly.)

A cursory examination of the Contract with America, however, reveals its most fascinating and potent feature: it is not a list of policy objectives but rather a promise of procedural reform. Consider the eight provisions (later recast as twenty pieces of legislation), slightly condensed here for brevity's sake:

- Require that all laws that apply to the rest of the country also apply to the Congress;
- Hire an independent firm to audit Congress for waste, fraud, or abuse;
- Cut the number of House committees, and reduce committee staff by one-third;
- Limit the terms of committee chairs;
- Ban proxy voting in committees;
- Open all committee meetings to the public;
- Require a three-fifths majority vote to pass a tax increase; and
- Implement zero-baseline budgeting for the federal budget.

The supermajority requirement for tax increases, the zero-base budgeting provision, and the waste and fraud provision promised a leaner, smaller government. But there was no specificity in the contract as to whose oxen were to be gored. It was not an indictment or even a set of positions on government policies, but instead an indictment of Congress's performance.

In developing the Contract with America, the Republicans took advantage of another post-1992 strategic insight: they could repackage Ross Perot's 1992 reform message, attach their party's name to it, and sell his ideas as Republican reformism. As Ronald Rapoport explains in his definitive account of the Perot movement, *Three's a*

Crowd, the Republicans used results from focus groups conducted with 1992 Perot voters to develop messages that would specifically entice them to vote Republican in the 1994 midterms. Republicans then targeted U.S. House districts won by Democrats in 1992 in which Perot had run well. According to Rapoport, they toned down the party's platform, replacing content dedicated to family and moral values with more neutral language. The Contract with America more closely approximated the rhetoric of Perot's "United We Stand, America" platform than of the GOP's own 1992 presidential platform.

Although Clinton pollster Stanley Greenberg and the Democrats were also trying to decode and attract the Perot voters, the Republicans understood them better. The Contract with America reflected the type of no-nonsense, party-neutral procedural reforms that specifically drew voters to Perot. "Republicans," writes Rapoport, "made a bid for Perot supporters in 1994 by sharpening their appeals to Perot and his adherents. . . . [I]n addition the national party's decisions about where to allocate money in House elections were based in part on the size of the 1992 Perot vote in the district." The strategy worked: the GOP won just 2 percent of House districts where Perot drew 10 percent of the vote or less in 1992, but 42 percent of districts where he drew 26 percent or more.[35]

Selling procedural pragmatism was electorally potent because Democrats had unified control of Washington and would thus be the primary targets of voter anger. The long-term problem with winning elections by offering procedural reforms, however, is that doing so is no guarantee that the reformers' policies will be popular with the voters initially attracted by the procedural pitch. *How* a government or party conducts its business is related, but not identical, to *what* business a government conducts. In the long run a corrupt, sclerotic, entrenched government that provides the goods and services the citizenry wants may be electorally preferable to a lean, mean, disciplined, and ethical government that is deconstructing programs the public expects its government to deliver—a lesson in the disconnect between politics and policy that Gingrich would learn the hard way.

Gingrich's coronation and the 1994 House results deserved—and got—the lion's share of attention, but the Senate results were almost as dramatic. Republicans captured key seats in postindustrial states—Ohio's Mike Dewine, Michigan's Spencer Abraham, Pennsylvania's Rick Santorum—and in the West and South, including two seats in Tennessee thanks to the special election to fill out Vice President Al Gore's vacated term. Winning the Senate catapulted Kansas moderate and 1976 vice presidential nominee Bob Dole into the majority leader's chair. Unlike Gingrich, Dole was known as a Washington fixer; in 1983 he spearheaded Ronald Reagan's Social Security reform efforts on Capitol Hill, and he'd had a hand in almost every major legislative deal over the previous two decades. He was no Young Turk, and he harbored no ambitions about deconstructing the welfare state that he'd helped solidify.

But the Senate Republicans Dole was to lead were not the same caucus he first joined in 1969. He would be flanked atop the Republican leadership by his conservative deputy Trent Lott, who coasted to his first Senate reelection in 1994 by more than thirty points—the sort of electoral win by a southern Republican that was unthinkable in Mississippi just a few decades earlier. Lott's victory was particularly notable because, like Gingrich and Armey, he used it to catapult himself into a leadership spot. The one disappointment on Election Night for Senate Republicans was the failure to defeat the ultimate liberal target, the surprisingly vulnerable Ted Kennedy, who broke free of a dead-even race in September to beat a telegenic, well-funded Mormon challenger who would be heard from again.

Downballot, dozens of Republican gubernatorial candidates and thousands of Republican state legislators pushed incumbent Democrats to the curb. Eisenhower, Nixon, and Reagan had all won landslide reelections, the latter two in forty-nine-state romps. But 1994 was altogether different: the greatest top-to-bottom Republican victory since before the New Deal. Gubernatorial victories by Christine Todd Whitman in New Jersey and George Allen in Virginia a year earlier had created the expectation that an anti-Clinton backlash would help sweep Republicans into offices across the country, and those expectations were wildly exceeded. No Republican incumbent lost, anywhere in the country, at the national or state level. The pack of new GOP governors included Fob James in Alabama, Frank Keating in Oklahoma, Tom Ridge in Pennsylvania, and New York's George Pataki, who ousted three-term Democratic powerhouse Mario Cuomo. Many incumbent Republican governors easily cruised to reelection, including some from states that had been turning Democratic, most notably California's Pete Wilson.

The major surprise on Election Night 1994—surprising to the punditry, the Republican Party, and the Bush family alike—was not only that just one of the two Bush brothers won his race for governor, but that it was George in Texas, not his younger brother Jeb in Florida. By unseating formidable Democratic incumbent Ann Richards, George leapfrogged ahead of Jeb in the Republican Party's presidential sweepstakes. This flipping of the Bush family script would have long-term portents, but in 1994 it was a sign of how quickly Texas had been transformed under Karl Rove's stewardship.

With Michel retired and Gingrich elevated to the Speaker's office, the majority whip's position became available. Tom DeLay had his eyes on it, but Gingrich feared letting him gain even more power. He favored Bob Walker of Pennsylvania, a veteran legislator who worked comfortably with the newer classes of more aggressive House Republicans. As Tom Edsall recounts in *Building Red America,* the new Speaker also worried that, coupled with himself and Armey, the addition of DeLay would give the new leadership a too-southern face. DeLay had spent the early 1990s cultivating the Washington lobbying establishment, cajoling trade associations representing insurance agents, beer wholesalers, wholesale grocers, and other industries to hedge their campaign contribution bets on the chance that Republicans might finally capture the House. Now he wanted to claim his political reward. Edsall explains that "DeLay appeared to be the certain loser [in the whip race], except for two developments that had gone largely unnoticed by Gingrich and Walker." The first was how much money DeLay and his K Street allies had funneled to Republican candidates, and the second was that DeLay promptly asked the winners to let the rest of the Republican House Conference know they wouldn't be there if not for his electoral efforts. The man they called "the Hammer" ballpeened Walker, winning 119 to 80 on the strength of his support from 52 of the 73 newly elected Republicans.[36]

Before he assumed power, Gingrich was already losing some control. As congressional historian Julian Zelizer explains, those newcomers didn't arrive on Capitol Hill content to merely see their names on office doors. "From the beginning, Gingrich's strategy was to depend on the freshmen voting as a bloc," writes Zelizer. "The 73 freshmen were an extremely cohesive group of individuals who were convinced they had a mandate and cared little about their political future."[37] In DeLay, the GOP was planting the seeds for an even more aggressive—and in his case corrupt—style of partisan governance that fused Republican rule on Capitol Hill within the permanent interest group community of K Street.

Chicken

On November 15, 1995—a year and a week after the heady triumph of the Republican Revolution—the federal government shut down. More than 800,000 "nonessential" federal workers, including 130,000 in the nation's capital, were furloughed—locked out of their jobs. Public services ranging from food safety inspections to Census Bureau data collection to bankruptcy oversight ceased or were reduced to a bare minimum. In the White House, unpaid interns—including a recent college graduate named Monica Lewinsky—filled in for staffers who had been sent home. Two days later, the Republicans revealed their seven-year plan to balance the federal budget by 2002. The government shutdown became a partisan showdown—and for Clinton and Gingrich, a personal battle—that made the 1993 economic plan and 1994 health care reform fights look like family dinners.

Congressional Republicans had reason to believe they could win again. Clinton and the Democrats had been rebuffed in the 1994 midterms. The president had made the tactically foolish decision to wave his veto pen during the health care debates, the kind of undisciplined brinkmanship the GOP figured he would repeat. Republicans also pointed out that when the budget debates stalled back in 1990, the Republican White House, rather than the Democratic Congress, had incurred most of the blame for the stalemate, because the Congress acts first in passing budget legislation and then the White House decides whether to sign or veto. So they were expecting Clinton to take the brunt of the criticism for any stalemate or consequent government shutdown. "It's the President who forces a shutdown of the government anyway if he vetoes legislation we send up," a Republican House Budget Committee staffer told the *New York Times*.[38] In this partisan game of chicken, Republicans believed they needed only to hold firm. The immature president would blunder or cave.

Clinton almost did cave. As presidential adviser George Stephanopoulos later recounted in his memoirs, had the GOP held on a few more days, the White House might have folded and given Gingrich and Dole the opportunity to declare victory.[39] But Clinton was not without weapons. He declared federal workers who distributed Medicare, Social Security, and veterans' benefits "essential" personnel, bringing into high relief the consequences of the shutdown for the nation's neediest citizens—not to mention those with the highest voting turnout.[40] Additionally, Clinton could act unilaterally, whereas Capitol Hill Republicans needed to keep together a heterogeneous coalition of members that still included many moderates, who were far less zealous about using brinkmanship politics to tear down the welfare state. Clinton held steady, curbing his impetuous tendencies and his personal distaste for Gingrich. The president suddenly looked presidential: composed and resilient in the face of repeated Republican attacks.

Congressional Republicans also forgot a lesson they should have learned two years earlier during the legislative battle over Clinton's first budget and economic stimulus program: the public likes tough talk about government spending in the abstract, but is uncomfortable tinkering with the major entitlement programs where real budget savings might be found. Clinton, still very much learning on the job, made a variety of tactical errors during those early budget negotiations. As Bob Woodward details in *The Agenda*, Clinton pushed too hard for an energy tax that was eventually scaled back to a per-gallon gasoline tax smaller than the one his Republican predecessor had passed; he had to promise budget-cutting and entitlement reform in order to get the votes of conservative Democrats in both chambers; and all the while, he had to handle internal White House staff problems, including leaks and ideological warfare between the liberal, Stephanopoulos-led "kids" and the new centrism epitomized by the moderate, "adult" inside player David Gergen, brought into the West Wing to handle communications.[41] Nevertheless, as they had done during the much-maligned 1991 George H. W. Bush budget deal, the young Republican Turks were advocating a politically impossible fiscal agenda: no tax increases and possibly tax cuts, plus budget reductions, without substantial cuts to entitlements or defense. Again, despite the purported demand for cutting back the size of government, many American voters are philosophically conservative but operationally liberal. They believe that somehow cuts in foreign aid or windfalls from waste, fraud, and abuse crackdowns will yield major savings, when in fact such programs are dwarfed by middle-class entitlements, particularly those for seniors. The illusion that public zeal for budget cutting trumped service delivery led Gingrich and his allies into a trap of their own making.

In the first two years of the Clinton presidency, conservative Republicans had the luxury of voting against the Democrats' agenda. They knew that any electoral blowback from raising taxes or from insufficient spending cuts would harm the Democrats, not them. The GOP could support deficit reduction without having to make the tough choices about raising taxes or cutting popular programs. The GOP could pillory Clinton without having to play chicken with a government shutdown and run the risks Gingrich and his new majority were about to suffer. But now the GOP had not only power, but responsibility.

In 2011, sixteen years after that fateful 1995 showdown between Clinton and Gingrich, House Republicans again contemplated shutting down the government as a way to force the Obama administration to meet their budget-cutting demands. Maryland Republican Bob Ehrlich, a moderate House freshman in the 1994 Republican class, used the anniversary to characterize the 1995 stalemate as a failure of will. "Our problem was twofold," Ehrlich wrote in a *Washington Post* op-ed. "Many moderate members of Congress had no taste for 'shutdown' politics; they began to leave the reservation in the aftermath of harsh media coverage and public union opposition. And, of course, there was the master manipulator Bill Clinton, always ready, willing and able to summon the 'courage' to stop mean-spirited Republicans. The unpleasant results? Political momentum was stopped, entitlement reform was postponed and Clinton was reelected."[42] (In 2013, without so much as a companion Senate majority, the House Republican majority actually did shut down the government.)

Perhaps Ehrlich and fellow Hill Republicans had a legitimate gripe about Clinton receiving more favorable media treatment during the 1995 stalemate. As many conservatives also complained, also with cause, only two years after Clinton talked tough about Medicare reform during the 1993 budget negotiations, the president suddenly reversed himself in 1995 and depicted the Republicans as heartlessly stripping seniors of their medical coverage. But note the causal inconsistency of Ehrlich's last sentence, which implies that postponing entitlement reform allowed Clinton to slip through to reelection in 1996. That's simply not true. Clinton may have played fast and loose with Medicare politics, and Gingrich may have been unfairly suckered by the president. But in the end it was the threat of tinkering with Medicare that undid the Republicans, not postponing its reform or failing to privatize it.

On the same day Ehrlich's op-ed appeared, Gingrich also took to the pages of the *Washington Post* to revisit the 1995 shutdown. He claimed that his efforts had been a huge victory for deficit reduction, for him personally as Speaker, and for House Republicans, who in 1996 reelected a House Republican majority for the first time in sixty-eight years—the *only* time in American history that had happened in an election in which a Democrat carried the White House. (Boehner's Republican House caucus repeated this feat in 2012.) "The lesson for today's House Republicans is simple," Gingrich advised. "Work to keep the government open unless it requires breaking your word to the American people or giving up your principles." He justified his party's actions by saying they had promised a balanced-budget amendment in the Contract with America, and after coming up one vote short of passing that in the Senate, were obligated to do legislatively what they could not accomplish constitutionally.[43]

The government shutdown game of chicken was partisan, ideological, and institutional, but it also devolved into a personal battle of wills between the parties' two youthful leaders. Clinton got the better of Gingrich, who overestimated his 1994 mandate. That mandate may have been rooted in voter apprehensions about expanding government, but the Contract with America didn't give Gingrich and his fellow Republicans a license to shrink the government—at least not the programs and services voters had come to expect. "After the government was shuttered for weeks, the Republicans had to finally give up on making Clinton buckle," writes conservative pundit Rich Lowry in *Legacy*, his critique of the Clinton presidency. "They had lost. The Republican 'revolution' was over." But the revolution did claim at least one casualty, notes Lowry: in three short years, Clinton had morphed from a politician who in his 1993 State of the Union address rebuffed Reagan's antigovernment mantra by promising that "government can do more" to one who declared in his 1996 address that "the era of big government is over."[44] As Gingrich argued in his *Washington Post* commentary, discretionary spending was curbed significantly during the Clinton-Gingrich divided government era. But revenues increased significantly as well—not just because of the tech market boom but also because of the higher marginal rates Clinton and the Democrats enacted over the objections of Gingrich and the minority congressional Republicans in 1993.

In the Clinton-Gingrich clashes, Clinton had lost something in his 1993 and 1995 budget wins, and Gingrich had won something. The broader lesson—one to which a first-term governor in Austin and his "boy genius" adviser certainly paid serious attention, at least initially—is that tinkering with popular social safety net programs was very, very dangerous political business. Gingrich was not the only Republican to pay for the party's Medicare gambits: as we'll see in Chapter 4, Bob Dole would be the next major casualty.

As for the agreed-upon narrative that Clinton and Gingrich misinterpreted their respective mandates in the 1992 and 1994 cycles, there is an important distinction between their supposedly similar fates. "Before the [1994] election and afterward, [Gingrich] boldly advertised his agenda: It was to remake the welfare state," writes political reporter John Harris in his book *The Survivor.* "He promised a 'revolution' that would eliminate large chunks of the federal government and ensure that whatever was left operated on new premises, designed to dethrone bureaucracy and empower free markets. Gingrich believed it was his mission to execute the next and most important phase of the conservative ascendancy that had begun under Ronald Reagan."[45] Clinton overreached in trying to reform and expand U.S. health care policy, but like Ronald Reagan—and unlike Gingrich—he understood that government entitlements such as Medicare touch the lives of millions of middle-class Americans and are therefore politically inviolable. Once the episode was over, a more reflective Gingrich came to terms with his failures. In conveniently first-person-plural language, the former Speaker continued to insist that Clinton had lied to Republicans by pretending to be serious about a deficit bargain that would include Medicare cuts. ("How naïve could we have been?" he lamented.) But he did admit to a fatal miscalculation. The American people, he wrote in his aptly titled book *Lessons Learned the Hard Way*, "want their leaders to have principled disagreements, but they want these disagreements to be settled in constructive ways. That is not, of course, what our own activists were telling us. They were all gung ho for a brutal fight over spending and taxes. We mistook their enthusiasm for the views of the American people."[46]

To this day, Gingrich continues to speak in glowing terms about Ronald Reagan and his legacy, but the blinding light from that glow prevented Gingrich from understanding the true meaning of Reagan's presidency. Presidential historians have compared Clinton's role in the post-Reagan era to that of Dwight Eisenhower after FDR: each president brought his opposing party more fully in line with the political zeitgeist. Eisenhower led Republicans toward acceptance of the New Deal society Roosevelt created, and Clinton steered Democrats toward acceptance of the post–New Deal society Reagan initiated. Gingrich presumed Reagan's work was incomplete because it had not gone far enough, whereas Clinton properly understood that it was incomplete only in that it had not spread *widely* enough to incorporate the moderate Democrats and independents he needed to recapture to win reelection.

The Tipping Point

The post–Gulf War period quickly turned from a George H. W. Bush victory lap into a struggle for Republican identity. With no Evil Empire or even what George W. Bush later termed "evildoers" available as a foreign foil, Republicans focused on domestic demons, most notably the devilish Baby Boomer inhabiting the Oval Office that the GOP had come to regard as its property. But if Bush Sr. had any doubts about his political security at the end of 1991, Buchanan's challenge from within the party and Ross Perot's third-party rumblings confirmed that his mandate was not his own. The four years from 1992 to 1995 saw the culmination of the intra-party warfare between paleoconservatives and a new generation of more fundamentalist conservatives. The early 1990s were the tipping point in the relationship between the conservative movement and the Republican Party. This is when conservatives stopped taking their marching orders from party leaders and instead began to issue them.

Not coincidentally, those conservative elements also reinforced the party's newly energized congressional wing, particularly on the House side under Newt Gingrich and his key adjutants. Even before George H. W. Bush's failed reelection bid ended the Republicans' twelve-year White House rule, and even while they remained the minority party, the GOP's congressional wing had begun to deploy a new, procedural-based strategy and a more aggressive set of tactics to attract public attention and assert power. Congressional Republicans proved they could win, especially on the House side, in otherwise bad Republican cycles. Capitalizing on Clinton's early missteps and aided by race-based redistricting and the rapid conversion of disaffected southern Democrats three generations removed from the New Deal, a new generation of aggressive and combative leaders on Capitol Hill began to assert its power.

The history books record 1994 as the key year during this period. Coupled with Reagan's 1980 win, the midterm elections of 1994—the so-called Republican Revolution—were no doubt a critical turning point for conservative politics. But 1994 was merely the reward for years of investments made by a group of upstart Republican legislators and their aggressive young staffers. The 1992 election was a critical table-setter, not only because of the relatively strong congressional showing but also because conservatives turned their backs on a Republican president, thereby helping elect a Democrat whose performance during his first two years was essential to the GOP's 1994 successes. The Democratic Party in 1992 made an important choice about its future in selecting a candidate from the party's Democratic Leadership Council wing, but the Republicans made an equally important choice about their future in abandoning George H. W. Bush's mainline Protestantism and budgetary centrism in favor of a new set of guiding principles.

In just four years, the partisan situation in Washington had reversed. National politics and the national electorate had pivoted from a Republican president and a Democratic Congress to a Democratic president and a Republican Congress. The result was a national Republican Party that was winning down the ballot in ways the once-dominant presidential wing of the 1950s through the 1980s could only dream about. But precisely because the party's national message and brand were now decoupled from the specific talents and flaws, victories and failures, of its parade of elected presidents from Dwight Eisenhower to George H. W. Bush, the American electorate had a clearer view of what the modern Republican Party looked like once the presidential mask was removed.

For some, of course, this new face was ever so pleasing to the eye. Conservatives had wrested control of Congress from the Democrats and were learning to use against Democrats the very tools of power that had for decades been used against them. Very quickly, however, the majority Republicans took on some of the very characteristics they despised in Democrats: the reliance on brinksmanship and obfuscatory tactics; the sacrifice of ideas and ideals in favor of polemics and partisanship; an inability to exert the will to shrink government; and a penchant for taking advantage of the privileges power affords, often by unethical or illegal means. The reversal on both ends of Pennsylvania Avenue caused growing pains for both the new Democratic president and the new Republican congressional majorities. By mid-decade, the Republicans were already discovering the perils of their new identity.

4

REFORMULATION

For Republicans, the great celebration following the capture of Congress in 1994 quickly evolved into a period of reformulation. At first, it looked like congressional Republicans were ascendant and the rube from Arkansas sitting in the Oval Office was destined to be bounced out after one term. Few would have predicted in early November 1994—or even in December 1997, when news of the Monica Lewinsky scandal first broke—that by the end of the decade Bill Clinton would still be in office and Newt Gingrich would not. But the contagion that beset the Clinton White House in the first half of the 1990s seemed to have spread to Capitol Hill, where Republicans who had cut their political teeth in the minority suddenly found themselves under assault, from forces both outside and within their coalition.

The Republicans maintained control of both chambers of Congress during the second half of the decade, but they saw their majorities steadily thinned during the 1996, 1998, and 2000 elections. Faced with the need to fill two power vacuums at the top of the party's congressional hierarchy—first, following Bob Dole's resignation as Senate majority leader in 1996 to run for president, and later by Newt Gingrich's downfall as House Speaker in 1998—the Republican caucuses on Capitol Hill became both more conservative and more combative. Meanwhile, outsiders led by George W. Bush and a coterie of neoconservatives reframed the national debate over foreign policy, in part by distancing themselves from congressional Republicans whose stridency alienated many voters.

The most important change for Republicans during this period was the recognition that, following Bill Clinton's reelection, they were now a Congress-based party in a presidency-centered American political system—that, in effect, they were *still* the opposition. After 1994, so much more seemed possible. Clinton had suffered wounds, many of them self-inflicted, and for a time the president looked ripe for defeat in 1996. Republicans also changed the way Congress conducted its business—reorganizing committees, changing procedural rules—and forced the self-styled centrist Democratic president to move further to the right on a variety of issues and to forgo the larger ambitions of his first term in favor of incremental wins in his second. The GOP did recapture the White House in 2000—but barely, and despite losing the popular vote and benefiting from not only the Electoral College's small-state advantage but a favorable Supreme Court ruling. Nevertheless, during this period congressional Republicans suffered from a variety of political and electoral growing pains.

San Diego: The Anti-Houston

Before the Republicans gathered in San Diego for their 1996 national convention, the word from party leaders had gone out: we will not have another disaster like 1992. The party will appear unified and the mood will be upbeat. The public will see a diverse convention featuring racial minorities, women, and ideological moderates to counter the party's growing image as an exclusively white, male, conservative club. The two overarching themes will be "opportunity and optimism," because those were the themes on which Ronald Reagan built his presidential majorities.

Several veterans from the Reagan administration—public relations guru Michael Deaver, former chief of staff Kenneth Duberstein, and Jim Baker's reliable aide-de-camp Margaret Tutwiler—were brought aboard to supervise the party's makeover. Managing the spectacle from on high was Republican National Committee chairman Haley Barbour of Mississippi. His top communications guy at the RNC was none other than Ed Gillespie, who ended his long stint on Capitol Hill to help refashion the party's national image after the 1992 convention debacle. Barbour and Gillespie both understood their mandate: avoid another Houston.

To that end, two potential land mines needed to be carefully defused. The first was the abortion question, and the second was the related, lingering problem of how to deal with gadfly Pat Buchanan. In 1992 Buchanan's "holy war" speech had bumped Reagan's address past prime time. That mistake would not be repeated, if only because the Gipper was too infirm to appear. (A video tribute by former first lady Nancy Reagan would have to suffice.) But Reagan or not, the objective was a smooth convention free of hostile takeovers from isolationist Buchananites or messy floor fights over social policy. It didn't help that Buchanan managed to further vex party leaders by inserting himself rather directly into the abortion controversy. He put the party on notice as early as March, when it became clear that Bob Dole was pulling away from the rest of the GOP presidential field, that if Dole selected a pro-choice running mate there would be trouble. On the Sunday morning television shows, Buchanan threatened a convention walkout if Dole chose either General Colin Powell or New Jersey governor Christine Todd Whitman as his running mate. Despite the trouble Buchanan had caused four years earlier, former Republican National Committee chair Rich Bond told Dole not to "take any shit" from him.[1]

Bond's comments echoed a preemptive chorus publicly warning Buchanan not to play the spoiler. After Buchanan announced his walkout threat, rookie Republican governors John Engler of Michigan and Tommy Thompson of Wisconsin answered. Engler, a pro-life Catholic, scoffed that "twenty things are more important at the convention than whether Pat Buchanan speaks," while Thompson sternly advised Buchanan to "start trying to unify the party instead of trying to tear asunder the party and its tenets." Capitol Hill Republicans, however, were less uniformly in lockstep behind Dole in pushing back against Buchanan. "House Speaker Newt Gingrich and other GOP legislative leaders privately . . . warn that the GOP and Mr. Dole would pay a high price for any decision regarding Mr. Buchanan that made the senator look like he did not control the Republican National Convention," reported Ralph Hallow of the *Washington Times*. "They also say that attacking Mr. Buchanan personally is foolish and that recognizing the relevance of his issues, if not his solutions, is wise."[2] The House GOP had once again poked its camel nose into the presidential campaign tent.

Meanwhile, the GOP didn't seem to fully comprehend its gender problems or how the party's strident position on abortion was creating an electorally punitive gender gap. "My big thing was to say, 'Women don't stop being people when they get pregnant to become nothing more than a vessel for a child,'" says Whitman. She felt then, and still feels, that the GOP's abortion stance is designed to attract a small core of the base at the expense of a broader appeal. Despite being a convention co-chair with new Texas governor George W. Bush, Whitman was scheduled in San Diego for a midday speaking slot when, she says, "nobody's really watching." She knew the party was trying to marginalize Republicans who were not in lockstep with its pro-life platform. Although she was frequently mentioned as a potential vice presidential choice, Whitman never really considered herself in contention and was not upset with how the Dole campaign treated her. The Dole campaign asked her to wait until later in 1996 to endorse him, she says, not because her abortion stance was a liability but in the hopes that her support would not get drowned out during the noisier stages of the primary. However much of a liability Whitman might have been at the convention, she was determined to put a line in her speech to the effect that the party "may disagree over issues of choice" but "we all agree that we want Bob Dole as the next president."[3]

When she turned in the draft of her speech, the reaction was immediate and fierce. "They gave me holy shit over that line, excuse the language," Whitman recalls. "And I had to fight and fight to put it back in. And they finally said, 'You can't have it in.' So I took it out and just said it, because it was ridiculous to me not to say it. I wasn't throwing down a gantlet or anything."[4] Some delegates stood and turned their backs as Whitman spoke. Her convention speech skirmish was a matter of principle to her but also part of a larger effort to get the GOP to make inroads with female voters the party was losing to the Democrats. As younger and more pro-choice women replaced their mothers and grandmothers in the electorate, some of these losses were attributable to the party's stance on abortion. "Obviously I wasn't getting much favorable reception," says Whitman.

"I kept reminding them that women are more than 50 percent of the vote."

The convention's planners managed to avoid the problems they had had in Houston. The lineup of speakers on stage was clearly more diverse. In addition to Nancy Reagan, future first lady Laura Bush, New York congresswoman Susan Molinari, Kansas senator Nancy Kassebaum, and Dole's wife, Elizabeth, all spoke during prime time. Colin Powell gave the closing speech on the first night of the convention, which also featured appearances by former presidents Bush and Ford. It is unclear whether Republicans intended such repackaging (past or present) to expand their reach to nonwhite and female voters, or merely to shore up wavering support from Republican-leaning independent and moderate white voters, including women, who might be turned off by the party's hard-edged rhetoric.

Despite the superficial changes, the roll call of delegates in San Diego was 90 percent white and two-thirds male.[5] The GOP's shift in emphasis and tone between Houston and San Diego was an implicit acknowledgment that—aside from rare exceptions like Senator Olympia Snowe or Representative J. C. Watts—a party still led almost top to bottom by white men would have to change if it wanted to attract a diverse set of new faces and compete electorally in a country where the share of white male voters was declining every year. The question was whether the party, anchored to a base that was strongly anti-abortion and whose national leadership was almost entirely composed of older, conservative white men, was capable of changing. Beginning what would become a familiar pattern, few members of the overwhelmingly white, male Republican congressional leadership were featured onstage in San Diego during prime time. Behind the scenes, of course, they remained the dominant force within the party.

Marital Bliss

The national debate over gay marriage began about as far from Washington as possible: in Hawaii's state supreme court, which ruled in 1993 that the denial of marriage licenses to three same-sex couples was an unconstitutional form of discrimination. In the next two years, more than a dozen states considered legislation or even constitutional amendments to define marriage as strictly between a man and a woman. Although many states rejected such measures, Utah and North Dakota passed them. Americans turned their sights to Washington, where President Clinton and Congress were expected to create a federal standard that would protect states with heterosexual marriage statutes or constitutional provisos from having to recognize gay couples married elsewhere.

With his reelection bid only months away, Clinton—whom gay Americans already viewed suspiciously following his imposition of "don't ask, don't tell" as a compromise standard for gays in the military—stated his personal opposition to same-sex marriage. But he initially avoided taking a position on whether he would sign federal legislation defending the rights of states to deny benefits to homosexual couples. May 1996 proved to be the critical month for the issue: within a few weeks, a bill denying federal benefits to same-sex couples was introduced in both chambers of Congress, Clinton declared his intention to sign it if it reached his desk, and the Supreme Court ruled in *Romer v. Evans* that an antigay marriage constitutional amendment approved by voters in Colorado violated equal protection standards.

In July, the House passed its version of a bill establishing the federal definition of marriage as strictly between a man and a woman. A majority of Democrats, and every Republican but one, voted in favor; sixty-five Democrats, independent Bernie Sanders, and the chamber's only openly gay Republican, Wisconsin's Steve Gunderson, opposed it. Gunderson, whose orientation was open only because, in a mean-spirited floor speech two years earlier, Republican representative Bob Dornan had outed him, expressed dismay after the bill's passage. "Why must we attack one element of our society for some cheap political gain?" he asked.[6] When the Senate brought the legislation to a vote in early September, just eight weeks before the 1996 elections, the partisan pattern was repeated: Republicans were unified in their support, and roughly two-thirds of Democrats joined them to forge a substantial bipartisan majority to send the bill to the president's desk. Only eighteen liberal Democrats opposed the bill.[7]

If the purpose of wedge issues is to divide the opposing party against itself, the Defense of Marriage Act (DOMA) worked precisely as Republicans had hoped. Congressional Democrats were divided and on the defensive throughout the summer and fall of 1996, with DOMA supporters anxiously defending their position to gay constituents and donors, and DOMA opponents coming under attack by critics for threatening the traditional family and America's Judeo-Christian value system. Many Democrats protested that the legislation would have almost no real-world effect and was little more than Republican-engineered electoral posturing—but voted for it anyway. White House press secretary Michael McCurry called it "gay baiting, pure and simple" and "a classic use of wedge politics designed to provoke anxieties and fears"—and then his boss signed the bill into law.[8] Despite complaining that the Republicans harbored cynical, self-serving motives, most Democrats were simply too scared to vote against the bill, and many of those who did provided electoral ammunition to Republican challengers. For Republicans in the mid-1990s, using gay issues to divide the Democrats made perfect sense.

But the national debate over gay marriage also exposed the vitriol of congressional Republicans, especially on the House side.

Members thundered about the "radical" and "extremist" homosexual agenda. Oklahoma's Tom Coburn called homosexuality "immoral" and based on "perversion" and "lust." Virulent abortion rights opponent Henry Hyde accused the "homosexual movement" of intimidating the psychiatric profession to such an extent that "people who object to sodomy, to two men penetrating each other, are homophobic." The House bill's primary sponsor, Bob Barr of Georgia, described homosexuality as "the flames of hedonism, the flames of narcissism, the flames of self-centered morality . . . licking at the very foundations of our society: the family unit." Never one to be outdone at such moments, Bob Dornan, the California Republican who had outed Gunderson, predicted that within a few years Congress would be discussing legalizing pedophilia.[9]

Representative Jim Kolbe of Arizona listened to all this and voted with the rest of his fellow Republicans to pass the bill. He explained his vote for the Defense of Marriage Act as a defense of states' rights. But two weeks later, upon learning that a newspaper was about to publish a story revealing his homosexuality, Kolbe confirmed what many Washington insiders already knew: he, too, was gay. Overnight, the caucus of openly gay House Republicans doubled in size.

What congressional Republicans could not have anticipated was how rapidly public attitudes about homosexuality were about to change. In a country that took two centuries to achieve a public consensus on the idea that African Americans were humans and therefore citizens, that women were the equals of their husbands and brothers, that workers should have the right to organize to seek fair wages and benefits, or that the handicapped deserve equal access to public and private spaces, public support for equal marital and other rights for homosexuals would effectively double, from about one-quarter to one-half the country, in less than two decades.[10] Either by change of heart or by the replacement of older members, Democrats in both chambers rapidly evolved into pro–gay rights caucuses. By 2012 not only did President Barack Obama reverse his previous support for civil unions as an alternative to gay marriage, but former president Clinton admitted that signing DOMA was a mistake. In 2013 the Supreme Court—composed of five Republican appointees, including Chief Justice John Roberts—agreed with both and ruled the law unconstitutional.

Republicans remained outliers. Although support for same-sex marriage and gay rights gained some traction with a few congressional Republicans, on Capitol Hill the GOP remained steadfastly and unapologetically antigay. And why not? For congressional Republicans, there was almost no political downside to maintaining this stance—and for members in most districts and states today, there still isn't. For Republican presidential candidates, however, the party's antigay policies and rhetoric have grown ever more problematic.

Doleful Performance

President Clinton, who at one point in 1995 felt compelled to remind Americans that his presidency was still "relevant," began in early 1996 to carefully reposition himself for reelection. He did so through a series of "third way" policies of triangulation, which is Beltway-speak for co-opting the opposing party's themes and positions. In Clinton's case, triangulation came with an infamously sly assist from consultant Dick Morris. Meanwhile, hard-line conservatives in 1995 and early 1996 were shopping for a presidential challenger other than rearguard "moderate" Bob Dole. In a thin field, wealthy businessman and chemical company heir Pete du Pont raised some eyebrows, and Jack Kemp was again in the mix. But the Republicans had not yet fully absorbed the idea that, suddenly, they were no longer the party of presidents. They were accustomed to a long roster of nationally and internationally recognized figures who were required by tradition to wait their turn. Eight years after he watched his longtime rival George H. W. Bush take the 1988 GOP nomination away from him, it was finally Bob Dole's turn.

The Kansan proved to be an uninspired nominee. With the economy clearly on the upswing, Clinton had little trouble deflecting his rival's economic criticisms. Ross Perot complicated the election by running again in 1996. But the Texas businessman's second presidential campaign turned out to be only half as effective as his first: his share of the national popular vote dropped from 18 percent to 9 percent. Even with Perot siphoning away fewer votes from the major-party candidates, Dole lost to Clinton by roughly the same margin in both the popular vote and the Electoral College that George H. W. Bush did in 1992. Dole's turn had arrived in the wrong cycle. He learned the same lesson in 1996 that Adlai Stevenson, George McGovern, and Walter Mondale learned before him: incumbent presidents are tough to beat.

The important backstory of 1996 was not that Dole did about as well as his old nemesis Bush, but that his party relegated him to secondary importance behind his new nemesis, Newt Gingrich. The bad blood between the two legislators went as far back as the early 1980s, when Gingrich infamously described Dole, then chair of the Senate Finance Committee, as the "tax collector for the welfare state." When both men rose to majority power in January 1995, their contrasting styles and mutual antipathies were obvious to anyone who covered Capitol Hill politics. Dole discounted Gingrich as "a politician with little or no appreciation for the art of legislating compromise." He also resented the rising Senate influence of former House Republicans, led by Mississippi's Trent Lott, who preferred Gingrich's politics-first style to Dole's less polarized worldview.[11]

In the two years between Dole's elevation to Senate majority leader and his presidential nomination, however, something changed that would further undermine his presidential chances: movement conservatives and establishment Republicans had become so enamored with their new congressional majorities that, when forced to choose between holding onto them and regaining the presidency, Congress prevailed. By the time of the 1996 elections, the dominant attitude among conservatives was the opposite of what it had been a quarter century earlier, recalls Americans for Tax Reform founder Grover Norquist. In 1972, says Norquist, Richard Nixon's campaign was identifying and mobilizing voters in key states who would support Nixon's reelection but vote for Democrats downballot. "Back then," he argues, "the idea was that you had to hold the presidency," and that overarching idea guided movement strategy for decades. But after the 1994 revolution, it was "interesting how quickly the attitude changed to 'the presidency would be nice, but the House and Senate are more important'"—particularly the House, because "you can run the country out of the House" where "team play," rather than the Senate's supermajority-dependent and go-it-alone ethic, makes absolute control possible.[12]

For Ed Gillespie, the decision in early 1996 to abandon Capitol Hill and take the communications job under Haley Barbour at the RNC was a tough one. Gillespie thought a new job might be fun, and he had a lot of respect for Barbour, but there was one concern to allay before he made the leap. "I was worried about keeping the House majority," Gillespie recalls. "And after such a hard-fought election in 1994, I was worried about losing it in '96." So he asked lobbyist and political friend Don Fierce, who was working with Barbour, "If it comes to a point where the RNC has to choose between salvaging the Republican nominee for president or saving the House, what would Haley Barbour do?" Fierce assured him that Barbour would save the House. "That gave me comfort to go there."[13]

Gillespie's communications job was broadened to include "congressional affairs," partly because of his background but also, he says, because "dealing with the Congress was so integral to the communications function of the RNC at that point."

Republicans would have loved to gain unified control of Washington for the first time since 1953–1954, but the smart money at the party's highest level was invested in keeping Congress rather than flipping the White House. So too were the campaign finance bets of interest groups. After 1994 most interest group money was donated to the Republicans, given that they ran both chambers and chaired all the key committees and subcommittees. For Dole, the insult on top of the injury of losing to Clinton was that he was forced to subordinate his presidential ambitions again, this time in favor of helping preserve the Republicans' new congressional majorities, including Gingrich's House speakership. As Election Day 1996 approached and defeating Clinton seemed increasingly unlikely, Dole took to the hustings, often in nonswing states, to support endangered Republican congressional incumbents. "He was campaigning in a lot of places that were not traditional because he was trying to help the Republican candidates across the country, and that was the sacrifice he made," remembers Christine Todd Whitman.[14]

In another bitter irony, Dole's presidential prospects were also damaged by Gingrich's politically risky bet, made the year before, that Medicare could be successfully used as a budget bargaining chip. Instead, Gingrich failed to appreciate how quickly antigovernment sentiment and Perot-inspired calls for fiscal austerity gave way to a defense of this popular program. In 1996 Clinton and other national Democrats repeatedly hung Gingrich and his Medicare gambit around Dole's neck.

As was often the case whenever Gingrich was involved, the story was more complicated than a political misstep on Medicare. In *Storming the Gates*, national political reporters Dan Balz and Ron

Brownstein argue that Gingrich had a significant impact on the 1996 election cycle because his House-based "antigovernment" re-branding of the Republican Party wasn't selling too well:

The Medicare fight alone put the party's fortunes in peril, and by late 1995 it was clearly damaging the GOP's standing with the American people. One poll in the heat of the debate showed only about a quarter of the people approved of the changes Republicans were making in their program, an anemic level of support substantially *below* the nadir of public back[ing] for Clinton's health care plan. Gingrich himself became as much a lightning rod for attacks from the Democrats as Clinton had been for Republicans in 1993 and 1994. . . . Republican strategists talked openly about their fears that in 1996, Democratic political ads would morph their candidates into Gingrich in the same way Republicans had morphed Democrats into Clinton in 1994.

The resolution of this debate [over taxes, the budget, and the shutdown] within the party framed the political dialogue with Clinton and the Democrats over the future of the country, but equally important, it demonstrated how tightly Gingrich and his generation controlled the party's agenda. . . . Gingrich had talked about 1995 as a year in which he and his followers would stamp their vision on the party, effectively *forcing the Republican presidential candidates to run on a platform established in the House.* In doing so, Gingrich created a political figure the country had not seen in generations: a congressional leader as powerful—as polarizing—as a president.[15]

A presidential candidate running on a House-inspired platform was a significant new development, and extremely problematic for the party's longer-term presidential prospects. A decade earlier, Kemp and Gingrich had influenced the Reagan administration's policy and rhetoric, but their impact paled against the influence the majority Republicans in Congress now exercised over national policy making, the party's image, and the positioning of its presidential candidates.

Republicans hadn't abandoned hope of recapturing the White House. But the period between 1994 and 1996 signaled a pivotal redirection of the party's objectives in ways that would make the Republicans a less competitive presidential party. Norquist doesn't recall Dole sacrificing his chance at the White House to help the GOP hold Congress. But he very distinctly remembers that his group of conservative activists embraced the new priorities. "We, as movement people, were clearly Congress-centered people," he comments. "We wanted Dole to win, of course; we all voted for him and worked with his campaign whenever and however we could. But when the house is on fire, you save the baby, not the Van Gogh. And the congressional majorities were our baby."[16]

Dole was triply cursed. First, the party establishment, conservative organizations, and business interests now valued the Congress more than the White House. Second, the Republican House, against which he had so often stood as a moderate bulwark, had poisoned the 1996 electoral well with Gingrich's shutdown politics and Medicare gambit. Third, and perhaps most galling of all, Dole had to sacrifice his presidential ambitions to save the very congressional majorities that had made him electorally vulnerable in the first place. There was little doubt that Gingrich's 1995 budget antics and political toxicity had wounded Dole. Yet the ever-loyal Dole sacrificed his ambitions to save Gingrich.[17] (Dole and George H. W. Bush exacted a small measure of revenge years later when they both endorsed Mitt Romney over Gingrich in the 2012 Republican presidential primary.)

Congressional Republicans and their supporters got what they wanted: the GOP would hold Congress for another ten years. Meanwhile, Clinton expanded the Democrats' edge among women, Latinos, and other elements of the emerging electoral coalition. After 1996 there was no longer any doubt that the center of gravity within the GOP had shifted. Republicans' presidential ambitions had taken a secondary and often subservient position to the party's congressional wing. Gingrich was king and Dole a tired old vicar whose presidential hopes had been dashed.

The House Captures the Senate

Dole suffered one more indignity from the 1996 election—although it came months before the votes were cast, and the political damage was a self-inflicted wound resulting from Dole's fateful decision to resign from the Senate in the middle of his presidential campaign. In the summer of 1996, with his prospects of beating Clinton looking as grim as Dole's furrowed brow, the Kansan gambled that resigning his Senate seat might make him look like a selfless patriot willing to risk the security of his present office to serve the nation in a larger capacity. The gambit failed, and his decision to step down as majority leader only opened the post for Trent Lott, who would import to the Senate the polarizing House style of politics Dole had stood steadfastly against. For the moderate wing of the Republican Party, the 1996 Dole campaign was in almost every respect a bitter surrender for an ideological dead-ender. Lott's ascension would be a lasting reminder.

Trent Lott was not some functionary who happened to rise to the top of the Senate hierarchy. As we saw in Chapter 3, the 1994 Republican Revolution also swept into Congress a new cohort of socially conservative senators, including Oklahoma's James Inhofe,

Arizona's Jon Kyl, and Pennsylvania's Rick Santorum. Yet the attention of politicians and the media focused primarily on Gingrich and the House. Two years later, however, the focus shifted to the Senate, where instead of losing net seats during a presidential cycle in which the Democratic incumbent won reelection, as Gingrich's House Republican Conference did, the Republican Senate caucus actually grew to fifty-five seats—the largest GOP seat share since before the New Deal. Lott was suddenly as powerful a figure in the Republican political universe as Gingrich—and, soon enough, *more* powerful.

Lott was no Bob Dole, and his new GOP caucus was unlike any that Dole had experienced during his long Senate career. "The new Senate more resembles the rebellious House of 1994," observed *New York Times* national political reporter Richard Berke in a lengthy profile about the new majority leader. "Forty-three Senators, including 25 Republicans, are alumni of the House, the largest proportion in modern history. During their long years in the minority many of those Republicans were schooled in partisan guerrilla tactics."[18] The Senate, especially on the Republicans' side of the aisle, was looking and acting more like the House for the simple reason that so many of the majority party had previously served there.

The tenor of the chamber was changing too, driven in part by state-level demographic changes that were expanding the number of safely Republican and Democratic states in presidential elections. The gradual disappearance of southern Democrats and northern Republicans purified and homogenized both parties' caucuses. As many pundits began to notice, the states were becoming not only more consistent across time in their partisan tendencies in presidential contests, but also more consistent in electing pairs of either Republican or Democratic senators.[19]

Consider just two pieces of evidence. First, when Dole entered the Senate in 1969, twenty-one states had split delegations (one Democrat and one Republican); when he yielded his majority leader's post to Lott in 1996, that number had fallen to nineteen; and by the time Lott resigned as majority leader during the 109th Congress of 2005–2006, there were just thirteen split delegations. Second, rising Senate polarization effectively eliminated almost all centrists of either party. As reported by the *National Journal*, in 1982 there were fifty-eight senators with ideological voting scores that fell in a wide middle area between the voting record of the Senate's most liberal Republican, Connecticut's Lowell Weicker, and its most conservative Democrat, Nebraska's Edward Zorinsky; that meant that just forty-two senators were either Democrats to the left of Weicker or Republicans to the right of Zorinsky. In 1994 the total number of "tweener" senators slipped to thirty-four, but they still constituted a third of the chamber. By 2002 their ranks had shrunk to just seven, and by 2010 there were none—*zero*.[20] Today, the most conservative Democrat is more liberal than the most liberal Republican. To say the Senate from which Bob Dole retired in 1996 was different from the one to which he was elected goes beyond nostalgic pining for an age of gentlemanly courtesy.

Lott intuitively understood these changes. Within a week of his selection as majority leader, he crossed the Capitol to pay a courtesy call on the House Republicans. He brought no staffers or fellow senators along with him. Many House Republicans were already upset with the way the Senate majority under Dole's stewardship had, in their view, too often caved to the Clinton White House; they expected Lott to be a force for change. "With pristine conservative credentials, Lott provides fellow Republicans with political cover on tough votes arguably not afforded by Dole, whose lukewarm reception of the Contract with America and jabs at the Republican freshmen alienated party purists, and contributed to his moderate reputation," wrote Capitol Hill reporter Sandy Hume in *The Hill*. "Lott's 16-year House tenure appears to make the senator permanently 'one of us' in the eyes of many representatives, elevating his credibility and trustworthiness."[21] Lott's House background also gave him greater legitimacy and leverage in bicameral negotiations with the House, and House Republicans especially. Again, it helped that more and more former House Republicans were serving alongside him. That November, in fact, several House Republicans were bidding to join Lott in the Senate. Tim Hutchinson of Arkansas, Colorado's Wayne Allard, and two Kansans—Pat Roberts in the regular election and Sam Brownback earlier in the year in the special election to fill Dole's vacant seat—all graduated to the Senate in 1996.

In a fascinating study, published in 2013 as a book called *The Gingrich Senators*, political scientist Sean Theriault examined the legislative careers of every Republican elected after 1978—the year Newt Gingrich was first elected to the House—who served first in the House before later winning a seat in the Senate. Starting with the 1984 Senate election of Phil Gramm of Texas—an especially interesting inaugural member of this group because he was once a Democrat—Theriault tracked the careers of the forty Gingrich senators as of the start of the 112th Congress. Theriault clarifies that his study assigns neither credit nor blame to Gingrich for the actions or voting records of these senators: the label merely describes a temporal cohort who came of age in Congress during the hyperpartisan era that Gingrich's generation of House colleagues helped to usher into Congress.[22]

Theriault was specifically interested in what ideological, policy, and even procedural effects, if any, these forty House-groomed senators have had on the chamber. His findings are remarkable, especially as they pertain to congressional polarization. Starting with Gramm alone in the 99th Congress, the number of Gingrich senators grew to fourteen by the 104th Congress, which took office following the 1994 election, and then to an all-time high (as of this writing) of twenty-five by the start of the 109th Congress. The Gingrich senators, Theriault explains, are most recognizable by their very conservative voting records and ideological ratings. In the Senate they vote together, and they are more likely to use procedural tactics—notably the filibuster—to prosecute their ideologically sharpened policy agenda. Most of all, the Gingrich senators have had a very polarizing effect on the chamber. Theriault writes:

> The Gingrich Senators have taken their more conservative voting record from the House to the Senate. In fact, almost the entire increase in party polarization in the Senate can be accounted for in the Gingrich Senators' increasingly conservative voting record and in their increasing numbers. . . . [T]he difference between the Gingrich Senators and the other Republicans can be compared to the differences between the Northern and Southern Democrats when they were most at odds with each other.
>
> The transformation of the Republican Conference in the House under the direction of Newt Gingrich was not a one-chamber phenomenon. Those House members elected in and after the Gingrich Era who go on to serve in the Senate are more polarizing than their Republican colleagues.[23]

Because he was elected to the House before Gingrich, Trent Lott is not a Gingrich senator, even if he shares a strong ideological kinship with them. That said, leading an increasingly polarized Senate was a far more comfortable role for Lott than it would have been for Dole, who chose an ideal moment to retire.

Foreign Policy Takeover

The mid-1990s brought another key development with long-term consequences for the Republican Party's presidential competitiveness: the party's foreign policy mind-set began to change. Neoconservatives articulated a set of new principles for the exercise of U.S. military power and promotion of American security interests. What's especially interesting about this development is its locus: even though Capitol Hill was now the power center for national Republican politics, none of the key figures driving this change were sitting members of Congress.

The Bosnian conflict brought into high relief the tensions within the conservative cosmos between the Pat Buchanan–led isolationists and a newly emboldened cohort of interventionists led by Elliott Abrams, Dick Cheney, Francis Fukuyama, Richard Perle, Donald Rumsfeld, Paul Wolfowitz, and a few others. To give their movement a name and a purpose, in 1996 these men joined with a dozen other signatories—including, interestingly, Jeb Bush but not George W. Bush—to form an organization called the Project for a New American Century (PNAC). Though not signatories, key conservative public intellectuals—primarily Robert Kagan and Bill Kristol, as well as Joshua Muravchik and John Podhoretz—helped develop most of PNAC's theoretical principles. Prominent media figures such as Fred Barnes and Charles Krauthammer also aligned themselves with the group.

Many of the ideas from PNAC's founding statement were drawn from a 1996 *Foreign Affairs* essay by Kristol and Kagan entitled "Toward a Neo-Reaganite Foreign Policy." In it, they criticized Clinton's multilateralism, Buchanan's isolationism, and Henry Kissinger's realism—and even took a swipe at Bob Dole, then in the middle of his presidential campaign. Noting that conservatives had issued mostly incoherent complaints about Clinton while vaguely calling for a more "adult" foreign policy under Dole's supervision, they wrote: "Bill Clinton has not vacillated that much lately, and Dole was reduced a few weeks ago to asserting . . . that there really are differences between him and the president on foreign policy, appearances to the contrary notwithstanding." Kristol and Kagan also obliquely criticized Newt Gingrich, if only because his congressional revolution was framed almost entirely around domestic issues. "The 1994 election is often said to have represented one last victory for Ronald Reagan's domestic agenda," they continued. "But Reagan's earlier successes rested as much on foreign as on domestic policy. . . . American conservatism cannot govern by domestic policy alone."[24]

Calling for a "Neo-Reaganist" alternative to what they saw as a muddled bipartisan foreign policy without theoretical or moral grounding, Kristol and Kagan invoked Reagan's name and that of his idol, Teddy Roosevelt, two presidents who "assumed cheerfully" a more assertive global posture. Although a number of countries were mentioned in statements by PNAC's founding members, one target invariably received more attention among the rogue's gallery of volatile nation-states demanding American attention: Iraq. Within a short time, this small, closely knit cadre of neoconservative politicians and intellectuals redefined American foreign policy and redirected America's attention toward Saddam Hussein. On October 31, 1998, a little more than two years after publication of the Kristol-Kagan essay, President Clinton signed the Iraq Liberation Act into law. During the late 1990s, with the economy roaring and low levels of unemployment, few people outside the Beltway's foreign policy community paid much attention. But after September 11, 2001, the neoconservatives' ideas would dominate the national conversation.

Until Bill Clinton's election, Republicans had controlled the White House for twenty of the previous twenty-four years. Republican presidents were thus the obvious and natural stewards of the party's defense and foreign policy agenda. The inversion of partisan control in Washington, as PNAC openly complained, had created a vacuum in Republican foreign policy. With congressional Republicans focused on domestic concerns, this policy void allowed a group of outsiders to redefine national defense and security policy for conservatives and the party. The twenty-five signers of PNAC's original mission statement included only four who had ever served in Congress: Cheney, Rumsfeld, and Minnesota's Vin Weber had served in the House, and Dan Quayle had been a senator before he was vice president. Cheney and Rumsfeld soon became vice president and secretary of defense, respectively. The Bush administration's response to the September 11 attacks would serve as a test case for PNAC's ivory-tower philosophies about American military might. Yet in the mid-1990s, when the most powerful Republican elected officials in America were on Capitol Hill, the party's soon-to-be-calamitous defense policy was being conceived in think tank conference rooms by an assemblage of academics and policy ideologues.

Neoconservative foreign policy ideas were not uncontroversial before 9/11. But as theoretical arguments about American military power gave way to real-world applications in Afghanistan and especially Iraq, this discussion moved from ivory towers to the nitty-gritty realities of war and peace. Although the GOP had long been regarded by most voters as the stronger party on national defense, the Republicans' foreign policy and security performance came to be viewed with a mix of suspicion and scorn. Within two election cycles of the September 11 attacks, polls already showed much public frustration with the Republicans' new foreign policy adventurism. This frustration contributed mightily to the GOP's disastrous showing in the 2006 midterms and John McCain's defeat in the 2008 presidential election. From the Reagan administration on, the congressional foreign affairs committees were led by Republican foreign policy realists like Senator Dick Lugar and Representative Benjamin Gilman—solidly conservative legislators, but not neoconservatives. Such figures were nowhere to be found on the Project for a New American Century's signatory list. This new foreign policy "project" originated very much outside the Republican corridors of Congress.

High Crimes in the Lower Chamber

The yearlong impeachment of Bill Clinton for lying and obstructing justice to cover up an affair with a White House intern was one of the most sordid episodes in modern American politics. Although many of the smaller details have been forgotten by most Americans, the key moments and participants are burned into our collective national memory: Monica Lewinsky and Paula Jones; Matt Drudge and Linda Tripp; Bettie Currie and Vernon Jordan; the cigar and the stained blue Gap dress; the Starr Report and the president's nationally televised admission that he'd had an inappropriate relationship with Lewinsky. The temperament and gusto for impeachment were decidedly different in the two chambers of Congress. The Republicans held majorities in both, but the fact that they had only fifty-five seats in the Senate—a dozen short of the two-thirds majority necessary for conviction—undoubtedly leavened the behavior of Republican senators in ways that did not constrain the House impeachment officers. But the bicameral differences were conditioned by more than head counts. In his book *Sellout*, David Schippers—a lifelong Cook County Democrat tapped by House Judiciary Committee chairman Henry Hyde to lead the committee's investigative process—laments the posture Senate Republicans took toward the impeachment process. Impressed by the House impeachment managers, who he says courageously set aside their reelection concerns, he was outraged by what he saw in the Senate:

> [The reelection concern] didn't apply to the House Managers. It didn't apply to the Republicans on the House Judiciary Committee. They did what justice demanded without thinking about reelection.
>
> Then I came to the U.S. Senate. It was pathetic and sickening. They would break each other's backs to get in front of a camera and announce how they'd vote—before they'd even looked at a word of our evidence. I was disenchanted, disgusted and frankly ashamed.[25]

House Republicans were not entirely unencumbered. Henry Hyde, who had been conducting an extramarital affair for decades, publicly fretted about being viewed as the "Larry Flynt of the House" if he published obscene material related to Clinton's indiscretions. Louisiana's Bob Livingston also had his reasons for caution in December 1998—just as he was poised to replace Gingrich—because he too had been unfaithful to his wife. Still, House Republicans, especially the impeachment managers on the Judiciary Committee, clearly applied themselves to the impeachment with greater zeal than did their partisan counterparts in the Senate.

Whereas Schippers saw House Republicans selflessly risking reelection, national political reporter John Harris noticed a more obvious explanation for their intensity: the asymmetrical electoral risks facing House and Senate members. Citing the impact of gerrymandering in reducing the number of politically competitive House districts, Harris argued that "any individual legislator did not worry about finding the political center. . . . To the extent politicians felt peril, it came from within the parties—from the threat of primary challenge, or from the fear of being ostracized by leaders in the party caucus for failing to show adequate devotion to the party line." Harris cites the example of Representative Jack Quinn of New York, a moderate Republican from a Democrat-heavy swing district in Buffalo who had occasionally supported Clinton administration policies. Quinn ultimately voted to impeach despite having signaled repeatedly to the White House that he would defect from the party line. "Facing political oblivion with his House colleagues, Quinn decided in mid-December that he would vote yes on impeachment."[26]

Likewise, as Peter Baker explains in *The Breach*, his definitive account of the Clinton impeachment, the House managers and a majority of House Judiciary Committee members were outliers within the House Republican Conference. But the Republicans on Judiciary were distinct in the opposite way from Quinn: they were more ideologically conservative and more insulated from electoral rebuke. They "tended to be more conservative than their House GOP colleagues," Baker writes, "just as the committee's Democrats tended to be among the most liberal." Representative Chris Cannon of Utah, for example, regularly boasted one of the highest ratings by the American Conservative Union. Committee members were from such safe districts that, despite the voter anger impeachment generated, not one was defeated in the 1998 election cycle; in fact, of the twenty Republicans on the committee who ran for reelection, nine had no Democratic challenger, and only three received less than 60 percent of the vote.[27] Even endangered Jack Quinn won reelection.

Throughout 1998, Newt Gingrich was something of a moving target. He vacillated between issuing criticisms of President Clinton and adopting an uncomfortable silence. When he did criticize Clinton, Gingrich focused more on the illegality of perjury and obstruction of justice than on the president's alleged infidelities. The reason, of course, was Gingrich's own sexual and marital history: he had twice left wives he had been cheating on, in the second case with a young Hill staffer, Callista Bisek, who later became his third and current wife. Gingrich had seen what the media had done a few months earlier to expose the moral and marital hypocrisies of House colleagues Henry Hyde, Idaho's Helen Chenoweth, and Indiana's Dan Burton. In fact, when Hyde came to Gingrich to personally offer his resignation once news surfaced of his five-year affair a few decades earlier, Gingrich "told him to forget it," recounts Baker in *The Breach*. "Gingrich could hardly afford to let adultery by itself become an offense meriting resignation." Rumors were already circulating on Capitol Hill about his affair with Bisek.[28]

The 1998 midterms delivered a bitter electoral rebuke for Speaker Gingrich. Impeachment fervor backfired: the GOP lost a net of five seats, the first time since 1934 that an incumbent president's party made House gains during a midterm cycle. More remarkably, not since 1822 had the party of a *second*-term president made midterm gains in the House. Yet earlier in the year, believing impeachment would harm the Democrats, Gingrich boldly predicted that his party in 1998 would gain a net of thirty seats—more than half the gains made during the GOP's historic 1994 cycle. He might as well have predicted that his hometown Atlanta Braves were about to start a run of World Series titles. Once the 1998 results came in, the countdown on Gingrich's days as Speaker began in earnest.

On the Senate side, the White House was cheered by news that Democrats Charles Schumer and John Edwards had unseated two vocal Clinton critics: Al D'Amato in New York and Lauch Faircloth in North Carolina. Despite the shadow impeachment cast over that year's election, there was very little congressional turnover. But the Democrats' small gains were magnified by the historical context and the heightened expectations Gingrich had created.

Down in Austin, as George W. Bush celebrated his reelection to a second term as Texas governor, his political mensch Karl Rove was paying close attention to the congressional results. Team Bush knew it needed to keep its distance from the congressional Republicans.

Two days after the election, Gingrich announced he would step down as Speaker and would not even serve the term to which he had just been reelected.[29] It was a stunning reversal of political fortunes for Clinton and Gingrich. Gingrich was now a lamer duck than Clinton. After serving for years as Clinton's political nemesis, and despite Republicans' finally having "Slick Willie" in what they thought was an inescapable trap, Baker writes, Gingrich "did not want [impeachment] to be his last act as Speaker." Nor did Bob Livingston, briefly Gingrich's replacement, "want it to be his first."[30] When Schippers and his team pulled together the impeachment evidence room, they were so worried that Democrats who had "successfully demonized" Gingrich would use the Speaker to "discredit" their work that Hyde had to personally ask both Gingrich and Dick Armey to agree *not* to access the room's information.[31] Gingrich had become a political liability and a target for scorn among his own colleagues, including many who owed their congressional careers to him.

In *The Death of American Virtue*, law professor Ken Gormley describes how the conservative House Republicans at this point repeatedly resisted overtures from the Clinton White House, moderate House Republicans, and Republican senators to find some sort of compromise measure that, given the electoral messages from the 1998 midterms, would provide political cover for all sides. Despite earlier declarations by the president and his legal advisers that they would not settle the Paula Jones harassment suit, Clinton took his lead attorney Bob Bennett's advice and settled the case shortly after the election. The legal rationale was that the perjury charges deriving from Clinton's deposition in the Jones case immediately disappeared, making the impeachment case tougher. As Gormley explains, the Clinton legal team could now ease "off the gas" in the hope that Republicans, with a strategic eye on the 2000 presidential race, preferred a wounded Clinton in office over an incumbent President Al Gore. "Yet the Clinton strategists," writes Gormley, "underestimated the strength of the Republican Party's 'Hezbollah wing,' those who hated Clinton so viscerally that they believed their divine mission 'was to end [his presidency] regardless of the consequences.' As for the White House peace offerings, the House Republicans regrouped, girding themselves for a bloody battle." Upstate New York's representative Amo Houghton, one of the few Republican moderates who did not bend to pressure from his House colleagues, told Clinton that his repeated warnings to fellow Republicans were falling on deaf ears because, as Houghton later described it, a "mob psychology" had taken hold within the House GOP caucus.[32]

Undeterred by the election results, House impeachment managers plowed ahead. An eleventh-hour gambit by the White House to get former president (and former House minority leader) Gerald Ford to persuade the House Republicans to join Democrats in passing a censure motion rather than proceed with impeachment had failed. The GOP was unified and determined. On December 19, 1998, for the first time in almost a century and a half, the U.S. House of Representatives voted to impeach an American president. The four articles of impeachment would now be tried by the Senate.

Newt and Bob and Denny

Newt Gingrich's troubles began well before the 1998 midterms. For all of his bombast and thinly veiled derision of his moderate Republican predecessors in the House leadership, just two and a half years into his speakership Gingrich was forced to contemplate his own ouster. Top leaders of the House Republican majority he brought to power—none of them old-guard moderates—were plotting a coup to replace Gingrich as Speaker.

The plotters were the most powerful House Republicans in the leadership under Gingrich: majority leader Dick Armey, majority whip Tom DeLay, Republican Conference chair (and future Speaker) John Boehner, and Republican leadership chair Bill Paxon. Paxon, a longtime loyalist from Buffalo, was appointed by Gingrich to a position created specifically for him; the other three had been elected to their posts by the House Republican Conference. As everyone in the Beltway knew, by the end of 1998 Gingrich had become a liability for the party and its agenda. President Clinton had led Gingrich into a trap on Medicare, and the Speaker's push for a government shutdown had backfired so badly that the vulnerable Clinton came out looking presidential—or at least enough so to win a second term.

The details of the plan remain in dispute. "The plan was to have Armey, DeLay, Boehner and Paxon present Gingrich with a fait accompli: step aside or be voted out by parliamentary maneuver," reported a then largely unknown junior reporter for *Time* magazine named Jay Carney, who would later serve as President Obama's press secretary. Although "what happened next is murky," according to Carney, Paxon appears to have been to blame: within thirty-six hours after news of the plot leaked out, Paxon offered his resignation to Gingrich, who promptly accepted it. Boehner claimed that he was acting as a mole on Gingrich's behalf and had helped foil the coup. Armey and Delay never admitted what their actions or intentions were. Whatever plan these four Republicans had hatched, the fact that top leaders wanted to overthrow Gingrich did not bode well for his future. "The Speaker was bolstered by the failed coup, albeit temporarily. . . . But dissatisfaction with Newt remains high, and a survivalist strategy won't satisfy his ego for long," Carney reported at the time. "Which is why Gingrich himself may be searching for a way to quit. He has a cover. According to several advisers, America's most unpopular politician is thinking about stepping down as Speaker—to run for President."[33]

The failed coup also poisoned the leadership well for the four Republicans rumored to have been involved in the scheme. (At least in the near term: Boehner became Speaker years later, but only after the GOP had lost and recaptured the House majority.) The stains on this quartet allowed two other Republicans, Louisiana's Bob Livingston and Illinois's Dennis Hastert, to position themselves to ascend to the speakership should Gingrich lose the confidence of his caucus—which is exactly what happened when the impeachment backfired against Republicans in the 1998 midterm elections. With House Republicans scrambling for a fresh face to lead them, Livingston initially emerged as Speaker-elect, but withdrew from consideration after news of his own infidelity broke; Hastert would be the beneficiary of Livingston's spectacular rise and fall. Both men were Republican veterans, but very different politicians.

Robert Linlithgow Livingston IV is an American blueblood whose family first arrived in the colonies in the mid-seventeenth century, when the first in a long line of Robert Livingstons bought 160,000 acres of prime Hudson Valley property and expanded it into a manor larger than Rhode Island. A Livingston signed the Declaration of Independence, another administered the presidential oath to George Washington, a third served on the Supreme Court.[34] Bob Livingston, born in 1943, married a senator's daughter and in 1976 ran for and won Louisiana's First District House seat, in the New Orleans suburbs. Aside from a failed bid for governor in 1987, his political career was the story of upward success in the

House GOP ranks. When Republicans took majority control in 1995, Gingrich made Livingston chairman of the Appropriations Committee. Colleagues regarded him as a serious, thoughtful legislator.

A year older than Livingston, John Dennis Hastert grew up in the rural Illinois town of Oswego, the son of a farm seed distributor father and a mother who had a Saturday morning egg delivery route. When young Denny graduated from Wheaton College, he was the first person on either side of his family to earn a four-year degree. He taught government and coached the local high school wrestling team, then ran unsuccessfully for state legislator. From there, his career blossomed thanks to his personal likeability and the failing health of those above him on the local political ladder. In 1980, a year after he lost that state legislative race, the incumbent became terminally ill, and local leaders drafted Hastert to replace him. One of the mentors who drafted him into politics, John Grotberg, won the local U.S. House seat in 1984 only to learn that he had terminal cancer; local leaders again cleared a path for the affable Hastert to run for and win Illinois's Fourteenth District seat in 1986.[35]

The familial and class differences between Livingston and Hastert were dwarfed by the common trait that put them in line to replace Gingrich—they were both demure, steady, and well-liked members of a House Republican Conference in desperate need of a striking departure from the bombastic and controversial Gingrich. After the Speaker resigned, the toxic duo of Dick Armey and Tom DeLay removed themselves from consideration and consolidated the caucus's support behind Livingston's candidacy. With Gingrich's resignation, the pending vote on the articles of impeachment against Bill Clinton, and Clinton's sudden announcement that the United States was launching targeted strikes against weapons facilities in Saddam Hussein's Iraq, December 1998 was one of the most tumultuous times anyone in the House could remember. Livingston seemed to be precisely the steady hand the House needed. Even most Democrats liked and respected him. "A first-rate human being," said veteran Democratic representative David Obey of Wisconsin.[36]

And then, so quickly that he never had a chance to drop the "-elect" from his title, Livingston resigned in disgrace. Aided by tips generated by *Hustler* publisher Larry Flynt, who was disgusted with the Republicans' impeachment antics and promised to pay a $1 million reward for information about extramarital affairs of Republican members of Congress, the media reported on Livingston's infidelities. A tearful Livingston admitted at a press conference that he had at times "strayed from" his marriage. Although most Republicans were personally supportive, a few fumed that, amid presidential impeachment hearings they continued to insist were not about sex or infidelity but about perjury and obstruction of justice, they were kept in the dark about Livingston's transgressions. "Bob should have told us" because it would have affected the search for a new Speaker, Tennessee Republican Zach Wamp complained to the media.[37]

Livingston's admission further rattled an already unstable House Republican caucus. In their political biography of Tom DeLay, *The Hammer Comes Down*, Texas journalists Lou Dubose and Jan Reid describe DeLay's reaction to Livingston's downfall. DeLay was dismayed but didn't miss a beat: "As Livingston collapsed, DeLay again tightened his hold on power. Even as he stood on the floor of the House with the eyes welling up with tears, describing Bob Livingston as 'this good man,' his deputy whips were locking up the votes to elect Denny Hastert Speaker. More quickly than DeLay had made Bob Livingston Speaker-elect, he cut him loose once he was damaged goods."[38] If he could not be Speaker, DeLay was going to be very close to whoever took the gavel next.

Lott to the Rescue

By December 1998, President Clinton was gaining confidence. Polls showed that a majority of Americans preferred censuring the president to removing him from office. The Clinton team also knew that minority leader Tom Daschle and his Senate Democrats had sufficient votes to prevent the two-thirds majority needed to remove the president. Meanwhile, the House Republican leadership was cannibalizing itself. So the White House and its allies repeatedly drilled home three key talking points: congressional Republicans were acting on behalf of an unrepresentative and radicalized subset of American primary voters; they were trying to reverse the will of the broader electorate in both the 1996 presidential election and the 1998 midterms; and they were ignoring the majority preferences of the public at large, as indicated by repeated poll results.

Federal judge Richard Posner, a prolific writer and a respected legal theorist at the University of Chicago, scoffed at all three claims. In *An Affair of State*, Posner argues that nothing about our constitutional design implies that members of Congress should be perfectly representative of the electorate or even the public at large; that the constitutional purpose of impeachment is precisely to remove a president who—Gerald Ford excepted—by definition had been elected to that office or at least the vice presidency; and that keeping presidents in office because of a popular majority makes no more sense than impeaching those who lack majority approval. But whether or not they had the public behind them, Posner argues, House Republicans made a very foolish error by ignoring the Democrats' request to limit the allegations and evidence to what was contained in the Starr Report.

Hoping to turn the public tide against Clinton, the House GOP leaked documents and videos of Clinton's grand jury deposition. Then, both after the Starr Report materials were made public and again after the articles of impeachment were sent to the Senate, House impeachment managers tried to pile new allegations, witnesses, and other materials onto the trial record, including Clinton's alleged sexual harassment of Kathleen Willey and Juanita Broaddrick. Had they been more restrained, writes Posner, complaints of "excessive partisanship leveled against the Republicans would have been largely defused, and the boomerang effects of hastily releasing the evidence that Starr had given the [Judiciary] Committee, including the videotape of the President's grand jury testimony," could have been avoided. Posner concludes that despite sufficient evidence in the Starr Report to bolster the perjury and obstruction of justice charges, the desperate attempts by impeachment managers to supplement the Starr Report—attempts that "fizzled"—were a very foolhardy gambit. In their passion to convict, House Republicans tainted their own indictment.[39]

Most senators, including many Republicans, did not want the constitutional responsibility of trying Clinton dumped in their laps. Because none of the four impeachment articles were likely to receive the required two-thirds majority, a scramble quickly developed to find an agreeable bipartisan solution that would keep the Senate from tearing itself apart. The task of navigating his colleagues through some of the most treacherous political waters the Senate had encountered since Vietnam fell to majority leader Trent Lott—the former House firebrand who would never have been in this position if Bob Dole had either lost the 1996 Republican presidential primary or won it and then defeated Clinton in the general election.

Lott was saved by two Senate titans. In a rare and quite extraordinary development, on January 7, 1999, senators from both parties met in secret—without reporters or even staff allowed—inside the hallowed walls of the Old Senate Chamber. After some initial discussion, the original "Gingrich senator" Phil Gramm and liberal icon Ted Kennedy stepped forward and agreed to work out a solution acceptable to both party caucuses. Although at first nothing was set down on paper and the specifics of a potential Gramm-Kennedy compromise remained unclear, the mere prospect of one of the chamber's most conservative and one of its most liberal members finding common ground produced widespread relief on both sides. Depending upon how one viewed the collegial nature of the chamber, this was the Senate either at its best or at its worst.

Yet Lott was far from in the clear. The House managers were pushing for an extended trial and the late introduction of new evidence, and they wanted their witnesses to testify live in the well of the Senate. Most senators wanted a quick, clean trial without salacious details or the cross-examinations of witnesses. They certainly didn't want Lewinsky trotted out to recount the tale of her soiled blue dress. But *most* senators did not equal *every* senator. "Lott was facing enormous problems on the Republican side. He and other senior members were being buffeted by 'cross-currents' driven by a recent sea change in Senate membership," recounts Ken Gormley, referring to one of the highest historical percentages of former House members in Senate history. "Lott was now confronted with a potential rebellion by twenty-two conservative senators led by [Oklahoma's Don] Nickles and Santorum, who believed that Lott was selling their party downriver and being too 'accommodationist.' The 'House-ification' of the Senate by many senators philosophically aligned with the thirteen House managers [made] it difficult for Senate leadership to implement the Gramm-Kennedy plan, even if they knew what it was."[40]

The House votes to impeach fell largely along party lines, testifying to the polarized nature of the House party caucuses. House Republicans were hungry for an extensive and very public trial. In his memoir *Herding Cats*, Lott said he knew he would never attain the two-thirds supermajority needed to convict, and thus a lurid and extensive trial might only damage the institution and his party, which was still digesting a dispiriting report about the 1998 election results from GOP pollster Linda DiVall, who warned that moderates had been soured by the House Republicans' impeachment fervor. Conservative senators including Santorum—who, like Lott, had graduated to the Senate from the House—were less concerned with electoral implications than with the judgment of history. "I was thinking of history, too," Lott remembers. "But many GOP senators failed to see that I also was trying to guide our part of the impeachment process with an eye on the 2000 elections."

Lott appeared jointly at an impromptu press conference with his Democratic counterpart Tom Daschle to announce that they had reached a deal for trial procedures that would not include live witnesses. When the press conference ended, the two leaders raised their hands together like presidential running mates. Seeing this, Santorum scowled, "There goes Lott again, caving to the Democrats." And yet it was Santorum to whom Lott turned for advice on the thornier task of explaining the compromise to the House impeachment managers, who continued to press for a longer trial and live witnesses. Arriving "uninvited and unannounced and unwanted" to visit the impeachment managers, Lott explained that each side would have twenty-four hours over five days to make its case for impeachment or acquittal—with no witnesses. Barr, Cannon, and Hyde called the plan a sellout. "I was in the House," Lott reminded them. "I was where you guys are. I sat on the Judiciary Committee during Watergate. I'm not against you guys."[41] One can only imagine how such a call for accommodation would have been received had it come from Bob Dole. But no matter the messenger, Senate Republicans didn't have the votes to convict. Clinton survived.

The impeachment of Bill Clinton was not an exclusively House-led political effort. Many Republican senators and other Republican politicians ardently supported removing the president from office. But ten Republican senators—a fifth of Lott's caucus—voted not guilty along with the forty-five unified Democrats on the perjury article of impeachment, and five also voted with the Democrats against the obstruction of justice charge. It is no exaggeration to say that the impeachment was largely conceived, spearheaded, and cheered on by House Republicans, in particular the electorally safe, ideologically conservative impeachment managers and their backers on the House Judiciary Committee. It may not have been entirely a House production, but Republicans in the people's chamber provided the starring cast, direction, soundtrack, and all the special effects.

Recounting Impeachment

The conventional political wisdom is that impeachment made Bill Clinton so politically toxic that it cost Vice President Al Gore the 2000 presidential election: Gore was damned if he embraced Clinton because of the president's scandalous behavior, and damned if he distanced himself from Clinton's successes. Circumstantial and even empirical evidence suggested that Gore was the favorite. The economy in 2000 was strong, receipts were flowing into the U.S. Treasury, and Clinton and congressional Republicans had just passed another balanced budget. Even Americans with antigovernment views were in a relatively good mood. Although George W. Bush offered undeniable appeal as a big-state governor with a potent family name running as an outsider against Washington, Gore boasted the stronger political and policy résumé. His eight years each in the House and then the Senate, plus eight more as Clinton's vice president, prepared him to assume the presidency.

Not that Republicans wanted Gore to have a head start: many were perfectly happy to keep Clinton in the Oval Office as politically damaged goods. As conservative pundit Rich Lowry later speculated, "If Clinton had left or been removed at any point . . . [Gore] would have taken over. . . . There would have been a nearly seamless continuity in the American government, and the Democrats probably would have had a better chance to hold the White House in 2000."[42] At a time when Nate Silver was an unknown consultant working for KPMG in Chicago, seven political scientists announced at the 2000 annual meeting of the American Political Science Association the results of their forecasting models for the two-party share of the popular vote. Relying on key predictive variables such as economic growth, six of the seven forecast that Gore would capture between 52.3 and 55.4 percent of the two-party vote nationally.[43]

But if short-term politics, economics, and even biography pointed to a Gore victory, history did not. With just one exception, parties in the postwar era have been unable to win three consecutive presidential elections. And since Martin Van Buren did it in 1836, only one sitting vice president has won the White House. Both of these exceptions occurred in the same year, when George H. W. Bush won in 1988. But the recency of that double exception also meant that political lightning would have to strike twice within a short period for Gore to win. And, again, Bush fils was an undeniably appealing candidate with a potent family name running an outsider's campaign. There were ample reasons to believe 2000 might be more favorable for Republicans than political science models suggested.

That said, might the belief that Clinton's impeachment was a net liability to Gore and the Democrats be—if not exactly wrong—at least overstated? The 1998 midterm losses clearly put congressional Republicans back on their heels. Pollster Linda DiVall's postelection memo confirmed that Republicans had been penalized for overzealous persecution of the president. Approval numbers for the party generally, and for congressional Republicans in particular, had taken a hit. The oft-repeated pledge by George W. Bush, Dick Cheney, and their surrogates that a Bush presidency would "restore honesty and integrity" to the White House was a thinly veiled attempt to drag Clinton's behavior into the race. The Bush campaign obviously believed Clinton posed problems for Gore. Less obvious is the fact that Bush's "compassionate conservative" pitch was the campaign's acknowledgment that voters harbored serious reservations about congressional Republicans' ferocious brand of reactionary politics. Bush and his political adviser Karl Rove knew there were risks to overplaying the morality card or focusing voters' attention too closely on congressional Republicans.

Perhaps the most compelling evidence that impeachment and the radicalism of congressional Republicans created electoral problems for Bush was the way the Bush campaign handled and packaged its candidate. Rove's fascination with the 1896 William McKinley campaign led him to an epiphany that doubled as an ingenious way to keep Bush from getting dragged down by his own party: in a modern version of the traditional nineteenth-century "front porch" campaign, rather than troop the Texas governor around the country, Rove brought conservative and religious leaders, Republicans officials, and other notable political figures to meet privately with Bush in Austin.

Bush couldn't stay cloistered forever, but even when he ventured to Capitol Hill to meet with fellow Republicans, as he did in June

1999, he treaded carefully. By then the Texas governor had racked up an impressive number of endorsements from Republicans in Congress: 23 of the party's 55 senators and 126 of its 233 House members. He was the establishment favorite and the certifiable front-runner. The goal of his visit was to signal his inevitability to party elites and donors who might be contemplating an endorsement of John McCain, maybe lock down a few more endorsements, and yet avoid associating himself with congressional Republicans in the eyes of voters. Reporting on Bush's Capitol Hill trip, veteran *Washington Post* reporters Dan Balz and David von Drehle described the potential trade-offs this way:

> Bush's relationship with the GOP-controlled Congress looks to be a long, delicate dance. The more support he commands from elected officials now, strategists from both parties agree, the more difficult it will be for any of his GOP rivals to deny him the party's nomination.
>
> But the Republican majority—with its legacy of impeachment, former speaker Newt Gingrich and a government shutdown—has proven not very popular with large numbers of voters. So the more Bush embraces Congress, the more he risks offending the moderates and independents he will need to win a general election.[44]

Bush stood for photo ops with several Republicans, including fellow Texans Kay Bailey Hutchinson and Tom DeLay. The Democratic National Committee quickly pounced, trying to hang congressional Republicans—DeLay specifically—around Bush's neck. "Attempts to tie me to DeLay and all that stuff, that's fine, but I don't think it's going to hunt," Bush replied. "We're running for the executive branch."[45]

For the rest of the campaign, Bush kept congressional Republicans—at the time, the party's highest-ranking officials—at arm's length. At the 2000 Republican National Convention in Philadelphia, only a few members of Congress spoke during prime time. Throughout the 2000 campaign, Bush avoided being seen too often alongside his partisan cohorts in Congress. "While Mr. Bush reveled in the support of the governors, he has studiously avoided any such display with members of Congress, whom he has associated with the gridlock and partisanship in Washington," *New York Times* reporter Alison Mitchell noted at the time. "In contrast, he called the governors pragmatic problem-solvers and said they would reinforce the message that he is a Washington outsider who can reach across party lines to get things done."[46] It's hard to sell the slogan "I'm a uniter, not a divider" while standing next to Tom DeLay.

While blame for the GOP's national image problems did not fall exclusively upon congressional Republicans, the fault was largely theirs, and House Republicans were especially culpable. Again, the most obvious evidence is the party's own internal choices, most notably the elevation of Dennis Hastert to Speaker. Compared to polarizing, off-putting southerners like DeLay or Armey, the avuncular former wrestling coach was a preferable choice to wield the gavel. When the congressional caucuses effectively admit to their own toxicity, it's hard to blame the party's presidential nominee for not wanting to poison his campaign by consorting with them. And therein exists a final irony in the curious relationships between the two Presidents Bush and the congressional Republicans of their respective eras: the congressionalization of the Republican Party and the rising influence of the party's House caucus made the younger Bush's capture of the Oval Office almost as difficult as they made the elder Bush's surrender of it.

Twilight of the Rockefeller Republicans

The late Jim Jeffords was always a political iconoclast. The Vermont senator's electoral career reflected the partisan changes that unfolded in his state, region, and nationally over his long career in public service. In 1972, as his state's attorney general, Jeffords lost the 1972 Republican gubernatorial primary because Vermont's Republican establishment, angry about the pressure Jeffords brought against International Paper Company to clean up Lake Champlain, backed another candidate.[47] He won Vermont's at-large seat in the U.S. House in 1974, the post-Watergate election that swept into Congress a new generation of Democrats—including Patrick Leahy, the first Democrat Vermont ever elected to the U.S. Senate—but only seventeen Republican House freshmen. The 1988 election was particularly sweet for Jeffords: he easily won the Senate seat of retiring moderate Republican Robert Stafford on the same day his state voted for blue-blooded Republican centrists George H. W. Bush in the presidential race and Peter Plympton Smith to fill Jeffords's vacated House seat. In the 1980s, moderate Republicans still dominated Vermont politics.

During the 1990s, Jeffords continued to bask in the partisan comforts of Republican centrism. He built strong relationships with both presidents he served with. He and Bush Sr. saw eye to eye on most issues. Bill Clinton regarded Jeffords as his favorite Senate Republican. To the dismay of conservatives, he frequently broke party ranks: on environmental issues, the Clarence Thomas Supreme Court nomination, Clinton's impeachment, gays in the military, and the Family and Medical Leave Act, among other key votes. Jim Jeffords was a RINO—Republican in Name Only—before the term became commonplace.

Both in Jeffords's home state and nationally, however, partisan currents were changing. Formerly a bedrock Republican state, the Green Mountain State was turning left so quickly it was mocked as the "People's Republic of Vermont." Meanwhile, the national Republican Party was heading in the opposite direction. Upon entering the Senate in January 1989, Jeffords likely took solace in knowing that Bob Dole, whom he regarded as ideological kinsman and responsible party leader, would lead the Republican Conference. But his position would steadily be undercut by rising polarization.

George W. Bush's election in 2000 was Jeffords's breaking point. If the elder Bush was Jeffords's ideal Republican, the son clearly was not. In the Senate, Jeffords pushed back against Bush 43's tax cut, exacting concessions from a displeased White House. But it was spending cuts to education that finally pushed him over the edge: at a press conference in Burlington on May 24, 2001, Jeffords announced that he was leaving the Republican Party. Although Democratic minority leader Tom Daschle had promised him the chairmanship of the Senate Environment and Public Works Committee if he made the jump, Jeffords dismissed any suggestion that he switched for political gain. "My decision . . . was to leave the Republican party," he said. "It was not based on aspirations for something else."[48] He didn't switch his partisan affiliation to Democratic, but pledged to caucus with the Democrats as an independent for the purpose of forming a majority. "I feel as if a weight has been lifted from my shoulders," he said.[49] Because the Senate had been split, with fifty seats apiece and Vice President Cheney's tiebreaking vote providing Lott and the Republicans with a majority, Jeffords's decision instantly replaced Lott with Daschle in the majority leader's chair.

Jeffords was neither the first nor even the most notable party-switcher during this era of American politics. But his was an exceptional case. Since the mid-twentieth century, most party-switchers had left the Democrats to join the GOP. Most famous among them was Ronald Reagan, a New Deal Democrat with a labor movement background who became the most beloved Republican since Teddy Roosevelt. Reagan didn't switch parties after being elected, but South Carolina's Strom Thurmond did, breaking open the dam for southern Democrats in 1964, when he declared himself a Republican. Following the Republican takeover of Congress in 1994, a spate of mostly southern conservative Democrats who had begun to feel ideologically disconnected from their party took an opportunistic leap to join the new Republican majority. Senator Richard Shelby of Alabama switched the week of the elections, and Ben Nighthorse Campbell of Colorado joined Shelby in Dole's new Senate majority shortly after the 104th Congress took office. Five House Democrats— Georgia's Nathan Deal, Louisiana's Jimmy Hayes and Billy Tauzin, Mississippi's Michael Parker, and Greg Laughlin of Texas—also switched by the end of 1995.

Some congressional moderates used the Jeffords defection as an opportunity to air their grievances with the party's leadership, blaming top Senate Republicans for ignoring the repeated warnings of caucus moderates like Jeffords, Maine's Susan Collins and Olympia Snowe, and Pennsylvania's Arlen Specter. "This was a very loud wake-up call and I think the caucus was awakened," said Specter, who a few years later would also abandon the GOP.[50] Moreover, blaming Jeffords for the Senate Republicans' losing their majority overlooked the far greater damage the caucus suffered by the traditional means. Six months before Jeffords's defection, the Republicans lost a net of four seats in the 2000 elections. Although they picked up an open seat in Nevada, and George Allen defeated Democrat Chuck Robb in Virginia, five nonsouthern Republicans lost their reelection bids—Delaware's Bill Roth, Michigan's Spencer Abraham, Minnesota's Rod Grams, Missouri's John Ashcroft, and Washington's Slade Gorton—and Democrat Bill Nelson captured the Florida seat vacated by retiring Republican Connie Mack.

Along with the appointment of Democrat Zell Miller to fill the seat left open in Georgia when Republican Paul Coverdell died in July 2000, the net loss of five seats in four months pared the Republican majority from fifty-five members to the bare minimum of fifty seats. Moderate House Republican Chris Shays of Connecticut called the 2000 election cycle "a humiliating defeat" for Lott and deputy majority leader Mitch McConnell of Kentucky. "If I were in the Senate," said Shays, "I would want new leadership."[51]

Lott and the Republicans would recapture their majority in 2002 and two years later build it back to the fifty-five seats they had attained in 1996. Jeffords, still caucusing with the minority Democrats, was undeterred. "The reasons for my switch, while apparent to me then," he said in a statement issued on the two-year anniversary of his leaving the GOP, "have become painfully clear to me now. The events of the past two years have only heightened my concern over the President's veer to the right, and the poisoning of our democratic process of government. Pundits asked after last November's election: will the President over-reach with his Republican majorities in the House and Senate? Well, President Bush hasn't just over-reached, he has set a new standard for extreme partisan politics that on many occasions has been supported by the Republican-controlled Congress."[52]

Jeffords would be vindicated by history. Thanks largely to the decision to invade Iraq, which Jeffords opposed but congressional Republicans supported almost unanimously, the GOP lost its congressional majorities in 2006, the year Jeffords decided to retire rather than seek a fourth term. His switch also will be remembered as a signature moment in the steady decline of Republican competitiveness in New England. By 2006, Vermont would be without a Republican member of Congress for the first time since the Civil War. New Hampshire, Connecticut, Massachusetts, Rhode Island,

and Vermont would all have two Democrats in the Senate. And Maine's two Republican senators, Olympia Snowe and Susan Collins, were rated among the most liberal members of Lott's caucus. Within a few cycles, Republicans would hold none of the twenty-two U.S. House seats from the six New England states. And whose seat in the region was the last to fall into Democratic hands? None other than the district represented by vocal Lott critic Chris Shays of Connecticut.

When Harry Reid became the Democrats' new majority leader in January 2007, he had a majority of fifty-five Democrats plus the backing of two independents: Connecticut's Joe Lieberman, who had left the Democratic Party and would eventually back John Mc-Cain in the 2008 election, but who still caucused with the Democrats; and Socialist Bernie Sanders, who took Jeffords's vacated Vermont seat. That working majority of fifty-seven senators was large enough that, even without the Senate's five remaining southern Democrats (Arkansas's Blanche Lincoln and Mark Pryor, Florida's Bill Nelson, Louisiana's Mary Landrieu, and newly elected Virginian Jim Webb), Reid still had enough votes to form a non-southern majority. Such was the state of the national Republican Party at the end of Jeffords's career: dominating the South, but struggling to compete in almost every other corner of the country except a swath of small, rural breadbasket and plains states. The Rockefeller Republicans were headed for electoral extinction, and with them the GOP's ability to maintain its Senate majority.

Republicans in Transition

For Republicans in the late 1990s, the replacements of Newt Gingrich and Bob Dole with Dennis Hastert and Trent Lott were signature transitions. They not only shifted leadership power but served as political and ideological barometers. Both chambers were becoming more polarized, which for Republicans meant increasingly conservative House and Senate caucuses. Where Hastert's rise differed from Lott's was in the signal their promotions sent to the national media and the broader public: the selection of Hastert as Speaker was an admission that Gingrich had quickly become politically toxic, whereas Lott's promotion to majority leader indicated that Dole's center-right moderation lagged behind the ideological shifts occurring within the Senate Republican Conference. The final moments of the Clinton impeachment were especially revealing of the leadership situation in the two chambers. The House was in disarray, plagued by its members' assignations and patent hypocrisy, whereas the Senate was finding its balance thanks to a new majority leader capable of demanding respect among the GOP's growing cohort of red-state Republicans.

The two Republican presidential nominees during this period lost one election and won the other, but George W. Bush's election was so narrow that he needed the Republicans' small-state Electoral College advantage to compensate for finishing with a half million fewer popular votes than Al Gore. More to the point, the Republicans in 1996 had consciously chosen to prioritize their congressional majorities over recapturing the White House. Four years later, Bush realized that those congressional majorities significantly impeded his desire to depict himself as a temperate, centrist, "compassionate conservative." It took less than six years for Republicans to admit that the congressional majorities that they fought for decades to attain were creating unanticipated problems for the party and its brand.

Bush's narrow victory gave the GOP an opportunity to refurbish that brand, or at least divert public attention from one end of Pennsylvania Avenue to the other. In 2001, with Republicans in control of the national government for the first time since the Eisenhower administration, there was talk of a rolling realignment that would lead to a generation of GOP rule. The only missing element was a dramatic, realigning moment like the stock market crash of 1929. Osama bin Laden was about to provide it.

5

PARALYSIS

On January 20, 2001, for the first time in nearly half a century, the Republican Party controlled the entire national government. The GOP's grip on government, however, was rather tenuous. The Senate was evenly split, with each party holding fifty seats and control determined by Vice President Dick Cheney's tiebreaking vote; but then Senator Jim Jeffords of Vermont abandoned the Republican Party and majority leader Trent Lott instantly became the minority leader. On the House side, Speaker Dennis Hastert's razor-thin 222-member majority was vulnerable to a mere handful of Republican defections. George W. Bush had won the White House, but unlike Ronald Reagan in 1980 or his father in 1988, he had finished behind Al Gore in the popular vote and pulled no net new House or Senate Republicans into office with him. This was not quite the overwhelming mandate that Franklin Roosevelt and his New Deal Democrats brought into office in 1933, or even what Dwight Eisenhower enjoyed in 1953—the last time Republicans exercised unified power in Washington.

It is difficult, from this vantage point, to remember the early criticisms of the Bush administration as seemingly aimless and unfocused. The political situation for both congressional Republicans and the president changed dramatically just nine months into Bush's presidency when terrorists attacked the United States on September 11, 2001. The GOP's advantage on security, defense, and military issues was immediately magnified. Fourteen months later, in the 2002 midterm elections, Republicans expanded and cemented their control of Congress. Although the gains were small, voters had clearly vested more power in national Republicans. A few days after the midterms, beneath a picture of key Democratic National Committee strategists with folded arms and glum faces, the *Washington Post* ran a story with a headline that summarized the Beltway's postelection verdict: "The Loser's Circle." Just two years later, after Bush won reelection and declared he had won "more political capital," pundits buzzed about the long-term Republican realignment Bush's political guru Karl Rove had been forecasting for years. Conservative wish lists moved to the fore; compromise and accommodation with moderates and liberals suddenly seemed passé. If the 2000 elections gave Republicans a taste of what they might achieve with unified control of the federal government, the 2002 and 2004 electoral results were an invitation to move all-in. For many Republicans, the long-awaited moment to expand and consolidate their power for the long term had arrived.

Still, public support for the conservative agenda lagged behind its adherents' ambitions, and the mandate provided by George W. Bush's narrow reelection—although legitimized this time by a popular vote majority—was thin. Yet the Bush-era Republicans at times governed as if they had been swept into office with an overwhelming electoral mandate. In so doing, the Bush White House in four short years completely destroyed the national security advantage the GOP had enjoyed for the better part of four decades. The first Bush term was a time for Republicans to rejoice and push for agenda items that had long been thwarted by their inability to capture the entire federal government at once—but also to sow the seeds for the party's mid-decade failures. The ideological and policy hubris of these years, both abroad and at home, was a recipe for overreach.

For Republicans, Bush's second term was a disaster. The party's twelve-year reign in Congress ended in 2006. By 2008 political observers would be describing Barack Obama's election as having closed the curtain on the Reagan era. The Democrats would have unified control of the federal government for the first time in sixteen years—and had made history by electing the country's first African American president. The GOP's congressional fortunes were bad, but its presidential performance was even bleaker. In just a few years, the GOP turned from talk of an emerging national majority to recriminations and predictions of permanent minority status.

Medicare, Part D(eLay)

By 2002 many of the party's 1994 revolutionaries were gone, having either lost reelection at some point, graduated from the House to the Senate, or retired to better-paid jobs as lobbyists. But Tom DeLay was still around, and more powerful than ever. When House majority leader Dick Armey announced he would retire at the end of 2002, DeLay was elected to replace him.

A former pest control businessman from Sugar Land, a suburb southwest of Houston, Tom DeLay began his electoral career by winning a seat in the Texas legislature at age thirty-two. In Austin, "Hot Tub Tom" developed a reputation as an ambitious, fun-loving, larger-than-life personality. Six years later, in 1984, he won election to the U.S. House seat that Ron Paul vacated to run for the U.S. Senate. (Paul lost the Republican primary to Phil Gramm, who went on to become the first "Gingrich senator.") Armey was also a member of that relatively small class of 1984 House Republican freshmen, and over the next two decades the two Texans would help transform both the House of Representatives and national Republican politics.

When Armey stepped down, DeLay became second in line to Speaker Dennis Hastert. The Texan was already known to for aggressive, even unscrupulous, behavior. He had referred to CNN as the Communist News Network and to the Environmental Protection Agency as the "Gestapo of government." He twisted arms on Capitol Hill and wrung dollars from K Street. While it's difficult to isolate DeLay's worst political moment, the floor roll call vote for Medicare Part D certainly makes any short list.

Prior to his reelection bid, President Bush wanted to create a major new benefit for senior citizens, a constituency he was counting on to deliver solid majorities for his 2004 reelection. So the administration proposed adding a new "Part D" prescription drug coverage benefit to Medicare. Many Republicans were conflicted: they wanted to help their party's president produce a tangible benefit to a key voting bloc, but they worried that endorsing the largest expansion of the nation's fastest-growing major entitlement program would harm their anti–big-government reputation. Fearing defections by congressional Republicans, the administration and Center for Medicare and Medicaid administrator Thomas Scully promised that the ten-year price tag for Part D would not exceed $400 billion. (It was later revealed that Scully's internal estimates, which the White House hid from fellow Republicans and the public, pegged this cost at more than $500 billion.) Despite these assurances, there were enough disgruntled House Republicans that Speaker Hastert had to keep very close tabs on the whip count to avert the embarrassment of a floor defeat.

By this time DeLay had acquired a new nickname. No longer "Hot Tub Tom," now he was "the Hammer." He was respected, even feared, because he was known to deliver two closely related commodities: floor votes for the House leadership in Washington and campaign resources for members' reelection efforts. The prescription drug bill was exactly the type of policy-meets-politics fight for which the Hammer was built. In fact, the original House version was nearly rejected when the GOP leadership first brought it to a roll call vote in June 2003. Only some last-minute maneuvering by DeLay and Hastert saved the day: the bill passed by a single vote, 216–215, after Republicans Butch Otter of Idaho and Jo Ann Emerson of Missouri were persuaded to change their votes to aye. Twenty Republicans voted against or present, and without the help of nine Democrats the GOP could not have forged a majority. Four of Indiana's six Republicans—Dan Burton, Steve Buyer, John Hostettler, and Mike Pence—accounted for one-fifth of the GOP's twenty defections.[1]

One day earlier and with far greater ease, the Senate had passed its version of the bill, and over the next three months the differences were rectified by a bicameral conference committee. House Republican leaders knew the floor roll call would again be close. They were scheduled to vote on the rectified bill the week before Thanksgiving, and that's when matters got interesting, thanks to a surprising double blast-from-the-past: two iconic retired House Republicans—former Speaker Newt Gingrich and recently retired majority leader Dick Armey—inserted themselves into the national debate.

A few days before the scheduled House vote, Gingrich spoke to House Republicans in a Capitol Hill legislative committee room. He implored them to vote for the legislation; he specifically touted the bill's creation of health savings accounts, a policy innovation the Bush administration was promoting vigorously. The speech was "very powerful" and "critical" to the bill's eventual passage, recalls John Feehery, then Hastert's deputy. Several Republicans who had voted no back in June specifically credited Gingrich's rousing speech with changing their minds. When Gingrich ran for president almost a decade later, episodes like his defense of Part D raised many conservatives' hackles. "I do think the combination of Medicare Part D and [No Child Left Behind] hurt Newt in that they both play into a narrative about big government conservatives that a lot of conservatives are trying to get away from," influential RedState.com blogger Erick Erickson wrote in late 2011.[2]

Upon learning of Gingrich's speech, Dick Armey quickly penned an op-ed for the *Wall Street Journal* urging Republicans to vote against Medicare Part D. In the years after they left Congress, the two men would move in decidedly different directions. Armey would stake out a position as an aggressive supporter of major entitlement reform. He co-chaired the David Koch–funded Citizens for a Sound Economy, which later split and merged with Jack Kemp's Empower America to form Freedom Works, under the motto "Lower taxes, less government, more freedom." Armey began his op-ed with the blunt language that had helped catapult him to national attention twelve years earlier, during the 1991 Bush tax fight.

"I have great respect for my friend and former colleague Newt Gingrich," he wrote. "But on the Medicare prescription drug legislation currently pending in Congress, he is dead wrong. The deal . . . struck this week is . . . bad news for senior citizens and possibly even worse political news for the Republican Party."[3]

When the bill came to the floor, Hastert and DeLay struggled to hold together enough of their caucus to pass it, with help from a handful of supportive Democrats. Michigan's Nick Smith was one of the Republicans who had voted nay on the first roll call back in June. Smith was retiring at the end of the term, and his son Brad was running in the Republican primary to replace him. At some point during the November deliberations—and before what turned out to be a rule-breaking three-hour vote, held open to give the leadership time to whip recalcitrant Republicans into line—the elder Smith was approached on the floor by DeLay. Smith claimed the next day that DeLay offered to contribute $100,000 (presumably from the deep-pocketed leadership PAC) to Brad's primary campaign. He later retracted this, but once the media got a whiff of the episode, DeLay's actions came under scrutiny as possibly violating not only House rules but legal statutes for bribery. An ethics committee was impaneled in early 2004 to investigate what violations, if any, DeLay, Smith, or others had committed.

Did DeLay only pledge to endorse Smith's son, or did he promise to deliver a contribution to the younger Smith's campaign? The ethics committee interviewed DeLay, Smith, Tom Feeney, and then–Republican National Campaign Committee chair Tom Reynolds, as well as several House Republican staffers. DeLay said he promised to endorse Smith's son as his "final offer," but also strongly implied that it was Smith who was fishing for more than an endorsement. After a six-month inquiry, and nearly a year after the incident, the ethics committee issued a sixty-two-page report. DeLay was admonished for violating House rules. The panel concluded that he had improperly offered "support for the personal interests of another member as part of a quid pro quo to achieve a legislative goal."[4] Democrats and the media howled that DeLay's actions went beyond rule breaking—that he had committed felony bribery.

But the larger Republican crimes were political and ideological. Many House members who would later cheerlead for the Republicans' austerity movement during the Obama era—including future Speaker John Boehner, future majority leader Eric Cantor, Iowa's Steve King, and the GOP's go-to man for fiscal responsibility, Paul Ryan—all voted for the entitlement. As *Slate*'s Matt Yglesias remarked in 2012, during the national debate over the affordability of Obamacare, those votes seemed to have "basically been eliminated from memory. Now all good Republicans are against spending money on anything, but nobody proposes to repeal the basic [Part D] benefit. It's as if the whole thing never happened."[5] And remember Christopher Cox and Jim Nussle, then junior House Republicans who in 1991 delivered stinging indictments of congressional norms in back-to-back lectures at the Heritage Foundation? Back then, Cox complained about massive spending bills, which few members bothered to read, being passed at late hours; Nussle called for members of Congress to be compensated on a merit system in which pay increases would be wedded to their ability to balance the budget. Given the unprecedented three-hour floor vote, not to mention the DeLay-Smith floor episode, you might suppose that Cox and Nussle stomped off the floor in protest of this massive entitlement bill—or at least voted against it. They did neither. Their fire-in-the-belly warnings about the collapse of congressional norms were also conveniently forgotten.

The controversy over DeLay's actions during the Medicare Part D roll call vote in November 2003 died down soon after the ethics committee report came out. Bush had just won reelection, the country was turning its attention to the holidays, and Washington was planning another presidential inauguration. And the Hammer was already embroiled in another scandal, involving allegations that he broke campaign finance laws in order to influence congressional re-redistricting in his home state of Texas. This one would prove far more damaging.

Pig Farming

American politics is replete with contradictions in terms: "military intelligence," "bureaucratic efficiency," "negative growth," and "congressional ethics." But by the midpoint of the Bush presidency, a new Washington oxymoron began generating nearly equal criticism from both left and right: "big-government conservatism." The federal budget grew by 30 percent in Bush's first three years in office, and fiscal hawks started to complain that Washington Republicans no longer valued limited government. If Medicare Part D was Exhibit A in the indictment against Republicans, Exhibits B and C were the 2002 farm bill and the explosion in congressional earmarks.

Farmers have historically supported Republicans, but farming districts and states today are redder than ever. The states of the central plains have voted loyally Republican in presidential elections since the rise of the Great Society and feature mostly Republican-dominated House and Senate delegations. Of the top ten states in U.S. Department of Agriculture (USDA) farm subsidy spending per capita—North Dakota, South Dakota, Nebraska, Iowa, Montana, Kansas, Arkansas, Minnesota, Mississippi, and Idaho—only Minnesota votes reliably Democratic in presidential contests, and thirteen of the states' twenty U.S. senators are Republican. Of the top twenty-five House districts in terms of USDA subsidies, nineteen are represented by Republicans.[6]

The Farm Security and Rural Investment Act of 2002 was thus a political bouquet delivered by congressional Republicans to a key constituency. To its credit, the Bush administration initially opposed the legislation; Agriculture Secretary Ann Veneman delineated the Bush administration's reservations about the proposed legislation.[7] The problem prior to 2002 was that loopholes in the 1996 law permitted large farms and corporate-owned agribusiness giants to apply for multiple subsidies. For example, a farm could be split into several separate corporations, each of which could apply for the maximum subsidy. This violated Congress's intent to subsidize small-farm families. Despite the Republican Party's incessant championing of free-market competition and the value of small and family-owned businesses, and its veneration of American farmers, the 1996 farm law—supported, it must be noted, by Clinton agriculture secretary Dan Glickman—turned out to be a giant corporate welfare subsidy for Big Ag. "Taxpayers are paying billions of dollars to subsidize prosperous farms," wrote Brian Riedl of the conservative Heritage Foundation as the new farm bill was nearing passage in early 2002. "Making matters worse, many of the large farms that receive subsidies have used these funds to buy out small farms and consolidate the agriculture industry."[8]

The 2002 bill was only going to make matters worse. Yet when some congressional Republicans in 2002 proposed floor amendments to clarify or enforce the subsidy limits, they were shot down by their own party. Michigan's Nick Smith—the same Nick Smith later embroiled in Tom DeLay's Medicare Part D bribery case—proposed two amendments to the House's version of the bill, both of which would have enforced the annual upper limits of $150,000 per farm. One amendment was defeated 238–157, with 70 percent of Republicans opposing it; the other was defeated by voice vote, with most Republicans presumably again opposed. And when an effort was made in the Senate to eliminate the subsidy bias toward large corporate farms, some Republicans even tried to amend the Freedom of Information Act to classify the amounts of farm subsidies and the identities of recipients as state secrets.[9]

The Cato Institute's Chris Edwards and Tad DeHaven reflected the dispirited mood among budget hawks, who had expected that unified Republican control of Washington would lead to budget cutting rather than more bloat. "The 1996 [Freedom to Farm] Act had sought to finally wean farmers off federal price supports and subsidies," Edwards and DeHaven wrote in 2004. "But the new farm bill embraced price supports and boosted farm subsidies. . . . Looking ahead, Republicans need to rediscover the reforming spirit that they brought to Washington after the landmark 1994 congressional elections."[10]

During their twelve-year congressional reign, Republicans' appetite for lavish, market-inefficient farm subsidies was matched only by their hunger for pork-barrel spending. Although scholars and budget experts differ on whether the terms *earmark* and *pork barrel* are synonymous, both refer to appropriations that target spending on a specific district, state, region, or industry. Compared to the government's total budget, the size of any single earmark is negligible; but taken together, such spending can be considerable.

By whatever label or however measured, spending on earmarks began to rise almost as soon as the Republicans took control of Congress in 1995. According to Citizens Against Government Waste, a nonprofit Washington watchdog group that reports on congressional earmarks, spending nearly doubled from $7.8 billion in 1994, when Democrats controlled Congress, to $14.5 billion in 1997—and then nearly doubled again to $29.0 billion in 2006, the final year before Republicans surrendered control of Congress back to the Democrats.[11] In their book *Cheese Factories on the Moon*, political scientists Scott Frisch and Sean Kelly point to the Republican chairs of the key appropriations subcommittees in each chamber—John Porter and, especially, Ralph Regula in the House, and Arlen Specter (with assistance from Democratic subcommittee ranking member Tom Harkin) in the Senate—as the legislators who opened the earmark floodgates once Republicans controlled Congress. But the larger motives came from the top. "The political pressure from the Republican leadership to maintain the House majority," write Frisch and Kelly, "was a frequent response when we asked insiders why earmarks grew so dramatically in the late 1990s and early years of the twenty-first century. . . . Newt Gingrich, Tom DeLay, and Dennis Hastert came to see earmarks as a tool for reelecting vulnerable members, and for helping members to raise money to fund costly reelection campaigns. . . . In spite of promises to root out wasteful earmarks . . . as Speaker, Newt Gingrich inserted himself into the appropriations process like no previous modern Speaker."[12]

Earmarks are not completely wasteful, and they have their defenders. According to Frisch and Kelly, despite the frequently sensational coverage earmarks receive, they sometimes serve the larger national interest. The early funding for developing predator drones and the Human Genome Project came from earmarks. Like the spoonful of sugar that helps the medicine go down, earmarks often help committee chairs and chamber leaders build and sustain the coalitions needed to pass important legislation. Frisch and Kelly contend that earmarks should be particularly alluring to Republicans, who routinely complain about the inadequacy of one-size-fits-all government programs and solutions. They even suggest that some of the dysfunction in the tea party–era Congresses may have resulted from the earmark moratorium established by House Republicans in 2011.[13]

Whatever their merits, it's difficult to see the doubling and redoubling of spending on pork-barrel projects during the Republicans' twelve-year hold on Congress as anything other than ideological heresy. This was the party that made so much noise—before 1994 and after—about the importance of ridding the appropriations process of earmarks. But even if earmarks were ideologically incongruous, election-minded Republicans quickly discovered the wisdom of exploiting their majority power to fund important projects and institutions in their home states and districts. "The new Republican majority may be full of ideas about shrinking government and strengthening America, but it has held onto the House by employing the same kinds of strategies that allowed the Democrats to be so successful for so many years," wrote political scientist Andrew Taylor in his 2005 book *Elephant's Edge*, citing earmark spending as one of the ways the GOP exploited its majority to stay in power.[14]

During the 1992 Oklahoma primary that cost him his House seat, Mickey Edwards's ill-fated response to James Istook was "It's not pork if you're bringing jobs that will be created anyway and you have them in Oklahoma rather than West Virginia." Although Edwards's comment reflected the view of many members, past and present, toward earmarking, his candid admission jeopardized his renomination. And what did Istook, who eviscerated Edwards in that primary by responding, "A pig is a pig no matter whose pigpen it happens to be in," do with his hard-won seat? Soon after arriving in Washington, he requested a $9 million earmark for the University of Oklahoma.[15]

Casino Jack and the K Street Crew

In the 1980s and early 1990s, congressional Republicans helped pave the way for the 1994 Republican Revolution by issuing withering indictments of the Democrats' sclerotic and corrupt four-decade rule over Congress. The Democrats had become permissive stewards of the House, as the check-kiting scandal showed. Some of the party's leaders were corrupt, as the Jim Wright scandal proved. But there's an old adage in Washington politics: the real scandals typically involve actions that are perfectly legal. By the late 1970s, political scientists and Beltway pundits had begun to document the entirely legal capture of the federal government by powerful, well-funded interest groups with a permanent presence in Washington.

Influential scholars such as Theodore Lowi (*The End of Liberalism*) and Mancur Olson (*The Rise and Decline of Nations*) argued that interest group growth inevitably paralyzes democratic governments because permanent, powerful interests promote specific agendas at the expense of the larger public good—and regardless of which party controls the government. Journalists and public intellectuals such as Jeffrey Birnbaum and Alan Murray (*Showdown at Gucci Gulch*) and Jonathan Rauch (*Government's End*) joined the fray, explaining concepts like "hyperpluralism" and "rent-seeking behavior" to nonacademic audiences who, of course, hardly needed esoteric social science terms to be instinctively cynical about the incestuous relationships between corporations or unions and the politicians who relied on them for information, endorsements, and contributions.

Republicans should have been repulsed by rising interest group influence. Hyperpluralism only leads to expansion of the functions and costs of federal government. Yet almost as soon as they took charge on Capitol Hill, Republicans began to cozy up to interest groups just as the Democrats had done. The GOP made interest groups' access to party leaders and committee chairs contingent on huge campaign contributions from corporations and trade associations. To solidify the bond between Congress and the so-called K Street lobbyists, congressional Republicans placed former members and top staffers with lawyer-lobbyist firms and trade groups—and prohibited these organizations from hiring former Democratic staffers. They often requested sample language for proposed legislation or regulatory rule changes from affiliated business interests like the Chamber of Commerce and lobbyist groups from key industries such as energy, manufacturing, defense, and finance—and even had them help whip the votes needed to pass legislation. Saying the Republicans didn't do anything that the Democrats hadn't done before them is valid only to a point because, again, the tightening grip of interest groups on national policy making is generally antithetical to conservative governing principles.

The rise of the Republicans' K Street connections was first brought to public attention in a widely discussed 2003 *Washington Monthly* article by Nicholas Confessore. By the middle of Bush's first term, congressional Republicans were systematically overhauling the lobbyist community. Once a week, Senator Rick Santorum of Pennsylvania convened a private meeting on Capitol Hill with roughly two dozen Republican lobbyists for the express purpose of determining which departing policy and committee staffers would be placed with which major interest groups. "Through efforts like Santorum's—and a House version run by the majority whip, Roy Blunt—K Street is becoming solidly Republican," wrote Confessore. "The corporate lobbyists . . . are being replaced by party activists who are loyal first and foremost to the GOP. Through them, Republican leaders can now marshal armies of lobbyists, lawyers, and public relations experts—not to mention enormous amounts of money—to meet the party's goals." Within a decade, he reports, the contributions from nineteen major industries had swung from roughly evenly divided between the two parties to a two-to-one ratio favoring the GOP.[16]

Republicans did not invent the political cultivation of corporate lobbies. Democratic representative Tony Coelho of California made a national name for himself by shaking down corporate interests for campaign contributions. But as Confessore explains, there is an inherent asymmetry between the two parties: the connections between Democrats and organized labor provide a built-in check against the Democrats' cozying up too closely with corporations. "When it came to the vastly bigger interests on K Street," writes Confessore, "someone like Coelho could aim only for financial parity and perhaps a slight advantage in jobs. The emerging GOP machine, however, is premised on a unity of interests between party and industry, which means the GOP can ask for—and demand—total loyalty."[17] And they did.

Tom DeLay understood how to exploit this partisan asymmetry, and he became the central figure of the Republicans' K Street project. Conservative author and pundit Matthew Continetti traces DeLay's role as the GOP's K Street consigliere back to the contest DeLay won in December 1994 to become House majority whip. With his connections to the business community, says Continetti, DeLay's elevation to the whip's position "was the first step in the creation of a new Republican machine—one that would keep Republicans in power by tightening the grip the business lobby had on the conservative caucus." DeLay specifically recognized that despite all the talk of free markets, most businesses and industries benefit from fixed markets and competitive advantages, which means passing legislation and tax laws and writing regulations that favor the industries that contribute to Republican campaigns. Because DeLay and like-minded House and Senate Republicans "viewed government as a business," Continetti argues, the revolution of the November 1994 elections gave way to a "December revolution" in which power shifted from Capitol Hill to K Street.[18]

Once congressional Republicans grew comfortable with majority power, it made perfect sense for them to cement themselves in Washington by cooperating with national interest group networks. There are ample philosophical and constitutional reasons for the GOP to relish its capture of Capitol Hill, especially if the party were forced to choose between ruling Congress and holding the Oval Office. Like the party's use of race-based gerrymandering or its embrace of earmarks, building permanent relationships with powerful Washington lobbyists and interest groups is just another case of partisan institutionalism's intoxicating lure. It's easy to criticize political behavior in the abstract, but difficult in practice to resist forces that aid members' reelection or increase the power of the party's congressional majority. Inevitably, however, some Republicans took a general principle too far—so far that they shaded into ethically questionable practices. Enter Jack Abramoff.

Born in Atlantic City, "Casino Jack" Abramoff moved with his family to Beverly Hills when he was a boy. He attended Brandeis University, where he became involved in College Republican politics and met another larger-than-life personality, Grover Norquist. In 1981 Abramoff was elected national president of the College Republicans, and in next few years worked for conservative nonprofits like Americans for the Reagan Agenda before moving to Hollywood in his late twenties to pursue what turned out to be a failed career as a film producer. After a short stint working as a lawyer, he returned to Washington in early 1995, after the Republicans took control of Congress, to dovetail his interests in conservative politics, law, advocacy, and Hollywood theatrics by becoming a lobbyist for Seattle-based Preston Gates Ellis & Rouvelas Meeds, a traditionally

Democratic firm that wanted to beef up its connections to the new Republican leadership.[19]

In Washington, Abramoff quickly established himself as some-one with connections to powerful people. He helped Preston Gates land major contracts representing the U.S. business interests of Saipan and the Northern Mariana Islands. He left the firm to join Greenberg Traurig, where he sought out Native American tribes with casino gambling interests as clients. Brash, confident, and tire-less in his quest to wring as many dollars as possible from his access to top Republicans—some of whom he helped set up on expensive junkets to exotic locations—Abramoff at one point owned two Washington restaurants, one of which he used to woo clients, cajole members of Congress, and host big-dollar political fund-raising events. "Dressed in expensive suits, he moved around the capital in a BMW outfitted with a computer screen, often headed to one of the countless fund-raisers he gave for Republican congressmen and senators at Redskins and Orioles and Wizards games in his private sky boxes," wrote Michael Crowley in a 2005 profile for the *New York Times Magazine*. "Jack Abramoff was a man in full."[20]

But Abramoff's hubris and his association with a number of shady individuals—including people eventually connected to the murder of a Florida cruise casino owner—caused both his meteoric rise and his spectacular downfall. The bilking of Indian tribes for lobbying fees, which Abramoff claimed were needed to protect the tribes' casino interests, and the playing of one tribe against another to extort money from clients he privately referred to as "monkeys," "morons," and "troglodytes" proved to be his undoing. The story of Abramoff's tribal shakedown broke nationally in February 2004, and soon federal investigators were hot on his trail. The Senate Committee on Indian Affairs held hearings. Abramoff's confeder-ate Michael Scanlon, a former spokesperson for Tom DeLay, soon confessed to the two men's involvement in bilking the Native American tribes, among other legal and ethical violations.

The Abramoff scandal reached in all directions: to the Bush administration, Congress, and Washington's lobbying community. When it was over, twenty-one people had been convicted, including Bush officials at the Department of Interior and the Office of Management and Budget, Republican representative Bob Ney of Ohio, several of Ney's deputies and other House Republican staffers, and two members of a Republican environmental organization. Though never indicted, Republican senator Conrad Burns and Republican representatives John Doolittle and John Feeney were also electoral casualties of the scandal.

Congressional experts Thomas Mann and Norman Ornstein acknowledge that members of Congress in both chambers, including prominent Republicans led by John McCain, took the allegations seriously. They wanted the ethics committee to perform a proper inquiry and, if it determined Republican members were guilty, sanction them accordingly. But McCain was an outlier. The vast majority of Republicans in Congress were not very interested in ethics investigations—or if they showed interest, they quickly learned what the consequences would be. Mann and Ornstein explain:

> The approach of Congress, however, especially in Tom De-Lay's House, was neither outrage nor embarrassment, but rather a concerted effort to put the lid on any investigations and to employ large-scale damage control by punishing or silencing those who wanted to sanction the miscreants. . . . The signals by the Speaker [Hastert] could not have been more clear: take your responsibilities as guardians of House ethics seriously and you will be the ones stigmatized. . . .

In effect, there was no ethics process in place to deal with a set of problems hitting the House with full force— and no acknowledgement of the problem, or the fundamental challenge to the integrity to the body, by the Speaker or any other major leader in the majority. Whatever the problems in the 1990s—and there were significant ethical issues then—at least the leaders in the majority under Speakers Wright, Foley, and Gingrich had made sure that the ethics process moved forward. . . . Not so the House of Speaker Hastert and Majority Leader (now former Majority Leader) DeLay.[21]

The prevailing attitude among congressional Republicans toward the pay-to-play and hire-to-play norms that DeLay, Santorum, and others established was similar to President Clinton's solution to the gays in the military controversy: don't ask, don't tell.

Although only a fraction of congressional Republicans initially knew about Abramoff's shadowy activities among DeLay's network of congressional allies—and even though the members caught up in the scandal were unknown to most people outside their districts or the Capitol Hill press corps—the connection to DeLay made it a major national story and left the Republican Party with a black eye. On February 10, 2011, a federal judge sentenced Michael Scanlon, the former DeLay aide, to twenty months in prison. Scanlon's conviction, which came after he served as the government's key witness in the prosecution of many of the other twenty defendants, gave federal prosecutors a perfect record for all twenty-one defendants and closed the books on one of the most destructive episodes in Republican politics since Watergate.[22]

The big fish that got away, as far as the media and Democrats were concerned, was DeLay himself. Although Abramoff regularly invoked his close relationship with the House majority leader for political leverage, DeLay was never indicted for his involvement with Abramoff. But the Hammer's avoidance of legal consequences didn't mean he escaped unscathed. News that DeLay had taken an Abramoff-sponsored golf excursion to Scotland added to the majority leader's reputation as an ethically challenged wheeler-dealer working to exploit his and his party's power for personal and political gain. Moreover, when coupled with news of Abramoff's frequent excursions with clients and members of Congress to the Marianas and other exotic locales, DeLay's Scotland junket brought significant and unwanted attention to another pattern of congressional excess during the DeLay era: the explosion in domestic and foreign junkets members of Congress were taking.

There is nothing inherently wrong with congressional delegation ("codel") trips, even if corporations and trade associations foot the bill—provided, of course, that members travel to locations in an official capacity and with some public policy–oriented agenda. But the number of visits to attractive destinations, plus the tagging along of staffers, friends, and especially spouses, suggested that too many of the trips were focused more on play than on work. In the peak year of 2005, members took an astounding 5,000 trips, at an estimated combined cost to sponsoring organizations of $10 million.[23] Congress had gone hog wild. Both parties were complicit. Members of the Congressional Black Caucus, all Democrats, came in for withering criticism for junket abuse, as did members traveling on the dime of the American Israeli Political Action Committee. Tales of lavish junkets made for great media stories and confirmed voters' worst suspicions about the corruption of elected officials.

Soon after Democrats took control of Congress in 2007, they passed an ethics overhaul that included new rules for junkets, earmarks, and lobbyist behavior. Republicans complained that the law was a toothless, recycled version of reforms the GOP tried to enact before it lost its majorities. They had a point: within a few years after the Honest Leadership and Open Government Act was passed in 2007, stories about members exploiting loopholes in the law to take fancy junkets began making headlines. But even if Democrats were guilty of assigning too much blame to Republicans and taking too much credit as reformers, the fact is that, not unlike the rise in earmarks and farm subsidies, junket abuse rose to unprecedented levels during the GOP's stewardship of Congress.[24] And as with almost every other rotten storyline emanating from Congress in those days, Tom DeLay was at the center of it.

Lazarus Lott

Trent Lott typifies the political arc of congressional Republicans in the post-Watergate era. Born during World War II, Lott comes from one of the deepest corners of the Deep South. He is credited with encouraging Ronald Reagan's 1980 presidential campaign to signal its desire to peel white southerners away from Jimmy Carter's coalition by holding its first campaign event after the nominating convention in Mississippi's Neshoba County, site of the infamous 1964 slaying of three civil rights workers.

In the late 1960s, Lott came to Washington as a young idealist. He worked for his home district's House member and eventually succeeded him in office in 1972, when southern Republicans were a small band of regional pioneers. He quickly impressed senior members and steadily rose into his party's leadership during his eight terms in the House—and then repeated the same path to power in the Senate. He reflexively supported all of the five Republicans who occupied the White House during his political career, and either took positions or cast votes on every notable political development during his nearly four decades of service: Watergate, the formation of the Departments of Energy and Education in the late 1970s, the 1981 Reagan tax cuts, the 1983 Social Security reforms, the Gulf War, the 1993 Clinton-Gore budget, the Senate trial of Clinton's impeachment, George W. Bush's 2001 tax cuts, and the 2002 Iraq War resolution. Though he once confided his presidential ambitions to close friends, he never declared himself a candidate for the nation's highest office.

The sad epitaph to Lott's storied career in Congress is that on-line searches of the phrase "Trent Lott for president" return a series of articles about the episode that will forever taint his political resume: his December 2002 remarks at a ceremony celebrating the one-hundredth birthday of a legendary Senate icon, South Carolina's Strom Thurmond. Praising the career of his fellow southerner, Lott spoke of Thurmond's 1948 run as the nominee of the segregationist States' Rights Democratic Party. "I want to say this about my state," Lott declared, in remarks that quite obviously were neither scripted nor vetted by his press deputies. "When Strom Thurmond ran for president, we voted for him. We're proud of it. And if the rest of the country had followed our lead, we wouldn't have had all these problems over all these years either."

For the Republican Party, Lott's three sentences quickly turned from a debate on whether the Mississippian was an apologist for segregation into a national conversation about the party's reliance on racial politics to appeal to southern (and nonsouthern) white voters. There's little doubt that post–civil rights era Republicans used race to convert white Democrats—particularly southerners and those with economically populist tendencies—into Republicans. But the GOP carefully avoided acknowledging that it was exploiting racial antagonisms for political gain. Even if Lott meant only to pay kind tribute to a colleague who was both the longest-serving and oldest-ever senator in history, his offhand remarks removed the party's carefully constructed race mask and put its national brand at risk.

It was expected that many Democrats would call upon Lott to resign. More surprising was that key Republican figures also turned against him. Secretary of State Colin Powell, who had given a powerful speech with strong racial themes at the Republican National Convention two years earlier, openly criticized Lott. Most notably, the Bush administration refused to come to Lott's defense. Top White House officials increased the pressure on Lott to resign by giving disparaging, unattributed quotes about him to the media. After Lott told the media he had spoken with President Bush by phone about the Thurmond incident when in fact he hadn't, White House press secretary Ari Fleischer promptly denied Lott's claim.[25] Bush, whose reelection campaign had already begun in earnest, once again needed to put some distance between himself and congressional Republicans.

Lott did not resign from the Senate, but within two weeks he succumbed to pressure and relinquished his post as majority leader. As House Republicans had done when choosing Dennis Hastert as Speaker over more-controversial alternatives, Senate Republicans recognized the need to distance themselves from their Mississippi colleague. Even the editors of *National Review*, the print conservative media's standard-bearer for nearly five decades and a magazine that had defended segregation in an infamous 1957 commentary, came down hard on Lott. Leading *National Review*'s critique was former Bush speechwriter David Frum, one of modern conservatism's most powerful intellects. "What came out of [Lott's] mouth," Frum wrote, "was the most emphatic repudiation of desegregation to be heard from a national political figure since George Wallace's first presidential campaign. Lott's words suggest that one of the three most powerful and visible Republicans in the nation privately thinks that desegregation, civil rights and equal voting rights were all a big mistake."[26]

Republicans chose Tennessee's Bill Frist as their new majority leader, a post he held for four years, until the GOP lost its Senate majority in 2006. A medical doctor who was President Bush's choice for the vacancy the White House helped create, Frist was not a natural legislator or chamber leader. Compared to Lott or even Bob Dole, he was regarded by longtime congressional observers as a "light touch" rather than the strong-arm type.[27] With no elective experience before being elected to the Senate in 1994, he was not a "Gingrich senator" in a chamber teeming with them. "From the start," observes congressional scholar Ross Baker, "Frist struggled under the burden of having been seen by his Republican colleagues as the choice of the Bush White House who was foisted on the Senate. Unlike Lott, a creature of both the House and Senate, Frist was innocent of any prior political experience and soon proved himself unequal to the task of managing the Senate floor. The contrast between the well-disciplined Hastert-DeLay vote whipping operation in the House and Frist's inability to follow suit became a source of House-Senate friction."[28]

Proving that there are second acts in Washington politics—and confirming that few congressional Republicans, even in the ungerrymandered Senate, are very concerned about backlash from minority voters—Lott partly resuscitated his reputation when, two weeks after his party's calamitous 2006 midterms, Senate Republicans chose him over Tennessee's Lamar Alexander to be their new minority whip. Ironically enough, Lott won by the same one-vote margin by which he had beaten Wyoming's Alan Simpson to become minority whip the first time, eleven years earlier. "There's nobody better at working with other folks, including across the aisle, than Trent," said Arizona Republican senator Jon Kyl.[29] When

President Bush—whose White House had left Lott to twist in the wind during the Thurmond episode—called to congratulate him on his victory, Lott answered the phone, "Hello, Mr. President. This is Lazarus."[30] In the modern GOP, southern Republicans are always on the rise.

Disorder in the House

The Republicans' control over the 107th Congress, installed in January 2001, was very tenuous. The GOP's Senate majority, dependent on Vice President Cheney's tiebreaking vote, was soon lost to a party switch. In the House, the cumulative effect of post-1994 seat losses reduced the GOP to a razor-thin majority of just 222 seats—4 more than the minimum needed for a ruling majority. But in the 2002 midterms that followed the September 11 attacks, Republicans converted a small but significant electoral wave into slightly more comfortable majorities on both sides of Capitol Hill. On the Senate side, Republicans now had a narrow but solid caucus of fifty-one members. Likewise, the House GOP majority added seven net seats at the start of the 108th Congress, which took office in January 2003, only two months before the start of the Iraq War.

Even before the 2002 electoral boost, the House majorities under Dennis Hastert's stewardship provided reliable support for Bush. Time and again, House Republicans delivered key legislative wins for the White House, even if it meant grinding out narrow floor roll call victories. On contentious legislation, the margins were often very thin. "Throughout Bush's first term," writes congressional expert Barbara Sinclair, "Speaker Dennis Hastert repeatedly mobilized his slim majority to pass Bush's priorities: tax cuts, education reform, the faith-based initiative, the Patriot Act, Medicare/prescription drug legislation, and use-of-force authorizations for Afghanistan and Iraq are only the most prominent instances. In a number of cases, Hastert had to rely almost completely on Republicans, and in some—the Medicare/prescription drugs bill, for example—he had to use all his procedural and party resources to pull out a victory."[31]

Hastert's leadership style was crucial. In a 2003 profile in the *New Yorker*, Jonathan Franzen explained how Hastert rose to the pinnacle of power in the U.S. House. Elected in 1986, he quickly developed a reputation for being likeable and a good listener. Coming from Illinois, a state that had already produced a long line of House Republican leaders, from Robert Michel to Edward Madigan to Henry Hyde, he had to wait his turn because there wasn't room for another Illinoisan to break into the leadership. A barrel-chested, plain-spoken midwesterner with nary a mistress in sight, Hastert was a Zelig-like character who appealed equally to good government watchdogs and K Street lobbyists, moderates, and conservatives. "If you listen to one of Hastert's funny, self-deprecating campaign speeches," Franzen wrote, "you can't help liking him. If you follow the bitter partisan contention in the House, you're ready to believe the worst about the man. He is an irrelevant, indispensable, modern, old-fashioned, moderate, archconservative nobody somebody."[32] Hastert's patience paid off when he was elected Speaker in 1998.

Sinclair's observations about Hastert's tenuous grip on the majority conference were borne out in the new Speaker's struggles to unify his caucus. By 2003 the divisions within the House Republican Conference were so problematic that Hastert quietly instituted an informal rule: legislation would reach the floor only if a majority of House Republicans supported it. He first alluded to this "majority of the majority" standard during a largely unnoticed 2003 floor speech written by his deputy, John Feehery. But he made a more public acknowledgment of the new rule in November 2004, after admitting he had prevented an intelligence bill supported by the Bush administration from reaching the floor because a majority of House Republicans opposed it. Had it come up for a vote, it almost certainly would have passed with the Democrats' help. Known thereafter as the "Hastert Rule," the majority-of-the-majority standard was intended to prevent a bipartisan coalition from passing legislation that most Republicans opposed. Feehery told the media quite matter-of-factly that previous House Speakers who failed to please a majority of their caucus hadn't held the gavel very long.[33] His observation was prescient: Hastert later retired as the longest-serving Republican Speaker in history, a title that, at this writing, he still holds.

Hastert wasn't the first House Speaker to impose the majority-of-the-majority standard. He was merely guilty of being honest about a standard he did not invent but chose to enforce. The real issue was how often Hastert invoked the rule. Critics noted that Democratic Speakers had allowed major legislation their president supported, but that a majority of their party's House Democrats opposed, to reach the floor and pass with the support of Republicans. An oft-cited example is the House vote in December 1993 to approve the North American Free Trade Act, which roughly three-fifths of House Democrats voted against, but which was passed by the remaining Democrats plus almost every Republican. If Democratic Speaker Tom Foley had enforced Hastert's rule, the pro-labor Democrats, though making up just a third of the chamber, could have blocked NAFTA.

Hastert's public admission of the rule drew many criticisms, most notably that the GOP was championing minority rule. "Hastert's position," wrote *Washington Post* national political reporter Charles Babington, "which is drawing fire from Democrats and some outside groups, is the latest step in a decade-long process of limiting

Democrats' influence and running the House virtually as a one-party institution. Republicans earlier barred House Democrats from helping to draft major bills such as the 2003 Medicare revision and this year's intelligence package."[34] House Republicans also instituted another rule change, while Tom DeLay was awaiting indictment for campaign illegalities, which permitted members to retain committee or leadership posts even if they had been charged with a felony.

Hastert's majorities were comparable to those Gingrich led during his brief reign as Speaker. So the calculus for how many party defections Hastert could absorb while maintaining a 218-vote majority was basically the same as for Gingrich. But the *number* of allowable defections isn't necessarily the same as the *likelihood* of defection. The reality is that Hastert frequently struggled to keep the House in order because the Republican Conference was changing. Newer members were more aggressive, more independent, and—despite DeLay's outsized influence—less reliant for their nomination on party leaders, their political action committees, or the National Republican Campaign Committee (NRCC). And gerrymandering assured that, once renominated, most incumbents would be reelected. This confluence of factors yielded an ideologically conservative, politically comfortable majority. "The House that he presides over is an increasingly angry and polarized place," wrote Franzen. "Moderate Republicans are angry because the party leadership and agenda are so hard-line conservative; hard-line conservatives are angry because, to them, even small compromises feel like defeats; and House Democrats are angry because they feel excluded from the legislative process altogether."[35]

Franzen quotes none other than Gingrich, who compared himself with Hastert this way: "I was the relentless, entrepreneurial, idea-oriented disrupter of the old order, and he is the organizer, codifier, and maintainer of the new order." The latter role sounds less politically perilous, and in fact Hastert ruled over the Republican House twice as long as Gingrich. But maintaining a revolution can be as difficult as starting one, especially when the new order is defined by disorder. In 2003 and 2004—almost a decade before the tea party emerged—the early hints of the intraparty factionalism that would define John Boehner's speakership were evident in the drastic moves Hastert relied on to keep his party's House coalition together.

Soft Money, Hard Realities

Political fund-raising by the four "Hill committees," the respective House and Senate campaign committees for each party, has passed through several historical phases. Until the 1980s, the sums raised by either party were relatively small, and most of the money gravitated to the Democrats because they ran Congress and were expected to continue to do so indefinitely. But the Republicans' capture of the Senate in 1980, along with the rise of the Gingrich-era House Republicans, signaled a possible end to the Democrats' dominance. By the end of the Reagan-Bush era, both parties were raising greater sums; the party splits, though still favoring the Democrats, became more balanced. The 1990s begat the era of "soft money"—large, uncapped sums donated by wealthy individuals, unions, and corporations that parties used for general party-building activities and issue advocacy, so long as they did not engage in direct activity on behalf of specific candidates.

Republicans past and present have tended to resist any attempt to restrict campaign finance. The GOP's opposition seems self-serving, given the party's connections to big business and its support from wealthier Americans. In 2001, when Republican John

McCain and Democrat Russ Feingold in the Senate joined with Republican Chris Shays and Democrat Marty Meehan in the House to yet again sponsor the Bipartisan Campaign Reform Act (BCRA), which would substantially limit big donor contributions, many Republicans reflexively opposed the legislation. Beyond Republicans' general disinclination toward campaign finance limitations, the cosponsorship of the bill by McCain and Shays—moderates who often bucked fellow Republicans—made BCRA even less attractive to conservative Republicans on both sides of the Capitol.

Yet congressional Republicans may have had reasons to support McCain-Feingold, as BCRA was commonly called. The legislation raised the nearly three-decade-old limit of $1,000 on hard money contributions to $2,000, and then benchmarked it to keep up with inflation. Because so many wealthy Republican contributors bumped into the hard money ceiling, raising the hard limit presumably helped the GOP more than it helped the Democrats. The law did not, however, raise the $250 maximum presidential campaign matching amount per donor that candidates who meet other fund-raising and spending restrictions could accept. Thus it might advantage presidential candidates from the party with more small-dollar donors, because with the dollar-for-dollar match of the first $250, raising $2,000 from one wealthy donor would now be worth $2,250, whereas raising $2,000 from eight individuals giving $250 each would be worth $4,000.

The bill's major provision banning soft money donations might also have appealed to congressional Republicans precisely because Democrats seemed petrified by its implications. Unlike hard money donations, which campaigns can spend directly on (or against) specific candidates, soft money could be raised without limit, but could be used only in party-building activities like voter registration and infrastructure spending, or to aid the party's candidates indirectly by funding issue ads that stop short of endorsing or opposing candidates. The national parties also exploited state campaign finance regulations to launder soft money through the state party treasuries. In 1998 and 2000, Democrats took advantage of these loopholes to maximize the impact of their soft money.

Because Republicans had outraised the Democrats in hard money for so long, in the late 1990s Democrats began to rely heavily on large soft money donations from unions and wealthy Democrats to close the fund-raising gap with Republicans. A Democratic Party internal analysis revealed that 20 percent of the party's $100 million-plus in soft money receipts in 1996 came from just 168 donors.[36] Although Republicans also had an advantage in soft money contributions, it was much smaller than their hard money edge, and in the 2000 cycle the Democrats actually surpassed Republicans in soft money receipts. Yet when Speaker Hastert exhorted the House Republican Conference not to waver in its opposition to McCain-Feingold, he did so by specifically reminding his fellow Republicans that six of them "would not even be here" if not for soft money.[37]

Easing restrictions on the total dollars that flow into parties and campaigns should, all else being equal, favor the party with stronger connections to corporations and wealthy donors: the Republicans. "Before the strategic environment changed in the 1994 election cycle, parties and interest groups did not commit great sums of money to election campaigns," explain campaign finance experts Diana Dwyre and Robin Kolodny. "Once the House Republicans proved that the national electoral environment was indeed competitive, the parties became more selective about targeting more money to the most competitive seats that could change party control of government institutions. This led to the parties' search for more resources— hence, soft money."[38]

When McCain-Feingold became law—with solid Democratic majorities in both chambers supporting it and solid Republican majorities opposed—the asymmetrical damage it was expected to cause Democrats led political analyst Seth Gitell to call it the "Democratic Party suicide bill."[39] He concluded that both parties seemed to have voted against their own interests. But election laws often have unintended consequences. One consequence of McCain-Feingold's soft money ban was that it forced both parties, the Democrats especially, to expand their small-dollar donor bases. Thanks to a giant assist from the Obama presidential campaign's record-setting outreach in 2008, within just six years the Democrats had identified millions of low-dollar donors they might otherwise have overlooked had they been able to continue relying on soft money donations. Brian Wolff, who in 2008 was executive director of the Democratic Congressional Campaign Committee, admitted that McCain-Feingold "forced us to do what we should have been doing all along, which was including more people in the political process."[40]

So perhaps, when they voted against McCain-Feingold and, following its enactment, challenged BCRA's soft money ban in the courts, Republicans were not behaving self-destructively. (They lost Supreme Court rulings in 2003 and again in 2010.)[41] Nor did the Democrats' vote to ban soft money turn out to be a puzzle at all. Once their New Deal congressional hegemony came undone, any legal change that allowed more money to flood into campaigns presumably conferred an advantage on Republicans. "When viewed from the perspective of risk-averse, victory-oriented parties, the positions taken by the legislative parties on BCRA appear puzzling," conclude political scientists Vincent Moscardelli and Moshe Haspel in their analysis of why Republicans and Democrats voted as they did on campaign finance reform. "When viewed through the lens of party difference, however, the behavior of the legislative parties comes into focus."[42]

Congressional Republicans fought McCain-Feingold and other attempts to limit campaign contributions because they believed—correctly—that it would hamstring the party's electoral competitiveness. In a few years, the Supreme Court would make it even easier to raise political money and to hide its sources.

Hammered

Most congressional scandals taint only the reputations of the politicians involved. But when a member of Congress has a history of repeat offenses, it begins to tarnish his party, too. If any member of Congress personified the excesses of House Republicans' twelve-year reign, it was Tom DeLay. He somehow managed to be involved in almost every congressional controversy during his final decade on Capitol Hill. Like few others, DeLay seemed to delight in the intrigue of insider politics played at the highest levels—and he often escaped just before the political noose was slipped around his neck. But even DeLay couldn't elude the hangman forever, and the mid-decade gerrymandering of Texas's U.S. House districts was the episode that finally brought him down.

Thanks to Karl Rove, in a span of two decades Texas had transformed from the land of Lyndon Johnson to a very red Republican state. Following the 2000 election, the state had two Republican U.S. senators, Phil Gramm and Kay Bailey Hutchinson, and a new Republican governor in Rick Perry, who replaced the one then in the White House. The state legislature had been trending Republican for years, but although the GOP flipped the state senate in 1998, there were still enough conservative white Democrats to join with the more liberal minority Democrats to prevent the Republicans from taking over the state house the way they had taken over almost everything else in the state. With blocking power over the 2000 redistricting process, Democrats were able to maintain a more favorable U.S. House map. The Republicans gained seats during the 2002 midterms, but Texas Democrats maintained a slight (seventeen to fifteen) edge in the state's U.S. House delegation—a result that infuriated DeLay. To change it, he needed the Texas state house.[43]

DeLay had been scheming for ways to flip the chamber for years. In the 1990s he supported the efforts of Republican state representative Tom Craddick, a close political friend and ally, to convert the house to the Republicans. When the state legislature convened in 2001, Texas house Democrats had a very thin (seventy-eight to seventy-two) majority, and Craddick and DeLay committed themselves anew to taking the chamber. But DeLay knew he had to gain more than four seats to get control, because Craddick, his choice to be Speaker in a Republican-controlled house, was disliked by so many of his colleagues that the Democrats might be able to build a governing coalition even if they fell slightly below seventy-six seats.[44]

In September 2001, DeLay used seed money from his federal political action committee, Americans for a Republican Majority (ARMPAC), to start a state political action committee called Texans for a Republican Majority. Donations were laundered to Texans for a Republican Majority (TRMPAC) from money collected in Washington by the Republican National Committee and the Republican National State Elections Committee. "One of TRMPAC's tasks was to provide a vehicle for recruiting candidates, evaluating candidates, and picking and choosing among potential Republican candidates in the Republican primary to find the best candidate," explains Steve Bickerstaff, whose book *Lines in the Sand* is the definitive account of the Texas re-redistricting episode. "The political action committee further was a means of paying for and providing help for selected candidates."[45]

DeLay did not hide his role in forming TRMPAC. He declared at a November 2001 news conference in Austin that Republicans were poised to control both state legislative chambers and every statewide elective office—and that TRMPAC would be integral in turning Texas state politics solidly Republican. DeLay initially considered supporting Texas Republicans seeking election or reelection to statewide office, but soon realized that the Democrats' house majority in Austin was too ripe a target to ignore. TRMPAC picked more than a dozen Republican candidates to challenge Democratic incumbents and provided funding for a few endangered Republican house incumbents. The key criterion, according to Bickerstaff, was whether the Republicans pledged to back Craddick as the new Speaker. Craddick personally disbursed hundreds of thousands of dollars to TRMPAC's chosen candidates.[46]

The plan worked. In 2002 Republicans took control of both legislative chambers for the first time in 130 years. With Republican governor Rick Perry's blessing, they promptly proposed a mid-decade re-redistricting of the state's thirty-two U.S. House districts. All hell broke loose in Austin. At one point, in an effort deprive Republicans of the chamber quorum necessary to adopt the new district lines, fifty-two Texas house Democrats fled to neighboring Oklahoma. But the maps were eventually redrawn, and in 2004 Republicans picked up six U.S. House seats—five by election of new Republicans replacing defeated or retiring Democrats, and a sixth when Democrat Ralph Hall, to save his political career, preemptively changed his affiliation to Republican. The Texas re-redistricting more than accounted for the House Republicans' five-seat increase nationwide in 2004. Almost single-handedly, Tom DeLay was responsible for the party's entire House gains in 2004.

In the process, DeLay attracted a lot of political heat. By summer 2004, when the Republicans convened in New York to nominate Bush for a second term, DeLay had become toxic. He effectively had to go into hiding. The Medicare Part D vote, the political fight in Austin, the developing Abramoff story—in each case his fingerprints, if not his hammer-wielding hand, were plainly visible. Even though he was the second-highest-ranking member of the House of Representatives, DeLay thus spent most of the convention week far from the official festivities and television coverage. He mostly attended private, high-ticket events where he schmoozed with corporate and trade association sponsors. He never spoke from the convention podium, formally addressed only the Texas delegation, and made only four official appearances during his five days in New York. "People close to DeLay, however, said his semi-exile was self-imposed, stemming mainly from disappointment that a firestorm of criticism had forced him in May to cancel plans for extravagant parties, cruises, dinners and fundraising," the *Washington Post* reported at the time. "If that had not happened, DeLay might have been the toast of Manhattan this week."[47]

Soon he would be toast. In early 2005, a Texas grand jury indicted DeLay and his confederates in the Texas re-redistricting episode. DeLay was charged with money laundering and conspiracy. Although he initially stayed in Congress, he eventually yielded to political pressure. He announced in January 2006 that he would not seek reelection to Congress, and that summer he resigned his seat after a former aide pled guilty to charges related to the Jack Abramoff investigation. The signature triumph of Tom DeLay's career—his brazen use of his national power to manipulate state politics to bolster the Republican House Conference's electoral clout back in Washington—led to his downfall.

DeLay's deteriorating public image had, by mid-decade, become a major liability. Fellow Republicans and the media turned on him, and President Bush remained as distant from his fellow Texan as he did back in 1999, when Bush visited Capitol Hill as a presidential candidate. Polls showed Democrats primed for major gains in the 2006 midterms, and DeLay provided a useful target for partisan attacks. The Hammer was getting hammered, and for liberals and Democrats his reckoning was long overdue. "If the system had worked," liberal columnist Michael Tomasky observed in 2005, just before DeLay's undoing, he "would have been exposed long ago— first by the media, which would have done far more to reveal the ethical and procedural corruption of this regime, and second by moderate Republicans, who could have made a difference if they'd had the nerve, en bloc, to stand up and say something. It's a shame, and an indictment of what's happened to the political culture, that if Tom DeLay goes down, it will be because of things he did to Tom DeLay. . . . A lot of people who could have said something about all this louder and sooner didn't bother to."[48]

Wide Stances, Hypocritical Stances

If power corrupts, there was every reason to expect congressional Republicans to fall prey to political and personal scandals similar to those that crippled the Democrats during the late stages of their rule in Congress. Tom DeLay, Duke Cunningham, Bob Ney, and others were forced from office because they used their power for political or personal gain. But other congressional Republicans, while not necessarily breaching any legal or even ethical standards of professional conduct, preached the importance of sexual virtue while demonstrating an inability to practice the morality they expected of American voters. These failings created their own credibility issues.

In June 2007, Senator Larry Craig, a three-term Idaho Republican, was in a men's room at Minneapolis–St. Paul International Airport in Minnesota, awaiting a connecting flight and unaware that airport authorities had set up a sting operation in response to complaints about sexual activity in men's bathrooms. According to the undercover officer in the stall next to the one Craig entered that day, the senator tapped his foot, slid it under the stall divider, and reached under the divider with his hand—signals the officer took as coded solicitations of a sexual encounter. Craig was arrested upon exiting the bathroom and given a citation. Attempting to bury the episode, in early August he pled guilty to misdemeanor disorderly conduct and paid the relevant fines and court fees. Three weeks later, news of the episode broke nationally.

To fellow politicians, voters, and the media, Craig denied the substance of the allegations, saying the arresting officer had misinterpreted his foot and hand movements. He claimed he was wide-bodied and, although he never used the words "wide stance," the phrase quickly became a punch line for late-night comedians. The airport incident was followed by reports of other alleged homosexual encounters involving Craig, some dating back to his college days and others occurring during his Senate career. At a Boise press conference, he denied being gay or having ever "been gay," and said it was a mistake to have pled guilty to the lesser charge in an effort to make the incident "go away."

It didn't go away: Craig was publicly denounced by a steady stream of fellow Republicans. Some joined his state's most influential paper, the *Idaho Statesman*, in calling on him to resign. "We cannot abide an elected official who didn't disclose a lewd conduct arrest until the story broke 77 days later—a lie by omission and a violation of the public trust," the paper editorialized. "We cannot believe Craig can effectively serve Idaho, under the shadow of his guilty plea on a lesser charge of disorderly conduct."[49] It didn't help Craig's party standing that the bathroom incident occurred in the very city where Republicans were scheduled to meet a year later for the 2008 Republican National Convention.

After Craig refused to resign, a Senate ethics committee was impaneled to review his behavior. Liberals and the media excoriated him for opposing Idaho or federal same-sex marriage provisions, as well as sexual orientation–based hate crimes legislation. Though he steadfastly insisted he was not gay, many doubted his protestations; the senator looked like yet another closeted Republican hypocrite. In February 2008, the ethics panel officially admonished him for discrediting the Senate.[50] He finished his third term but in 2008 opted not to seek a fourth, instead slipping quietly into retirement and fading from the national political discourse.

The 2004 case of U.S. Representative Ed Schrock made far fewer headlines than Craig's arrest, even though the details were equally salacious. A Virginia Republican, Schrock had served in the state legislature before being elected to Congress in 2000 and re-elected in 2002. Then in August 2004, gay rights activist Mike Rogers—later featured in the Kirby Dick–directed documentary *Outrage*, about closeted antigay politicians—released a tape of Schrock allegedly posting an audio advertisement on a site where gay men solicit for sexual partners. Schrock was a military veteran, husband, and father whose Virginia Beach–based district was home to televangelist Pat Robertson's media empire, and his spokespeople initially denied the story, but within two weeks he abandoned his reelection bid and resigned his House seat.[51]

Revelations of alleged homosexuality among staunchly antigay Republican politicians create electoral headaches for the party. In

December 2013, Schrock's former colleague in the Virginia house, Randy Forbes, made national headlines when he stated his opposition to spending NRCC money to support two openly gay Republican House candidates with decent chances to pick up seats in California and Massachusetts. Forbes justified his position by saying that other House members, who pay membership dues to the NRCC to help fund the party's House campaign activities, might have trouble explaining these expenditures to their constituents. House Speaker John Boehner rejected Forbes's position, saying that the party should support competitive gay candidates.[52]

Then there was Republican senator David Vitter, who was cleared of ethics violations in 2007 stemming from his alleged use of prostitutes. What's fascinating about Vitter's political career is how marital infidelity paved the way for him to reach the Senate in the first place. He was elected to the U.S. House seat that almost-Speaker Bob Livingston vacated after revelations of his assignations forced him into early retirement. And Vitter ran for the U.S. Senate in 2004 only after he abandoned his 2003 Louisiana gubernatorial campaign when a Louisiana paper reported that he had an ongoing relationship with a female prostitute. A husband and father of three, Vitter admitted to troubles in his marriage—a confession that might have come with more permanent consequences than merely the end of his political career. In the wake of the Clinton and Livingston infidelity scandals, but before the rumors of her husband's alleged infidelity surfaced, Vitter's wife described herself to the New Orleans *Times-Picayune* as "a lot more like Lorena Bobbitt than Hillary [Clinton]. If [my husband] does something like that, I'm walking away with one thing, and it's not alimony, trust me."[53] Vitter won an open seat race in 2004, becoming Louisiana's first Republican senator since Reconstruction. Presumably, he arrived in Washington in January 2005 with his anatomy intact.

When the "DC Madam" scandal broke in early 2007 and Vitter's name was discovered in the client logs of Deborah Jeane Palfrey—the woman eventually convicted of running a high-end prostitution ring in the nation's capital—his political career and personal history again collided. Despite rumors that the senator sometimes liked to wear diapers during his encounters with prostitutes, his wife, Wendy, stayed with him, even after his connection to Palfrey prompted a Senate ethics inquiry. The ethics committee eventually ruled that, because Vitter's alleged activities predated his election to the Senate, he would not be sanctioned. Vitter's colleagues in the Senate Republican Conference gave him a standing ovation. Some of these same Republicans declared in 1999 that they voted to impeach Bill Clinton not because of his sexual infidelities but because the president had committed the crimes of perjury and obstruction of justice. Of course, in most states, including Louisiana, sex with another consenting adult is not a crime, but soliciting prostitutes is. If Vitter had been sanctioned and resigned his seat, however, Democratic governor Kathleen Babineaux Blanco would have been able to nominate Vitter's replacement. Republicans seemed to have a separate set of rules for sexual indiscretions when the punishment for those transgressions meant surrendering a seat in Congress.

Gay or straight, congressional Republicans caught in sex scandals were tarnishing the GOP's national image. The party already had a strained relationship with American voters on issues of sex thanks to the GOP's opposition to abortion, certain forms of birth control, and sex education for children—not to mention Republicans' prurient prosecution of President Bill Clinton. Plenty of prominent congressional Democrats over the years, from Ted Kennedy to Barney Frank to Gary Condit, got ensnared in sex scandals. But Democrats generally don't preach about sexual morality from political pulpits, nor do they rely on conservative evangelicals for electoral support. In matters of sex and scandal, the asymmetries of partisan politics cause more damage for congressional Republicans than for their Democratic counterparts.

All Is Lost

For congressional Republicans, the 2006 elections were catastrophic. A dozen years after the glorious 1994 midterms, the Republican majorities in both chambers were obliterated. Democrat Harry Reid would be the Senate majority leader in the 110th Congress. His House Democratic counterpart, Nancy Pelosi, would be the new Speaker and the first woman ever to lead either chamber. Republicans still held the White House, but only because President Bush didn't have to stand for election in 2006. With approval ratings in the mid–30 percent range, he almost certainly would have been rejected by the American electorate had he been on the ballot.

More than anyone else, Bush was responsible for the Republican losses. By 2005 the long war in Iraq was going horribly wrong. The president's war approval was even lower than his overall approval ratings. Congressional Republicans had backed the Bush administration's preemptive war policy and suffered the electoral consequences. American voters in 2004 had begun to doubt the wisdom of invading Iraq, and by 2006 their opinions had soured to the point that it affected their congressional votes. Although there was no relation between county casualty rates and George W. Bush's 2004 county-level performance, casualty rates did contribute to the decline between 2000 and 2006 in the county-level performance of Republican Senate candidates. "Senators do incur political costs from deferring to the president, even tacitly, in an unpopular war, even when casualty totals are orders of magnitude smaller than those

sustained in Vietnam," concluded political scientists Douglas Kriner and Francis Shen in their study of the war's effect on the 2006
Senate races. In a similar study of 2006 House contests, Christian
Grose and Bruce Oppenheimer found that higher-than-average district casualty rates from Iraq, combined with Bush's approval rating, sank the reelection bids of many Republican House incumbents.
"The swing percentage in a number of districts with large war deaths
was the difference between a Republican or a Democratic victory,"
the authors concluded.[54]

In most presidential cycles, domestic politics outweigh foreign
policy, defense, and security issues; domestic concerns take on even
greater salience in midterm cycles because the presidency is not on
the ballot. Yet a remarkable 51 percent of voters surveyed in late
September 2006 by Pew Research who cited national concerns as
most important in their vote choice specifically cited Iraq as their
top issue. "Iraq has become the central issue of the midterm elections," Pew's summary report explained. "There is more dismay
about how the U.S. military effort in Iraq is going than at any point
since the war began more than three years ago."[55]

Typically, heightened attention to national defense favors Re-
publicans. But increased voter attention to Iraq worked against the
GOP in 2006. In a *New York Times*/CBS poll taken the week be-
fore the election, President Bush's approval rating on handling the
Iraq War had fallen to a new low of 29 percent, and 80 percent of
Americans said he had no plan for ending the war.

Amid these unsurprising results was this shocker: the Democrats were now more trusted on terrorism.[56] Their advantage was
within the margin of error, so effectively the two parties were now
viewed equally by the American public on the defining issue of
the moment. But given both the long-term and post–September
11 advantage the Republican Party had enjoyed on defense and

security—and just two years after President Bush went into his re-election enjoying a solid advantage on terrorism over Democratic nominee John Kerry—the poll results were remarkable. Republicans had squandered their most important electoral advantage of the post-Vietnam era. Without the security advantage, the 2006 Republican congressional candidates were pinned down and running out of electoral ammunition.

A central theme of this book is that congressional Republicans have repeatedly and systematically undermined their party's presidential competitiveness. Although by 2006 congressional Republicans had largely forfeited their control over U.S. foreign and military policy to neoconservative outsiders, and although they did vote in lockstep with Bush on the October 2002 Iraq War resolution, the president's decision to invade Iraq is an important counterexample to this general pattern. Here, it was a presidential action that undermined the party's congressional competitiveness.

Still, congressional Republicans couldn't blame the Bush administration's Iraq War management for *all* of their electoral woes. Republicans on Capitol Hill were dealing with their own self-inflicted wounds, most notably the congressional page scandal that ended the career of six-term Republican representative Mark Foley of Florida. Foley, who at the time was a deputy whip to Speaker Hastert and chaired the House Caucus on Missing and Exploited Children, had to resign his seat in Congress after news broke in October 2006 that he had sent sexually explicit e-mails to underage male congressional pages, and later had sex with two former pages, aged eighteen and twenty-one. The damage to Republicans might have been limited to Foley's own seat, except that a number of House Republicans or their staffers had known about the e-mails several months, if not years, earlier. Those members included Speaker Hastert and his top deputy,

John Boehner, who in January 2006 had replaced Roy Blunt as House majority leader. Boehner admitted that he learned about Foley's alleged behaviors in spring 2006, months before the story broke.

The revelation that top congressional Republicans—including many who had spoken out and voted against homosexual rights throughout their political careers—had ignored or tried to cover up the activities of a gay pedophile within their caucus in order to save one House seat was simply too much for many voters to bear. According to an October 2006 poll by *Time* magazine, two-thirds of Americans who had heard about Foley's e-mails believed House Republican leaders had attempted to hide the scandal, and one-fourth said the scandal made them less likely to vote for Republican candidates in their district. Describing the episode as a "disgrace for every Republican member of Congress," the conservative *Washington Times* called for Hastert's resignation. "Mr. Hastert has forfeited the confidence of the public and his party, and he cannot preside over the necessary coming investigation, an investigation that must examine his own inept performance."[57]

The American electorate was fed up with the Republicans. While other congressional decisions, plus stories of the political co-optation if not outright corruption of House members, undoubtedly contributed to voter dissatisfaction, the Iraq War led to the party's worst midterm performance since 1986 and the first time since 1954 the GOP lost both chambers simultaneously. Their twelve-year rule on Capitol Hill—the party's longest period in control of Congress since before the New Deal—was over. The Democrats ran on their usual kitchen-table domestic issues and against the war. But the election wasn't so much about policy alternatives as the mere fact that Democrats were the alternative to a Republican Party that had lost the public's confidence.

The Next Wave

The opening of the 110th Congress presented an important dilemma to congressional Republicans as the new minority party. Should they work cooperatively with the new Democratic majorities, and if not, what should their legislative strategy be? With Dennis Hastert and Bill Frist gone, Republicans were now led by Representative John Boehner and Senator Mitch McConnell, neither of whom seemed to instill much fear in Democratic hearts or much hope in the House and Senate Republican conferences. The most obvious example on which they could draw was the last time Republicans held the White House but not Congress: the final years of the Reagan-Bush era, from 1987 to 1993.

That period coincided with Bob Dole's elevation in 1987 to Senate minority leader. Although Dole's Senate Republican Conference was neither as conservative nor as committed to obfuscation as McConnell's later turned out to be, the Republicans had significantly ramped up their use of the filibuster after 1987. To frustrate the Democrats' new congressional majorities twenty years later, House Republicans counted on their Senate peers to do the same. "House Republicans are fast learning a number of tough lessons during their early days as the minority in this new Democratic-controlled Congress," *Politico*'s Patrick O'Connor wrote in early 2007, just two months after Speaker Pelosi took over. "And one of the most striking—one that members and aides are loath to admit—is the newly acquired respect for the Senate. . . . After working in lockstep with the White House to push President Bush's agenda through Congress during his first six years, Republicans now are—more often than not—intent on blocking legislation advanced by the Democrats." House Republican Tom Feeney of Pennsylvania told O'Connor, "If you're on offense, trying to get something passed, the Senate cloture rules become a big obstacle. When you're in the minority, constantly getting rolled, thank God for the Senate."[58]

By December 2007, with more than a full year left in the 110th Congress, Senate Republicans had already set the record for a two-year Congress with sixty-two filibusters—and this was with a Republican president still in office. Republican use of the filibuster during Obama's presidency would eventually cause Reid to invoke the so-called nuclear option, changing the rules to end the use of the filibuster on presidential appointments. Meanwhile, in the House, John Boehner spent the next two years trying to regroup. His biggest challenge would actually begin after the 2008 elections, when Democrats captured the White House and unified their dominion over Washington. Boehner came to Washington in 1991, in the middle of the pre-revolutionary era defined by Newt Gingrich's block-stall-investigate-and-obfuscate brand of House minority politics, an experience that gave him insight into how to battle a unified Democratic government. But he wouldn't be in the minority for long. What neither he nor any Republican knew was how to manage a House majority when that was the only branch of government in Republican hands.

During the last six years of the Bush administration, congressional Republicans imploded along with their president, whose foreign policy adventurism contributed mightily to the party's decline. Aside from the Iraq War—supported by all but seven Republicans in the two chambers—the damage Republicans suffered on Capitol Hill was entirely self-inflicted. They spent money as if they hadn't controlled Congress in four decades: on entitlements as well as defense, on earmarks and subsidies. They took expensive foreign junkets, and some brought shame upon the institution and their party—either because they were literally in bed with people they weren't married to, or figuratively in bed with lobbyists to whom the party was increasingly wedded. At a time when the party wanted to project an image of fiscal responsibility and ethical governance, not to mention racial, gender, and geographic diversity, an arm-twisting white male Texas hustler known for his strong connections to corporate America and weak appreciation for the law had become the Republicans' most prominent face on Capitol Hill.

During the first decade of the new century, both chambers of Congress saw record-breaking levels of partisan polarization. The Democratic caucuses, to be sure, became more liberal. But the House and Senate Republican conferences were moving farther to the right than Democrats were moving to the left. President Bush won election and reelection by running away from his party's congressional wing. In 2008 one of the Senate's few remaining Republican moderates was nominated to replace him. But the fact that John McCain—one of the Senate's most conservative members when he arrived there in 1985—by 2008 was considered a moderate testified to just how far right congressional Republicans had moved. They were about to go even farther.

6

A CONGRESS-CENTRIC PARTY

In many respects, Mitt Romney was the ideal Republican presidential nominee. He was the patriarch of a picture-perfect family that
included a devoted wife, a quintet of square-jawed sons, and a growing brood of grandchildren. With his confident gait and flawless
haircut, Romney looked like he had arrived straight from central
casting to play the role of president. In other respects, however, the
former Massachusetts governor's record was problematic. Once a certifiable moderate, Romney had steadily flip-flopped his way from the
center to the far right on policies ranging from health care to abortion
to gay marriage. His personal wealth—and the fact that he got rich
as owner of a private equity firm that bought, repackaged, and then

sold businesses for a profit, often laying off blue-collar workers along the way—proved a biographical liability at a moment when many Americans were still struggling to recover from a horrible recession. Romney's Mormon faith also complicated his party's long-standing relationship with evangelical conservatives.

From the outset of the 2012 campaign, Romney was clearly the front-runner in a Republican field that many political observers, including some conservative pundits, deemed historically weak. He was the best-funded and best-organized candidate. He was also the most skilled, consistent, and mistake-free debater in the GOP field. For the most part, Romney hired quality advisers and consultants. Along with the Republican National Committee and affiliated center-right groups, he raised and spent as much in 2012 as President Obama and allied center-left organizations did—an unprecedented feat for a challenger running against a sitting president. And along with only Ron Paul, Romney had more or less been running for president continuously since 2007, when he launched his unsuccessful effort to win the 2008 Republican nomination. In 2012 it was Romney's nomination to lose.

At times in the run-up to the Iowa caucuses, it looked like he might lose it. He struggled to consolidate the party behind him. Except when one of the "anti-Romney" candidates momentarily surged to catch him in the polls, he led the field with somewhere between 20 percent and 30 percent support among Republicans for more than a year prior to the start of the primaries—but he struggled to break that 30 percent ceiling. His support was wide but not deep. Romney knew he needed an early win to separate himself from the GOP pack and prove he wasn't the 2012 Republican version of Hillary Clinton in the 2008 Democratic primary: the "inevitability" candidate who turned out to be not so inevitable. Like Obama's four years earlier, Romney's fate thus hinged on securing a once-deemed-improbable win in Iowa, a state he lost in 2008 to the disorganized and poorly funded former Arkansas governor Mike Huckabee.

Romney won Iowa by a sliver, with slightly less than 25 percent of the vote. Well, technically he *didn't* win Iowa. The results declared on caucus night gave him a narrow victory over former Pennsylvania senator Rick Santorum, but the official tabulations announced a week later showed Santorum winning by thirty-four votes. As the nomination contest continued, the surprisingly scrappy Santorum hung around long enough to become the last in a long parade of "not Romney" Republican challengers that included Paul, Minnesota congresswoman Michele Bachmann, Texas governor Rick Perry, businessman Herman Cain, and former House Speaker Newt Gingrich, each of whom tried but failed to sidetrack Romney from his inside path to the nomination.

The overlooked result from the Iowa caucuses was the performance of the four members of the Republicans' congressional wing. Combined, Santorum and, in order of finish, Paul, Gingrich, and Bachmann, attracted 64 percent of the votes cast by Iowa Republicans.[1] That this unusual quartet of congressional Republicans claimed almost two-thirds of the support from Iowa caucus-goers was a telling barometer of the party's electoral health. Santorum was an ex-senator a full six years beyond the devastating seventeen-point defeat that ended his two-term tenure as a polarizing, geographically misplaced conservative from the Northeast in a Republican Party that had nearly vanished from the region. His strong Catholic faith put him in good standing with the party's Christian evangelical base but made him a tough sell to moderates, suburban women, and libertarians. The iconoclastic seventy-six-year-old Paul was making his third presidential bid, having first run in 1988 as the Libertarian Party's nominee. He hailed from a more traditionally red state (Texas), but his gadfly politics, which combined fervent isolationism with support for drug legalization, proved unacceptable to large swaths of the modern Republican primary electorate. Bachmann, the field's only woman, held out the promise of reconnecting the party to female voters who felt increasingly isolated by Republican policies and rhetoric. But as the vocal and often virulent head of the congressional Tea Party Caucus, she sometimes came across as tin-eared and shrill.

And then there was Gingrich, the politician who more than any other embodied the rise of the congressional Republicans. Fourteen years after losing his speakership and resigning his House seat in disgrace, here he was, returning to the national stage to compete for a nomination he was rumored to have been considering way back in 1996, two years after masterminding the Republican Revolution. It was as if he had been thawed, Austin Powers–like, from a political deep freeze and brought to electoral life again. Many conservatives, however, were unenthused about a Gingrich presidency. "It's Newt's misfortune to want a high-pressure executive job with monarchical trappings where steadfastness and dignity matter. When he was Speaker of the House, he alienated his colleagues . . . and dragged himself, his family, and his party through a psychodrama," *National Review*'s Rich Lowry wrote in spring 2011 as Gingrich was gearing up to run. "If he were to replicate that performance in the White House, it'd be a formula for a LBJ- or Nixon-style meltdown."[2] Following Gingrich's victory in the South Carolina primary, which rattled the Romney camp because Gingrich had almost no field organization, New Jersey governor Chris Christie delivered a pep talk to Romney that summarized how most of the GOP establishment viewed Gingrich. "He's a joke," Christie grumbled. "And you're allowing him to be taken seriously."[3]

Indeed, chances were slim that Gingrich or any of the other three congressional contenders would become president. Major parties often nominate senators, but only two incumbent senators had won the White House since the 1920s—John Kennedy and Obama. The record of U.S. House candidates is even more dismal: the last House incumbent to win the presidency was James Garfield, in 1880. Even if Bachmann, Gingrich, Paul, and Santorum had been beloved incumbents with widespread respect within the Republican establishment—rather than polarizing candidates with mixed legislative records and glaring liabilities—none was likely to win the presidency. Yet together these four nonstarters amassed more than two and a half combined votes in Iowa for every vote for Romney. Gingrich and Santorum, winning a combined thirteen state primaries and caucuses, later posed serious threats to Romney's coronation.

It's tempting to dismiss the Iowa results as an aberration that contrasts sharply with Romney's more dominant performances later in the 2012 nomination contest. But along with their peers in New Hampshire, Iowa's rank-and-file Republicans enjoy the most direct personal exposure to the candidates; the pressure of national party expectations compels them every four years to provide their reasoned judgments as to who shall best bear the party's standard. This quartet of congressional candidates may have been running in a weak 2012 field with an uninspiring front-runner. But the weakness of the field only testifies to the dearth of presidential-caliber candidates in the GOP.

Despite having ample resources to spend against an endangered incumbent president, Mitt Romney lost the general election. The GOP also lost a net of two Senate seats and seven House seats. Yet not even six months earlier, many pundits believed Republicans would take enough seats from the Democrats—who, thanks to their huge 2006 freshman class, were defending a remarkable twenty-three seats—to recapture the Senate. And amid an otherwise gloomy night of electoral results, Speaker John Boehner maintained the Republicans' House majority, which electoral forecasters never believed was in jeopardy anyway. If it was not already obvious before Romney's defeat, by Election Night 2012 two realities about the national Republican Party were evident: national Republicans were a Congress-bound and especially House-strong political party; and the party's presidential fortunes were suffering.

The Rise of Congressional Republicans

Even casual observers of American elections are now versed in the Republicans' declining presidential fortunes. Between 1952 and 1988, the Republicans won seven of ten presidential elections; since then, they've won just two of six and, more damning, lost the popular vote in five of those six. Although Republican presidential candidates since 1992 have consistently carried fifteen to twenty states, many of these are small states, including five of the seven with populations so small they get only the constitutionally guaranteed minimum three electors. In the days following Obama's reelection—and nearly a decade after analysts including John Judis, Ruy Teixeira, Todd Estes, Phil Klinkner, and myself, among others, forecast the electoral impacts of America's changing demography[4]—political pundits seemed to finally recognize that it is growing harder for Republican presidential candidates to assemble winning coalitions.

The GOP's performance in congressional elections during the same period has been strikingly different. From 1952 to 1994, Republicans controlled the House for only two years, during the Eighty-Third Congress that opened Dwight Eisenhower's presidency. In the same period, they held the Senate for only eight years: those same two years at the start of the Eisenhower administration, plus the first six years of Reagan's presidency. To put the Democrats' mid-century congressional hegemony into perspective, consider that an American had to be at least forty-nine years old in 1980—far less than half the country, given the 1980 census's median age of thirty—to have been eligible to vote when the Republicans last won control of the House and Senate. Since 1994, however, the GOP has controlled the House for eighteen of twenty-two years and the Senate for ten years, plus briefly during the opening months of the 107th Congress at the 2001 start of Bush's presidency.

Today's partisan landscape is remarkably different. Four years after losing both chambers to the Democrats in 2006, the Republicans in 2010 recaptured the House but not the Senate. They retained the House in 2012 despite losing the presidency and losing ground in the Senate. The present partisan split in Congress—Republican House, Democratic Senate—inverts the pattern during the last sustained era of a divided Congress, the six years at the start of the Reagan administration. This inversion is no coincidence, and not without complications for today's GOP.

Figure 1 depicts the two-party share of the presidential and congressional vote during the nine presidential election cycles from 1980 to 2012.[5] The two-party vote is an imperfect measure. Ross Perot's third-party candidacies in 1992 and 1996, the wide variations in Senate populations, and the fact that many House candidates run unopposed in general election races all complicate the statistics. But the two-party results provide a reasonable baseline for comparing party performance in presidential and congressional elections every four years.

The figure reveals two patterns. First, the Republicans' two-party shares of the presidential and congressional vote since 1980 move in

A CONGRESS-CENTRIC PARTY

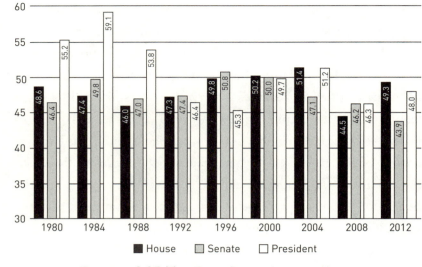

Figure 1. GOP Two-Party Share of National Vote,
Presidential Years 1980–2012

opposite directions. In the Republicans' three presidential victories during the Reagan–George H. W. Bush years, GOP presidential nominees outperformed their House counterparts by substantial margins. But in five of the six cycles since—2008 excepted—House Republicans outperformed their party's presidential nominees. The pattern is less clear for the Senate. Republican presidents easily outperformed Republican Senate candidates from 1980 to 1988 but did so in only half of the six cycles since. GOP Senate candidates have really struggled in recent cycles.

Second, House Republicans generally outperform the party's presidential nominees regardless of the presidential outcome. The GOP's House share was higher during all four cycles of the Clinton and Bush 43 administrations, as House Republicans captured a higher percentage of votes not only when Bush 41 and Bob Dole lost to Clinton, but also when Bush 43 beat Al Gore and John Kerry. The results were mixed during Barack Obama's two victories: despite losing by more than 7 percent nationally to Obama, John McCain ran ahead of his party's House candidates in 2008; despite losing by a narrower margin to Obama than McCain did, Romney in 2012 ran behind his party's House candidates.

While almost every American pundit can recite the fact that Republican candidates have lost the popular vote in five of the past six presidential elections, few have noticed that Republican presidential candidates have also been outperformed by their House Republican counterparts in five of the past six presidential cycles, and by their fellow Senate partisans in half of those six cycles. This is a testament to the enduring strength of the party's congressional wing. Republican congressional candidates do not always have a strong cycle, but of late they almost always have a stronger cycle than their party's presidential nominee.

These statistics are for presidential cycles. Some empirical studies and ample circumstantial evidence further suggest that Republicans benefit from voter turnout drop-off in midterm elections, when the presidency is not on the ballot, thus potentially exacerbating the congressional-presidential performance differences. Political scientists Martin P. Wattenberg and Craig Leonard Brians concluded that when voter turnout falls below 40 percent, it can result in partisan bias in midterm cycles, and more so when it dips close to 30 percent. For example, turnout in the 1992 election, won by Democrat Bill Clinton, was 55 percent, but fell to 39 percent in the 1994 midterms that swept Republican majorities into Congress. Although turnout decline does not entirely explain such divergent partisan results, Wattenberg and Brians estimated that if the 1992 voters had turned out in 1994, the Republicans would have gained twenty-one fewer than the fifty-two House seats they picked up that year. That would have left Gingrich and the Republicans with 209 seats—9 short of a majority.[6] Turnout expert Michael McDonald attributes some of the House Republicans' success in 2010 to the drop-off in the turnout of Democratic-leaning younger voters, who fell from 18 percent of the electorate in 2008 to just 12 percent in 2010, while Republican-leaning senior citizens jumped from 15 percent to 21 percent. These differences in turnout, McDonald writes, were surely a factor in the Republicans' gaining sixty-three seats.[7]

Republicans do not always have better midterm cycles than presidential cycles: the GOP posted landslide presidential victories in 1972 and 1984; Democrats had strong midterm cycles in 1986 and 2006. National issues and partisan waves also can drown out the effects of turnout differences among cycles.[8] But given the greater turnout among older, whiter, and more affluent Americans during midterm elections, once issues and waves are held constant we should expect Republicans to perform better when the presidency is not on the ballot. In the past half century, in fact, the two midterms that featured the largest voter drop-off from the preceding presidential cycle were 1994 and 2010—during which Republicans flipped the House twice and the Senate once.[9]

To understand more clearly the electoral fortunes of the modern Republican Party, it is useful to begin with Richard Nixon's 1968 victory. Just four years earlier, Lyndon Johnson had won in a landslide and Democrats boasted comfortable two-thirds majorities in both chambers of Congress. The New Deal coalition had changed during the three decades since Franklin Roosevelt assembled it, but LBJ's 1964 election seemed to confirm the coalition's resiliency. Then the GOP started chipping away.

First, with Nixon's defeat of Hubert Humphrey, the Republicans proved that someone other than a war hero could win the presidency for them, albeit narrowly. Nixon's victory also signaled the onset of partisan dealignment: he was the first president in American history who, in his initial election, failed to carry into office a majority for his party in at least one chamber of Congress. The Republicans made another advance in 1980, when Ronald Reagan won his first term by a much wider margin than Nixon did twelve years earlier and Republicans built their first Senate majority in twenty-six years. Then in 1994, the tenacious Newt Gingrich produced the Republicans' first House majority in four decades, while the GOP recaptured the Senate it had lost in 1986. Finally, six years after that, George W. Bush put back into place the original piece of the puzzle—the White House—and in January 2001 Republicans enjoyed unified control of the national government for the first time since 1953–1954. By 2008, they would surrender it all.

Note the temporal symmetry between the Republicans' postwar progression toward becoming a national majority party—the presidency first, then the Senate, finally the House—and their surrender of these institutions in essentially the same order. Although Bush was still in the White House when the Republicans lost both chambers of Congress in 2006, it's important to qualify this fact. Remember that in 2000 Bush lost the national popular vote and the Republicans held the Senate by a single seat that, thanks to a party switch, they momentarily gave back to the Democrats in early 2001. In almost any other presidential election system, Bush was not even supposed to be in the White House, and their Senate grip was weak, whereas the Republicans' House majority was never in much jeopardy in 2000 or the two elections that followed. And although the Senate and House fell in 2006 before Bush's presidency ended, that's only because Bush didn't have to stand for reelection himself that year. Given his plummeting approval ratings, he almost certainly would have lost. The presidency-then-Senate-then-House pattern also shows in the GOP's 2010 reclamation of the House, making it the last piece of the institutional puzzle not to fall into place for the Democrats because, well, the Republicans haven't fully let go of it—and may not for some time.

The GOP's House domination may be strengthened by the Supreme Court's June 2013 opinion in *Shelby County v. Holder*. The ruling ended the special preclearance requirement of the 1965 Voting Rights Act (VRA) for states and jurisdictions with a history of voting rights violations—a requirement, it should be mentioned, that prior to the *Shelby* ruling had three times been affirmed and amended by Congress, in laws signed by three different Republican presidents. *Bloomberg BusinessWeek* columnist Joshua Green assessed the ruling's implications for congressional elections. "The Supreme Court's decision to strike down a central provision of the Voting Rights Act will make it easier for Republicans to hold and expand their power in those mainly Southern states. That will, in turn, make it easier for them to hold the House," wrote Green. "It will also intensify the Southern captivity of the GOP, thereby making it harder for Republicans to broaden their appeal and win back the White House."[10] This trade-off—a Republican Party that dominates House elections but is dominated by its House caucus—poses a variety of problems for the national Republican Party.

Given that the *Shelby* ruling significantly limits electoral oversight by the U.S. Department of Justice, during the coming 2020 round of redistricting, state Republican political operatives will, wherever possible, continue to pack African Americans and Latinos into a few districts. They have, after all, been doing that since 1990 under the *stronger* version of the VRA. "In theory, southern legislatures could now seek to dismantle several minority-majority districts that routinely elect Democrats. But why would they?" *Cook Political Report* electoral analyst David Wasserman wrote in the wake of the *Shelby* ruling. "Minority-majority districts are the best thing that ever happened to Republicans, because they effectively quarantine Democratic voters into a handful of districts. . . . From 1992 to the present day, it's no accident that the partisan breakdown of southern seats has flipped from 96–43 in favor of Democrats to 108–41 in favor of Republicans."[11] *Shelby* thus reinforces the GOP's advantage in House elections. And if Green and Wasserman are correct, the GOP should continue to enjoy greater competitiveness in House races—but at the price of electing House Republicans who, with a few exceptions, hardly know how to communicate with and represent nonwhite voters.

But for the quirks of the Electoral College and the staggering of presidential and congressional cycles, the pattern of capture and surrender is this: first to be won, the presidency was effectively the first to slip the grasp of post-Nixon Republicans; last to be won, the House remains the party's final and most resilient stronghold, with Senate control falling in between. This pattern makes intuitive sense as a partial explanation for why the GOP has steadily—at times rapidly—turned to the right in recent decades.

Are the GOP's presidential ambitions doomed? Hardly. Despite its recent fortunes, the polarized and dealigned state of today's partisan politics still favors the Republicans in the 2016 presidential race. Only once during the past sixty years has a party won three consecutive presidential elections, in 1980, 1984, and 1988. (Democrats Bill Clinton and Al Gore won the popular vote three times consecutively between 1992 and 2000.) Other factors held aside—including the state of the economy and the quality of each party's nominee—the Republicans should be favored to win the next presidential election. That said, if in 2016 the GOP loses for a third straight time, the party's presidential prospects may be even worse than imagined.

Conservatism and Congressional Rule

There is a strong case to be made that conservatism, and by extension the modern Republican Party, are better suited to rule Capitol Hill than to occupy the Oval Office. Indeed, the congressional tilt of today's Republican Party ought to satisfy conservatives who subscribe to the theory of constitutional originalism, because the founders envisioned a national government dominated by Congress. Republican control of Congress squares neatly with these ideals.

Mid-twentieth-century conservative thinkers, most notably Willmoore Kendall and James Burnham, advanced this interpretation of constitutional intent in defense of their belief that Congress was critical to modern conservatism. In his 1959 book *Congress and the American Political Tradition*, Burnham argued for "legislative supremacy." Four years later, in *The Conservative Affirmation*, Kendall expanded upon Burnham's thinking with his "two majorities" thesis.[12] George W. Carey, a Kendall collaborator and disciple who still teaches at Georgetown University, summarizes Kendall's interpretation of the framers' vision for majority rule:

> He argued persuasively that the framers intended Congress to articulate the popular will through consensual processes, but that, over the decades, liberals had staked out a claim for the president as the most authentic representative of the people's values and aspirations. Thus, he saw a tension within the American system, a tension he described in terms of "two majorities": the congressional, which collects the sense of structured communities in terms of the hierarchical values and interests of those communities, and the presidential (necessarily cast in terms of lofty principle), which speaks for the people as an undifferentiated mass. According to his

analysis, *Congress was, as an institution, inherently more conservative than the presidency.*[13]

Burnham and Kendall were writing at a time when New Deal Democrats dominated Congress. But the words resonated with one self-styled student of political history: Newt Gingrich, who later wrote an approving foreword to the 1999 reissue of Burnham's book.[14] In an interview about the same time, Gingrich defended Congress-centered government: "For most of American history, the House and Senate were equal to, and sometimes slightly more important than, the White House," he said, citing the rise of the national economy, Woodrow Wilson, two world wars, and the Cold War as factors that led to a more presidential-centric system. "And I think that . . . as we leave the Cold War era, you're going to see a reassertion of Congressional initiative not because of partisanship but because of the natural pattern [of] the *Federalist Papers* . . . [which] say quite clearly you will normally in peacetime see the bias toward the legislative branch. . . . I think frankly that this is the correct model and I think in peacetime that the bias ought to be in favor of the legislative branch."[15]

Kendall predicted that presidents would try to transform "the American political system into a *plebiscitary* political system, capable of producing and carrying *popular mandates.*" The institutional objectives of presidents or those (especially liberals) who favor the plebiscitary model, Kendall warned, would include eliminating the Senate filibuster, ending committee seniority rules, and "iron[ing] out the inequalities of representation in Congress, since these, theoretically at least, are capable of substituting the will of a minority for that of the majority." Kendall then added parenthetically that "in the executive departments the animosity against the filibuster, the seniority principle, and the alleged 'over-representation' of rural folk and white southerners is both intense and deeply rooted." He scoffed that Congress "clearly regards as their particular virtue" the use of such impediments as the filibuster, while liberal intellectuals and other defenders of presidential power lament that Congress has a "peculiar vice, namely, that they *are* capable of frustrating an alleged majority mandate."[16] Were he alive today, Kendall might have been pleased to learn that the 112th Congress will be remembered as the least productive in seven decades—passing fewer laws than even the infamous "Do Nothing" Eightieth Congress of 1947–1948 that triggered President Harry Truman's ire.[17] He might also have been tickled to learn that Republicans held their House majority in 2012 despite attracting more than a million fewer votes than House Democratic candidates. And surely he would have been delighted to hear Republican Speaker John Boehner tell *Face the Nation* host Bob Schieffer in July 2013 that Congress "should not be judged on how many new laws we create. We ought to be judged on how many laws we repeal."

It's interesting that Kendall's arguments predate the Supreme Court's 1964 *Wesberry v. Sanders* and *Reynolds v. Sims* verdicts, which outlawed the perverse malapportionment that still prevailed for U.S. House districts and in many state legislatures. Although he is entitled to his normative defenses of malapportionment, as a strictly empirical matter the "overrepresentation" of white, rural Americans prior to the Court's two landmark rulings was no mere allegation—it was a reality, in some states, for their entire history. Kendall's defense of the "congressional majority" is thus oxymoronic, or at least anachronistic, for he validated it by dismissing those who defended the one-person/one-vote standard that today applies to every American legislature except the one exempted by the Constitution: the U.S. Senate.

Kendall's and Burnham's views of congressional power dovetail rather nicely with the institutional arguments of political scientist

Stephen Skowronek in his influential book *The Politics Presidents Make*. Skowronek begins by noting that the founders intended for the government to impart a special vitality and energy to the presidency. Because the office gives a single individual the power to act unilaterally, among the three otherwise coequal branches the presidency is uniquely capable of disrupting the political order. "Presidential action in history is politicized by the order-shattering, order-affirming and order-creating impulses inherent in the institution itself," Skowronek argues.[18] He then offers a four-case typology of presidents based on whether they were, first, either regime-affirming or regime-shattering in their ideological orientations, and second, whether the existing regime is strong or weak when a president first wins office. The most influential presidents, he contends, are those who ran against and defeated a weak regime. Ronald Reagan's 1980 election during the dying moments of the New Deal is a perfect example. Barack Obama's 2008 election may someday be regarded as having had the same regime-shattering effect on the debilitated Reagan-era coalition.

By disposition, American conservatives abhor rapid change; they favor politics and policies that change or accrete slowly, if at all. True, if the current regime is prosecuting a liberal agenda, conservatives may momentarily prefer a regime-altering Republican president. Reagan's 1981 tax cuts and deregulatory agenda are a perfect example: these policy shifts were an effort to return some aspects of government to their pre–New Deal arrangements. Such exceptions aside, conservatives generally believe a government that governs disruptively and energetically is not one that governs least. Indeed, the preferred Republican model of presidential restraint is not Reagan but the president he most revered, Calvin Coolidge. Amity Shlaes, an author praised by conservatives for her critiques of the New Deal, has dubbed Coolidge the "great refrainer." For conservatives, he is the presidential gold standard.[19]

Kendall died in 1967. His and Burnham's philosophical trea-
tises on congressional conservatism are mostly forgotten today. And
as congressional historian Julian Zelizer wryly observes, beginning
with Nixon's capture of the White House, conservatives and Republicans quickly learned to "stop worrying and love presidential
power."[20] But contemporary conservatives who value smaller and less
active governments ought to be ardent cheerleaders for a Congress-
centered national government. Of the two majoritarian branches,
the Congress is better suited to prosecute an agenda of blocking and
forestalling government action.[21] The allure of congressional rule
should be especially powerful whenever the GOP finds itself unable
to construct "plebiscitary" presidential majorities in support of its
agenda—exactly the situation in which the party finds itself today.
A half century after Kendall and Burnham published their theories
about congressional power and conservative ambition, their ideas
seem reborn: in 2013, Senator Ted Cruz and tea party–aligned
House Republicans employed extraordinary measures to prevent
what they viewed as regime-shattering efforts by the Obama administration to reform the American health care system; other Republicans are calling for the end of popularly elected U.S. senators;
and House Republicans are unapologetic about retaining their majority in 2012 despite collectively receiving fewer votes than their
Democratic counterparts.

Whether American conservatism is inherently predisposed to
congressional rule raises two related questions: First, is the Republican Party better suited to run Congress today than to control the
presidency? Second, insofar as Americans prefer divided partisan
government, might American voters actually prefer divided governments in which Democrats control the White House and Republicans the Congress?

On the first question, recent research by Northwestern University political scientist Kenneth Janda provides an important insight into how the current Republican coalition differs not only from the Democrats but from the Republican Party of the recent past. In his book *The Social Bases of Political Parties*, Janda examines the demographic composition of the two parties for the sixty-year period from 1952 to 2012. Using data from national election surveys on party identifiers, Janda develops composite portraits of the two parties based on their supporters' attributes, including occupation, education, region, urbanization, religious identity, and ethnicity.[22]

Janda argues that analyses of the demographic composition of political parties tend to focus exclusively on the *levels* of support the major parties derive from different groups. For example, a television graphic might report a poll showing that 60 percent of union members identify as Democrats or that 80 percent of white evangelicals identify as Republicans. This focus on levels of party strength, Janda argues, tends to obscure the equally important social *attraction* and social *concentration* of the parties. Social attraction he defines as "the extent to which the party attracts its supporters evenly from each significant group within any dimension of social cleavage." For example, if Democrats attracted 40 percent support from every religious subgroup and Republicans attracted 60 percent, both parties would exhibit uniform attraction for the social dimension of religion—the only difference being that the Republicans would be the majority party, given their higher levels of support from all subgroups. Social concentration is "the extent to which party supporters are concentrated within any dimension of social cleavage." If voters were classified into three equal-sized age categories—young, middle-aged, and old—and Republicans received all of their support from elderly voters but none from young and middle-aged voters, the party's concentration score would be a perfect 1.0, whereas if the Democrats received all of their support from young and middle-aged voters but none from the elderly, the Democrats would have a concentration score of 0.67 and would be the majority party.

The social attraction and concentration scores Janda computes for the postwar Democratic and Republican parties are complex and important, but not as important as his overall conclusions. Janda found that neither party is particularly concentrated on occupation, education, region, or urbanization, but both parties are highly concentrated in terms of ideology, ethnicity, and religion. More specifically, he found that the Republican Party today is the *much more concentrated party* with respect to its composite groups. It is more conservative, more white, and more evangelized than ever. Although Democrats exhibit a certain degree of concentration, they are the more broadly based party. When they advertise their diversity and multiculturalism, it is not a misrepresentation. "Increasingly, the Republican Party looks more like an interest group than a party," Janda remarked during an April 2013 presentation of his findings.[23]

How does Janda's conclusion relate to Republican congressionalization? The scholarly literature on national interest group behavior includes studies of how political groups lobby the White House, the federal bureaucracy, and even the courts. But most interest group behavior focuses on Congress, because it's the institution that is most amenable to interest groups' lobbying efforts. It features 535 elected officials scattered throughout all fifty states, representing both parties, featuring a range of policy agendas and political ideologies. Its members are relatively accessible. By comparison, the president is a single elected official from one party who is difficult to access, and federal judges are appointed, presumably nonpartisan, apolitical officials who are even harder to access. As interest group scholars say, there are far more "points of entry" in congressional politics, which is why so much interest group activity is focused on getting Congress to propose or block various legislative proposals and amendments. It is also why the vast majority of federal money raised by interest group–affiliated PACs goes to congressional races. For lobbyists, the Hill is home.

A party that has come to look more like a narrowly concentrated interest group than a broad-based party coalition ought to feel quite comfortable on Capitol Hill, practicing congressional politics. Put simply, the national GOP may have evolved into a congressionalized party because Congress is exactly where the party can best prosecute an interest group style of politics—especially for modern Republicans whose agenda, as Speaker Boehner boasts, is based on blocking and repealing legislation rather than passing it. For today's very conservative Republican Party, Capitol Hill provides a politically more comfortable home than the White House.

Which leads to the second question: Might American voters also prefer that Republicans run Congress? The answer is less clear because it is difficult to interpret survey data about Americans' attitudes toward divided government.

The preference for divided partisan government waxes and wanes. Survey results suggest that it also matters whether Americans are asked whether they *prefer* unified or divided government, or whether they believe one or the other is *good* for the country. Harris Interactive polls taken in 2006, 2008, and 2010 showed that roughly 40 percent of Americans said divided government is good for the country, around 15 percent to 20 percent believe it is bad, with the remainder either unsure or having no opinion.[24] Meanwhile, a Gallup poll taken on the eve of the 2012 election showed a marked decline in the number of people saying they prefer divided government. Gallup attributed this decline to a spike in support for unified government among Democrats, who in 2012 had an incumbent president seeking reelection—a result eerily similar to the rise in support for unified government among Republicans in 2004, when their party's president was seeking a second term.[25]

This pattern of presidential party identifiers preferring unified government at higher rates than out–presidential party identifiers emerges in the run-up to midterm elections, too: in the summer of 2006, with Bush still in office, only 15 percent of Republicans preferred divided government, compared to 38 percent of Democrats, with independents at 36 percent. Four summers later, with Obama in office, Republican support for divided government nearly tripled to 44 percent, Democratic support plummeted to 13 percent, and independents held steady at 34 percent.[26] It appears that, by sizable margins, members of the out–presidential party conveniently oppose having the White House and Congress in the same partisan hands. That pluralities within each party basically want the Congress when they already control the White House, but don't want the other party to control both Congress and the White House, isn't surprising. Partisans on both sides want unified control for themselves but not their opponents. More electorally relevant is the fact that support for divided government among crucial independent voters tracks closely with partisans of the presidential out-party. This also makes sense, given that many of these Americans self-identify as independents precisely because they dislike the performance or platforms of both major parties, and therefore wish to counterbalance each one's agendas and excesses with those of the other. If those who say it makes no difference are held aside, the ratio of Americans who say they prefer divided to unified government—particularly in polls taken before midterm elections—runs about two to one.

The shared preference among independents and the out–presidential party for divided government also helps explain the recent history of elections that have created both unified and divided national governments. In the past quarter century, the 1992, 2000, and 2008 elections created unified governments from previously divided governments; the 1994, 2006, and 2010 elections created divided governments after very short periods of unified government. Notice that the first three were presidential election years and the latter three were midterm cycles. Because the partisanship of the presidency is fixed during midterm cycles, voters have an unadulterated opportunity to end unified government by giving the out–presidential party control of one or both chambers of Congress. During presidential elections, however, especially those when the incumbent is ineligible to run (for example, 2000, 2008), the next president's partisan identity is unknown.

Unfortunately, pollsters do not ask respondents what their preferences would be if forced to choose between specific modes of divided government—Democrats in the White House with Republicans in Congress, versus the reverse. It's possible that partisans on both sides would prefer the presidency, given the power of presidents to appoint federal judges and Supreme Court justices, and their greater influence over foreign policy. But given the Democrats' recent domination of presidential contests, along with the fact that the combined support from independents and out–presidential party partisans (Republicans, at present) yields pluralities favoring divided government, the best way for contemporary voters to divide the national government is to offset Democratic presidents with Republican majorities in Congress. Put another way, in the post–Reagan-Bush era, preferring divided government has generally meant preferring Republican rule in Congress. And the best opportunity to effect this outcome is during midterm elections. Voters did exactly that in 1994 and 2010.

If the GOP increasingly acts like an interest group, and pluralities of American voters want divided government, it may be that

Republicans and the American electorate agree that, all else equal, the best solution is for Republicans to run Congress—or at least one chamber. Willmoore Kendall probably would have been delighted.

The Calculus of Congressional Republicans

Although the 535 members of Congress do not exercise equal influence, each holds a minimum reserve of power. This reserve is especially potent in the Senate, where the filibuster empowers a senator from even the least populous state to unilaterally block the wishes of the remaining ninety-nine members. But there is something unique about the parceling of power in today's Congress that goes beyond the structural capacity of numerical minorities to thwart majority will. Vexingly for liberals and Democrats, the minority power of Congress is exaggerated in ways that favor conservatives and Republicans. As a by-product of constitutional design and demographic happenstance, minoritarian rule is no fault of Republican politicians. But its effects alter the political calculus on Capitol Hill, and Republicans and conservatives are wise to take advantage.

The minority-majority Republican Senate. Because each state gets two senators even though state populations vary widely, a minority of the national population has always in theory, and often in practice, been able to control a majority of Senate seats. As of the 2010 census, for example, a combined 50.4 million people—about one-sixth of the U.S. population—lived in the twenty-five least-populous states. The remaining five-sixths of Americans lived in the twenty-five most-populous states. Were one party to control all of the seats from the twenty-five smallest states, plus one other, it could thwart the will of five-sixths of the country despite representing just the remaining one-sixth.

Of course, neither party's caucus has ever been made up like this. But by definition one or the other of the parties, whether in the majority or the minority, *always* represents a smaller share of the national population than its share of Senate seats. Because it dominates the states with smaller populations, the modern Republican Party has consistently been overrepresented in the Senate.

Consider the Republicans' two recent Senate majority eras. The first, when they were led by Tennessee's Howard Baker and then Kansan Bob Dole, extended from 1981 to 1987. With a brief interruption caused by the 2001 party switch of Vermont senator James Jeffords, the second GOP reign essentially lasted a dozen years, beginning with the historic 104th Congress, elected in 1994. Jeffords's switch complicates this history, but based on the preceding November's election results, the GOP opened all six Congresses with an absolute majority or tied. These Senate majorities were led by Mississippi's Trent Lott and Tennessee's Bill Frist. During these nine Congresses and eighteen years, the GOP enjoyed inflated representational power; because it was in the majority, one might say it wielded minority-majority power.

Figure 2 shows the minority-majority phenomenon with two percentages. The first is simply the number of the one hundred Senate seats (and thus the percentage) held by Republicans at the start of all nine Congresses during the two Republican majorities.[27] The second, rounded to the tenths place, is the share of the national population in the states represented by Republican senators, computed as the sum of the population of states with two Republicans (or Republican-caucusing independents) plus half the population of partisan-split states, divided by the total U.S. population. As the figure shows, the two recent Senate Republican majorities benefited

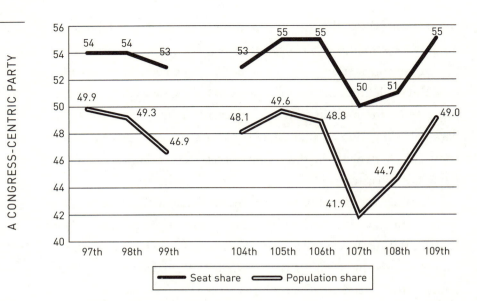

Figure 2. Senate Republican Apportionment Advantage, 1981–2007

from inflated representation. (Although not depicted in the figure, the intervening Democratic majorities never enjoyed inflated representation. Even in the minority, the modern GOP has enjoyed inflated Senate representation.)

Notice, too, that the apportionment advantage meant greater inflation during the Lott-Frist majorities of the Clinton-Bush era than during the Baker-Dole reign. Between 1981 and 1987, the seat-to-population inflation ranged between four and six points; the Baker-Dole Republicans held an average of just under fifty-four seats and represented about 49 percent of the national population. By contrast, seat-to-population inflation during the Lott-Frist era averaged six points, never fell below five points, and at the start of the 107th Congress in 2001 peaked at eight points. The Republicans' small-state advantage in the Senate has become more magnified. At its apogee—the fifty-five-member Senate majority that Republicans forged after netting four seats in the 2004 election—

the total combined votes cast for Republican candidates in the com- posite three cycles (2000, 2002, and 2004) that elected those Senate majorities were 2.5 million *fewer* than for Democratic candidates.[28] Empirical research confirms that the small-state advantage ac- counted for the Republicans' Senate majorities during the first six years of the Reagan administration and has continuously benefited Republicans—whether in the majority or the minority—since 1978. Small-state Senate elections also tend to be less competitive than those in larger and often more heterogeneous states, and cheaper to finance because advertising and field outreach expenses are lower. These factors help lock in the Republicans' Senate advantages.[29]

Republicans have not always been the apportionment-advantaged Senate party. Mid-twentieth-century Republicans regularly won Senate seats in large states like California, New Jersey, New York, and Pennsylvania, making the Democrats the advantaged Senate party. The Senate majority that controlled the 83rd Congress of 1953–1954 was led by just forty-eight Republicans—exactly half the total of ninety-six, good enough for a majority with the help of Vice President Nixon's tiebreaking vote—yet those Republicans represented 52.8 percent of the U.S. population. But the pattern today is clear: whether in the majority or the minority, the modern Republican Party's advantage in small-state Senate elections consis- tently inflates its representational power. Moreover, because each state's electoral vote is based on its total number of seats in both chambers, Republican presidential candidates also benefit slightly from the party's small-state advantage.[30]

If both parties were equally competitive in states both large and small, the one-state/one-vote Senate apportionment standard would wash out. But in recent decades, Republicans have dominated small- state elections for the Senate and in the Electoral College. Just ask President Al Gore.

House party. National Republicans are not only more Congress-centered, they are also becoming a party dominated by their House caucus. The "House-ification" of the GOP is evident on many levels. The party is presently experiencing the only sustained period since its founding in the 1850s when it has controlled the House but not the Senate, and the current ratio of House to Senate seats is at near-record highs. Speaker John Boehner maintained his majority despite 2012 Republican House candidates receiving a minority of votes cast nationally in House elections; Paul Ryan and other self-styled "young guns" in the House produce many of the GOP's policy ideas, political vitality, and press headlines. The prominence of the House Republican Conference is often a political liability for Republican senators and Senate candidates.

Let's start with House elections. Following the 2012 midterms, despite having been outvoted nationally, Republicans controlled 234 House seats, 16 more than the 218 needed to forge a majority. FairVote.org's Rob Richie and Devin McCarthy explain how the Republicans built their minority-majority in the House:

> In House races, Democratic candidates won about a million more votes nationwide than Republicans and would have increased that margin substantially if all races had been contested. After controlling for factors like vote inflation for incumbents and uncontested races, the data suggests voters generally preferred Democrats for Congress by a 52 to 48 percent margin.
>
> . . . That disparity in voter preference compared to seats did not result from ticket-splitting; in fact, there were only 24 districts in which one party's nominee carried the presidential vote and the other party's nominee won the congressional race, all but four of which were won by an incumbent.

The real problem for Democrats was that in a year in which Barack Obama won a decisive presidential election victory, he carried only 207 of 435 congressional districts.[31]

Gerrymandering alone did not deliver a House majority to the Republicans in 2010 or permit it to hold that majority two years later. But it helped.

National Journal's David Wasserman explains how the skewing of the House districts—partly but not entirely the result of strategic gerrymandering choices—creates a built-in advantage for Republicans. After the strong 2010 cycle in which they picked up key governorships and hundreds of state legislative seats, in 2011 the Republicans controlled the redistricting process in states with four times as many districts as Democrats did. But the Republicans are also aided by the increased clustering of Democratic voters into densely packed population centers. Wasserman points out that when 1988 Democratic presidential nominee Michael Dukakis lost the national popular vote, he carried 819 counties—129 more than Barack Obama carried in 2012 when he *won* the national popular vote. The clustering of Democratic voters in urban and inner suburban areas thus facilitates Republican gerrymandering objectives. "Welcome, then, to the new normal," Wasserman writes. "A growing coalition of young, nonwhite, and college-educated voters is now sufficiently large to allow Democrats to win statewide elections, and conveniently for their party, America votes for both the White House and the Senate on a statewide basis. But, just as conveniently for Republicans, this same coalition is way too clustered in too few districts to allow Democrats to win the House in the absence of a huge anti-GOP wave."[32]

However much population concentration or strategic gerrymandering contributed to his retention of the House in 2012, by January 2015 Speaker John Boehner will have presided for four years over a

House majority with no companion Senate Republican majority. When is the last time a Republican House and a Democratic Senate coexisted for that long? *Never.* Since the Republican Party's founding in 1854, there had been only two Congresses featuring a House Republican majority and a Senate Democratic majority: the 34th and 36th Congresses in the late 1850s, before the Republicans had even elected their party's first president. Boehner's four-years-and-counting majority provides powerful confirmation that the Republicans have become a House-heavy party.

Simple majority or minority control, however, is a crude indicator of a party's relative strength in Congress's two chambers. I compared the ratio of Republican House and Senate seats to create a more precise measure of the party's bicameral strength, regardless of whether the GOP controlled either chamber. Figure 3 depicts what I call the "bicameral party strength ratio" since the start of the Eisenhower administration. The horizontal line down the middle of the figure indicates interchamber parity which, given 435 House seats and 100 senators, is 4.35 to 1.[33]

The figure shows how House-heavy the congressional wing of the Republican Party is today. During the long period from 1954 to 1980, when comfortable Democratic majorities ruled both chambers, the Republicans steadily progressed from a House-heavy congressional party to a more balanced one—and even, by the late 1970s, became slightly Senate-heavy. In 1980, when they won control of the Senate for the first time in twenty-six years, the ratio was well below the 4.35 to 1 threshold, reaching a modern low in the 98th Congress of 1983–1984. Since then, however, the GOP's bicameral party strength ratio has steadily risen, attaining near-record highs during Boehner's speakership.

After the 2010 elections, in which Republicans recaptured the House, the ratio reached 5.14 to 1. As I explained in 2011 in the

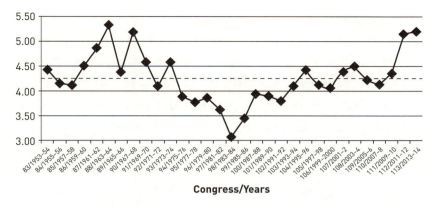

Congress/Years

Figure 3. Ratio of Republican House Seats to Senate Seats, 1953–2014

New Republic, this figure is historically unprecedented: "In fact, the 5.14 House-to-Senate tilt for the GOP today is greater than for all but six Congresses since the party's founding. In all six prior cases, however, one party controlled both chambers of Congress, thereby muting or even mooting the disparities because Republicans either controlled none or both chambers. Speaker John Boehner, for his part, leads a House-heavy Republican Party that controls only the House. His is arguably the GOP's most House-dominant coalition in the party's 158-year existence."[34] In 2012, after they lost a net of seven House seats but a slightly higher proportion of Senate seats (two), the ratio inched up to 5.20 to 1. And so, an update: Speaker Boehner now leads the most House-dominant coalition in the party's *160*-year existence—and, again, the only one since its founding to boast a House majority for four consecutive years without an accompanying Senate majority.

Mitt Romney's choice of Representative Paul Ryan as his running mate also shows how Congress-centered—and House-tilted—the national Republican Party has become. Romney didn't select just any House backbencher. Ryan was and remains the national party's brightest young star, having emerged as the Republicans' de facto national policy leader. As profiled by the *New Yorker*'s Ryan Lizza, the ambitious Wisconsin congressman aspired to become his party's point person for national fiscal policy soon after Obama's 2008 election. In response to the new administration's first budget, Ryan crafted a ten-year alternative that included severe cuts in entitlements and social spending. Initially, almost no congressional Republicans publicly supported his plan. After declaring his presidential candidacy in spring 2011, Newt Gingrich—perhaps feeling upstaged by the young congressman, whose House career somewhat resembles his own—criticized Ryan's plan to overhaul Medicare as "right-wing social engineering" and "too big a jump" for entitlement reform.[35]

But over the next three years, Ryan doggedly won over almost all Capitol Hill Republicans and most conservative think tanks and organizations. "Nearly every important conservative opinion-maker and think tank has rallied around his policies," wrote Lizza. "Nearly every Republican in the House and the Senate has voted in favor of some version of his budget plan."[36] By mid-2012 the entire field of Republican contenders, including Romney, was supporting Ryan's plan. Feeling an angry backlash from tea party conservatives, Gingrich retracted his criticisms and apologized to Ryan. On fiscal matters, Ryan had transformed himself from a representative mostly unknown outside his state to the politician setting the fiscal and social welfare policy agenda for the party's congressional *and* presidential wings. He is only the latest of many House Republicans in the past three decades—including former Ryan mentor Jack Kemp, Dick Armey, and Gingrich himself—to assert significant policy influence over the party's presidential nominees and presidents.

That Ryan could so thoroughly capture his party's policy agenda and be considered vice presidential timber so quickly only shows the GOP's lack of veteran policy leadership. His meteoric rise testifies to the lopsided power wielded by the party's congressional wing. But most of all, his emergence as a top-tier national figure demonstrates that the House Republican caucus is the party's backbone and the source for much of the national party's ideas and energy.

House-ifying the Senate. Of course, winning House elections and controlling the House are generally positive developments for Republicans. Difficulties arise when House Republicans' successes adversely affect the party's performance in Senate and presidential contests. A House-centric party can be politically and electorally problematic. Yet in a very literal sense, the Senate Republican Conference has also become House-ified because the share of Republican senators who served previously in the House has risen dramatically over the past six decades.

Table 1 shows the legislative backgrounds of Republican senators in the first Congress of each of the past four Republican Senate majority eras. In the 83rd Congress of 1953–1954, about a fifth of Senate Republicans had House backgrounds; by the start of the 97th Congress in 1981, the share had jumped to one in three; and by the time the 108th Congresses convened in 2003, after the GOP regained the majority it lost to Jeffords's 2001 party switch, nearly *half* of all Republican senators had served previously in the House.[37] This is an astonishing change.

Lately, the problems associated with a House-ified Senate have become worse. In his book *The Gingrich Senators*, political scientist Sean W. Theriault attributes the rising polarization of the Senate over the past three decades to the capture of the Senate Republican Conference by the generation of Republicans first elected to the House after 1978—the year Newt Gingrich first won his House seat. The forty "Gingrich senators" include some of Capitol Hill's

Table 1. Senate Republicans with Prior House Service, 1953–2004

	Total	Prior House Service	Percentage
83rd Congress (1953–1954)	48	10	20.8
97th Congress (1981–1982)	52	17	32.7
104th Congress (1995–1996)	53	24	45.3
108th Congress (2003–2004)	51	25	49.0

most polarizing figures: Colorado's Wayne Allard, Kentucky's Jim Bunning, Oklahoma's Tom Coburn, South Carolina's Jim DeMint, Oklahoma's James Inhofe, Arizona's Jon Kyl, and Louisiana's David Vitter—all of whom have had very conservative voting records in both the House and, later, the Senate. "The voting behavior of the Gingrich Senators may help explain why the modern Senate more closely resembles the U.S. House, where partisanship has been more prominent since at least the breakdown of the conservative coalition in the 1960s," Theriault and coauthor David Rhode concluded. "As the Gingrich Senators become more numerous and more powerful in the Republican caucus, the polarization trend will continue."[38]

The rise of the tea party movement has further complicated the GOP's Senate problems. Tea party–endorsed Senate candidates like Rand Paul in Kentucky and Marco Rubio in Florida—both of whom are possible 2016 presidential candidates—have enjoyed political success. The rub for Republicans is that candidates whose policy agendas and personal profiles please rabidly conservative primary voters in the spring may offend general election voters come autumn. In very conservative, highly gerrymandered House districts, the disconnect between primary and general election voters matters little, if at all. But in 2010 and 2012 some tea party Republicans who won Senate primaries in swing or blue states self-destructed in the general election. The 2010 list of candidates included Colorado's Ken Buck, Delaware's Christine O'Donnell, and Nevada's Sharron Angle. Angle's defeat represented a lost chance to scalp none other than the Democrats' Senate majority leader, Harry Reid.

Some of the 2010 Senate losses came in blue or purple states, which is easier to explain because Senate partisanship increasingly aligns with presidential partisanship.[39] The really crippling defeats came in 2012. Radical GOP candidates Todd Akin and Richard Mourdock blew what should have been relatively easy opportunities in, respectively, Indiana and Missouri—states that Mitt Romney carried—after they expressed polarizing and politically tone-deaf views about rape. Their policy position on "legitimate rape" was actually no different from the one supported at roll call by many fellow House Republicans, including vice presidential nominee Paul Ryan. But party-line votes on complex bills passed by Congress go mostly unnoticed, whereas gaffes recorded on radio or television during highly visible campaigns generate headlines. "To their dismay," the *National Journal*'s Alex Roarty wrote shortly after the 2012 elections, "Senate Republicans are discovering that their chances of retaking the chamber might rest as much with their House GOP brethren as with their own efforts. Increasingly, it's the lower chamber that defines the Republican Party brand—particularly during high-stakes fights like the fiscal-cliff and sequester standoffs in which House Republicans play a central role. This prominence is problematic because the House GOP doesn't live in the same political universe as the rest of the party; the congressional map . . . leans to the right."[40]

If there were any lingering doubts about the connections between ideological orientation and the demographic composition of the two parties' House caucuses, the 2012 election results provided a powerful reminder. Nancy Pelosi's Democratic minority caucus in the 113th Congress is quite literally a *minority* caucus: a majority of its members are either nonwhite, female, or both—the first time in American history that white men have been a numerical minority in the congressional caucus of either party in either chamber. By contrast, nearly nine out of ten House Republicans are white men, and in 2012 the caucus actually *lost* a net of two nonwhite and five female members.[41] In an election in which the Senate for the first time reached twenty female members (sixteen of them Democrats) and a record 28 percent of all voters were nonwhite, the House GOP actually became more white and more male.

Demography also explains this paradox: Despite the Republicans' built-in Senate malapportionment advantage, why does the GOP now control the House but not the Senate? As *New York* magazine's Jonathan Chait argues, it's not just that Republicans tend to fare better in the less-populous states, but that these states tend be differently populated from the rest of the country:

> The [Senate] doesn't attempt to represent America, exactly. It represents an approximation of America that is whiter and more rural than the real thing. This makes the Senate naturally more fertile territory for the Republicans, and while the Democrats have managed to hang on to majority control of the Senate since 2007, the way they have done so points to the forbidding odds they face. Republicans have thrown away easily winnable races in states like Delaware, Nevada, Indiana, and Missouri by nominating oddballs or cranks when perfectly loyal, more palatable Republicans were available. Democrats, meanwhile, have managed to hold seats in deep-red states only by carefully husbanding the political capital of their members. If liberals attempted to impose

anything close to the sort of partisan discipline on their Senate candidates that tea-party activists deploy against Republicans, the GOP might have a filibuster-proof majority.[42]

This tea party–enforced discipline likely caused Republicans to lose some otherwise winnable races, preventing the party from fully exploiting its small-state Senate advantage. The fact that Senate Republicans are the minority despite their small-state constitutional advantage is further evidence of the party's House-heavy tilt. Radical, House-style Republican candidates for Senate—and in Akin's case, actual incumbent House members—are creating electoral headaches for the party. Even those who do win in conservative states may take positions or make comments that other Republican nominees must either endorse or reject—either of which carries risks.

Like Senate contests, gubernatorial races are statewide elections free of gerrymandering effects. Here, however, contemporary Republicans boast a majority of state chief executives—thirty in 2014. But gubernatorial races tend not to devolve into arguments about the polarizing national issues that complicate matters for Senate candidates. As Republican media consultant Chris Palko observed in *Campaigns and Elections*: "In the 1960s and 70s, Democrats had lopsided advantages in representation in state executive offices. In the past two decades, possession of a majority of governor seats has seesawed between both parties, but Republican gubernatorial candidates have generally avoided the pratfalls that have occurred to their Senate candidates in recent years, and the distribution of gubernatorial seats more accurately demonstrates the small state advantage Republicans have."[43]

Senate elections have increasingly taken on the features of the winner-take-all statewide contests for presidential electors. That's why the number of split-delegation states in the Senate declined sharply between the Baker-Dole leadership era and the Lott-Frist era just two decades later. In effect, explains party polarization expert Alan Abramowitz, Senate elections have become more nationalized. "Fewer senators represent so-called swing states . . . while more senators represent states that are relatively safe for their own party," Abramowitz writes. ". . . Voters have increasingly come to see a Senate election as a choice about not just who will represent their state but which party will control the chamber. Therefore, in choosing a Senate candidate, voters are increasingly influenced by their opinions on national political issues and especially their assessment of the president's performance."[44] Given Democrats' recent dominance in presidential contests, this parallel effect on Senate results does not bode well for Republicans.

The final complication for the Republicans' Senate ambitions is the Constitution. Because the terms of each state's two senators are staggered and both are elected statewide, there are no Senate districts to draw and no maps to manipulate for partisan gain. What the Constitution giveth in the form of Senate malapportionment, it taketh away in the inability to gerrymander. Given that malapportionment may confer far greater partisan advantage to the small-state-advantaged party—and at present there's no doubt the Republicans *are* that party—it's truly surprising that Republicans hold the House without the Senate.

Partisan Institutionalism

Parties attain power by winning elections. Particularly during divided partisan governments, or when a party is faring better on either the national or state level, strategic partisans rationally attempt to shift power to the institutions over which they have greater or more consistent control. Political scholars call this phenomenon *partisan institutionalism.*

Since 1952, divided government was characterized, first, by mostly Republican presidents and either Democratic or split-control Congresses, and after 1994 by Democratic presidents and either Republican or split-control Congresses. When Republicans control the White House but not Congress, we should expect them to try to magnify the power of the executive, and when they control Congress we should expect the reverse. Since they are unable of late to construct Kendall-like "plebiscitary" presidential majorities, we should expect today's GOP to search for ways to expand its legislative power. Both before and after 2012, the Republican Party has done exactly that. Many of these efforts are forms of political retrenchment, aimed at maximizing the party's political-electoral power given a fixed or dwindling level of voter support.

Voter and voting restrictions. The American electorate is changing because the nation's demography is changing. Women have become more politically active. A majority of adult Americans are unmarried. More people live in large cities and coastal states. And, of course, America continues to become a nonwhite majority nation. Given that these trends make it harder for Republican presidential and statewide candidates to win, there is a strong temptation to limit these groups' electoral clout. Republican-affiliated organizations have tried to make ballot access more difficult, either by advocating strict voter identification laws, opposing states' early voting provisions, pushing to reverse Voting Rights Act protections, or calling for a reversal of the Seventeenth Amendment's requirement that U.S. senators be popularly elected.

Although the Voting Rights Act was extended in 1970, 1975, 1982, and 2006, many Republican politicians were already calling for it to be gutted even before the Supreme Court's 2013 ruling in *Shelby County v. Holder.* When the final 2006 reauthorization bill passed overwhelmingly in both chambers, Georgia congressman Charlie Norwood sponsored an amendment that would have removed the VRA's special classification for southern states.[45] The amendment failed, yet ninety-five of the ninety-six aye votes came from Republicans. Almost every southern Republican voted for it.[46] Undeterred, the Project on Fair Representation, a legal advocacy group funded by a consortium of wealthy conservatives, challenged the VRA's constitutionality in federal court. They were a powerful force in pushing for the Court to invalidate parts of the VRA; they provided legal counsel to the *Shelby* plaintiffs; and they publicly lauded the Court's ruling.[47]

Running alongside the push to repeal the Voting Rights Act are efforts to restrict ballot access. With model legislation and financial support provided by the American Legislative Exchange Council, a conservative nonprofit that raises tens of millions of dollars from corporations, Republican state legislators have pressed for more stringent voter identification requirements—even though repeated studies show that voter fraud is extraordinarily rare. Because younger, transient, poor, nonwhite, and urban voters are less likely to have driver's licenses or other government-sponsored picture IDs, the American Legislative Exchange Council's efforts appear designed to deter voting by demographic groups who vote overwhelmingly Democratic.[48] Republicans are also leading the push to restrict or eliminate early voting. "Both parties could put their energy into increasing turnout for their side," writes *Slate*'s legal expert Emily Bazelon. "Instead, the Republicans who litigate against early voting—and in favor of voter ID—talk about following the rules, even though the rules they are crafting have such self-serving ends, and inveigh against voter fraud, even though in-person vote stealing almost never actually occurs."[49]

Another creative response to America's changing electorate is to remove voters from the equation altogether. The 2014 midterm cycle marked the centennial anniversary of popular voting for U.S. senators, as mandated by the Seventeenth Amendment. Although only a small fringe of conservatives advocate returning the selection of senators to state legislators, the movement broadened after several tea party–affiliated candidates in 2010 and 2012 proclaimed their support for the idea. Defeated 2012 Republican Senate candidates Pete Hoekstra, Todd Akin, and Richard Mourdock, plus failed 2010 candidate Joe Miller of Alaska, all expressed support for repeal. Mike Lee, Republican senator from Utah, has described the Seventeenth Amendment as a mistake, and Texas governor Rick Perry also suggested he might favor returning the selection of U.S. senators to state elites.[50]

Electoral College tinkering. A party excelling in House elections but struggling in presidential elections might also seek ways to make presidential results more closely approximate House results. What better way of doing so than to literally House-ify the assignment of Electoral College votes?

In all but two states, electors are awarded on a winner-take-all basis to the presidential candidate who captures a plurality of a state's popular votes. Maine and Nebraska, however, use the congressional district model for allocating electors: they award two electors to the statewide popular vote winner, and one to the winner of each of the state's House districts. (In 2008 Barack Obama won Nebraska's Omaha-based First District, but John McCain won the other two and statewide to take four of the state's five electors.) Obama in 2012 captured 332 electors, yet carried only 207 House districts, plus twenty-six states and the District of Columbia, good enough for only 262 electors if all fifty states used the Maine-Nebraska model—8 shy of the 270 majority needed to win in an election in which he beat Mitt Romney by 3.9 percent in the national popular vote.[51] He would have lost reelection.

Almost as if on cue, a few months after Obama's reelection Republican state legislators in Ohio, Pennsylvania, and Virginia proposed converting their states to either the Maine-Nebraska model or a proportional allocation system. A similar attempt to convert Michigan to the Maine-Nebraska model was thwarted by Republicans in that state's legislature prior to the 2012 election—but only because Republicans there presumed that the son of former Michigan governor George Romney would carry the state and therefore want all sixteen of Michigan's electors.[52]

Not long ago, the Democrats were trying to persuade states to adopt the Maine-Nebraska model. Remarkably, Florida Democrats introduced a bill in 1992 that would have awarded their state's electors by House district; had Republicans not thwarted this effort, there might never have been a 2000 presidential recount, because Gore carried enough districts (ten) to give him more than 270 electors. Now the partisan shoe is on the other foot. Unfortunately for Republicans, post-2012 Electoral College "reform" efforts have mostly stalled, in large part because prominent state Republicans spoke out against attempts to break with their states' traditions. Advocates of this change do, however, have the blessing of the nation's top party official, Republican National Committee chairman Reince Priebus, who has said red states "ought to be looking at" Electoral College rule changes.[53]

Filibuster abuse. There was a time when Senate filibusters were as uncommon as the fictional one portrayed in *Mr. Smith Goes to Washington*. Filibusters were rare until the early 1970s, when usage suddenly spiked from a few times per two-year Congress to about two dozen times per Congress. It spiked again in the late 1980s, after Republicans lost their six-year Senate majority during the 1986 midterms, and again after they lost their Senate majority in the 2006 midterms. To be fair, Democrats responded with their own increased use of the filibuster once they fell back into the minority. But Republican minority caucuses have clearly ratcheted up the use of the filibuster to forestall legislation and, more recently, the confirmation of political appointees. A procedural option that was employed once per legislative session is now a daily occurrence.[54]

Beltway policy wonk Ezra Klein explains that no president has had his agenda so frequently filibustered as Barack Obama. "If not for the filibuster," he writes, "the Affordable Care Act would include a public option, the stimulus would have been hundreds of billions of dollars larger, and a plan to cap and trade carbon emissions would likely have passed the Senate." But the "apotheosis" of the current Republican Senate minority's use of the filibuster, Klein argues, came in December 2012, when Republican minority leader Mitch McConnell proposed legislation that would authorize presidents to unilaterally raise the debt ceiling unless two-thirds majorities in both chambers of Congress voted otherwise. McConnell was bluffing, but he didn't expect President Obama and Democratic majority leader Harry Reid to call that bluff. When Democrats asked for a roll call vote, McConnell caused a stir by initiating a filibuster to block his own proposal.[55]

McConnell's Senate minority has used the filibuster to create unprecedented delays in confirming Obama's judicial appointees:

78 percent of district court appointees and 42 percent of circuit court appointees waited at least one hundred days for confirmation, compared to 15 percent and 8 percent, respectively, for George W. Bush's appointees.[56] Finally, in November 2013, a frustrated Reid invoked the so-called nuclear option and eliminated filibusters for executive appointments and all judicial nominees except those for the Supreme Court.

A Senate caucus majority generally wants to pursue its agenda, while the minority caucus seeks to obstruct and dilute that agenda. But conservatives' orientation toward governmental activism contrasts sharply with that of liberals. When governing philosophy is taken into account, the capacity to block inverts the normal assumptions about the value of majority and minority control. Why? Because an underappreciated feature of the bicameral Congress is that the blocking power of House majorities is *greater* than that of Senate majorities. This difference has always existed: the Senate's more inclusive and individual-protecting norms put the majority and minority parties on a more even footing than in the House. The proliferation of the filibuster in the past four decades has further cemented this imbalance, because a single minority party senator— with forty colleagues backing her—can hold the entire chamber hostage, just as a single majority party senator can. Trent Lott, who served as both Senate majority and minority leader, has said that "being majority leader is much different and much more difficult than being minority leader," because while both parties can forestall action, only the majority party is expected to carry forward an agenda.[57] Lott's lament is even more true today.

In contrast, a highly disciplined House Speaker with a one-vote majority can thwart even the unified efforts of the entire minority party. The House is far less likely to be bogged down with thorny negotiations between the party leadership and a few petulant members; and there are few bipartisan "gangs" of self-styled moderates joining to resolve stalemates between the parties. So long as party loyalty is strictly enforced, a Speaker with a House majority of 50.1 percent wields more power than a majority leader with fifty-nine of the Senate's one hundred seats. Such a Speaker and his or her majority can paralyze the rest of the government. "You can govern with just the House," asserts conservative stalwart Grover Norquist, without any hint of irony.[58] The corporate community, to which Republicans are closely tied, often concurs in this view. Referring to the oil industry's "blocking strategy" during the Obama administration, one industry consultant said: "Whoever's in power in the House has almost dictatorial power. If you control what's going on in the House, you have huge influence over the final legislation, as well as over the budgets and spending mandates that shape regulation."[59]

If forced to choose a majority in one chamber and a minority in the other, the Republicans' preference should be for a House majority, because a House majority has absolute blocking power in a bicameral legislature. That's been exactly the situation in the 112th and 113th Congresses. The current electoral situation could be far worse for Republicans—and *was* during the first two years of the Obama presidency, when Democrats ruled both chambers. But if they had to pick just one of Washington's three elected institutions, given their ideological priorities, controlling only the House is their best option.

The Partisan Costs of Congressionalization

Still, conservatives and Republicans should be careful what they wish for. A Congress-centered national party with a House-heavy tilt comes with a variety of political and electoral costs. The GOP's congressional successes during the Clinton era were cause for great celebration among conservatives. But congressional Republicans quickly narrowed the party's political and policy focus and made it more beholden to its more self-destructive elements. This new strain of congressional Republicanism represented a striking departure from the nationally dominant presidential wing, which reached its zenith in 1984 with Ronald Reagan's forty-nine-state Electoral College victory. The congressional wing gave national Republican politics a sharper, more parochial, often reactionary tone.

The problems began soon after the 1994 victories. As the following year's federal government shutdown demonstrated, the antigovernment fervor that conservative members brought to Washington was neither conducive to effective governing nor electorally attractive. "So much of what went wrong in the 104th Congress came down to the fact that the Republicans just hadn't given enough thought to how they were going to run things once they took over," concluded journalist Linda Killian in her study of the freshmen who arrived in Washington as members of the new Republican majority. "They came up with a nifty campaign plan, some good slogans and buzzwords, some basic tenets about balancing the budget and cutting government. But Gingrich and company had no real game plan for what came next."[60] Congressional Republicans had long been in the business of opposition, of tearing things down and railing against Washington. Once in power, their policy and leadership shortcomings became apparent. And still, that 1994 freshman class did not move the Republican caucuses as far to the right as the tea party–inspired newcomers did in 2010. In 1994 the bigger rightward shift for congressional Republicans was still to come.

An ironic complication is that congressional Republicans were often *less* capable of pushing back against their own party's president. Because their political power initially derived from tactical superiority and rhetorical savvy rather than policy expertise or governing experience, when the headstrong executive tandem of George W. Bush and Dick Cheney came to power, Capitol Hill Republicans saw little reason to push back against their policies so long as the electoral benefits looked promising. "To me, the [Bush income] tax cut was a stalking horse," laments former Rhode Island senator Lincoln Chaffee, a moderate Republican who made national headlines when he announced that he would write in former president Bush's name on his 2004 presidential ballot. "The White House was out to neuter Congress, and the minute Congress rolled over for the cuts, it set the stage for one-branch rule."[61] The plebiscitary Republican presidency had arrived.

Many Republicans who served in Congress during this period—not just liberals like Chaffee but also conservative House stalwarts like Paul Ryan, Bob Ney, and tea party champion Dick Armey—later regretted that congressional Republicans so often capitulated to the Bush White House. With near-universal support, GOP Congresses passed the USA PATRIOT Act and the Medicare Part D drug plan expansion, neither of which can be considered limited government. Veteran Congress-watchers Thomas Mann and Norman Ornstein also noticed the congressional Republicans' sudden servility. "The arrival of unified Republican government in 2001," they write, "transformed the aggressive and active GOP-led Congress of the Clinton years into a deferential and supine body, one extremely reluctant to demand information, scrub presidential proposals, or oversee the executive. The uncompromising assertion of executive authority by President Bush and Vice President Cheney was met with a whimper, not a principled fight, by the Republican Congress."[62]

Comparing the twelve years of the Reagan-Bush era with George W. Bush's two terms, it is clear that Democratic Speaker Tip O'Neill and his successors had a moderating influence on Reagan and the elder Bush that Republican Speaker Dennis Hastert and majority leader Tom DeLay did not have on the younger Bush. In part, this difference reflects Bush 43's more conservative agenda. Republicans also controlled only the Senate, for six years, and never the House during the Reagan-Bush era, whereas the younger Bush had Republican majorities in the House for six years and in the Senate for four. A further distinction must be made here: Reagan swept that Senate majority into office with him in 1980, whereas Bush inherited his majorities. They had been slowly eroding in size and power after 1994, but they had also established their own leaders and agenda prior to Bush's inauguration in 2001. Whatever Bush's initial posture toward his Republican partisans in Congress, or theirs toward him, there is no doubt that the Republican majorities in both chambers—especially the fervent House majority—were more radicalized than the Republican Senate majority led by Howard Baker in 1981.

Moreover, because the two parties' ideological realignment eliminated both conservative southern Democrats and liberal Rust Belt Republicans, the congressional Republican agenda faced fewer internal constraints. When the GOP lost both chambers of Congress in 1954, a mere 5 percent of surviving House Republicans came from southern states; when they lost both chambers in 2006, fully 42 percent of surviving House Republicans were southern. As fellow political scientist Phil Klinkner and I forecast the month after the 2006 elections, this regional shift posed obvious risks for the GOP: "The Republicans face the challenge of overcoming the perils of regional over-representation. Parties too narrowly based in one region, especially a region that is ideologically out of step with the rest of the country, confront the political equivalent of Gresham's law as ideologically extreme views tend to become increasingly predominant within the party. That growing ideological purity threatens to further narrow the Republican appeal to other regions, which could, in turn, make the GOP an even more regionally concentrated party."[63]

By almost any measure, the congressionalization of the national Republican Party since Reagan left office has shifted the party's agenda and brand rightward—and has done so at undeniable political-electoral cost to the party. George W. Bush's presidency only magnified the congressional wing's radicalism in assent, rather than dissent. In retrospect, it is perhaps unsurprising that some of the worst abuses of congressional power occurred during this period, including Tom DeLay's attempt to re-redistrict Texas's congressional maps and the Abramoff lobbying scandal. Such is the partisan-institutional death spiral in which the national Republican Party presently finds itself: it is moving rightward and becoming more of a rump, House-based party, a process that in turn pushes the party even further toward the ideological margins.

The final problem for any party associated with running Congress is, well, the risk of being associated with Congress, an institution Americans hate. Regardless of which party controls it, Congress consistently is held in lower regard than the presidency or the Supreme Court. Although Congress's approval ratings have never been high, during the 1970s and 1980s they generally hovered in the low-to-mid-thirties. But since the early 1990s, following the House banking scandals that tarnished the Democrats' brand and the government shutdown that tainted the Republicans', public approval of Congress has plummeted. The last decade has been brutal: between 2002 and 2011, a period that includes unified Republican, unified Democratic, and split control, the share of citizens who said the current Congress had "accomplished less" than "recent Congresses" steadily climbed from 20 percent to 50 percent.[64] By June 2013, Gallup recorded its lowest approval rating ever—just 11 percent—and other polls have registered approval figures in the single digits.[65] Amid the October 2013 government shutdown and debt ceiling crisis, a remarkable 78 percent of Americans said they would like the *entire* Congress to be thrown out and replaced.[66]

The scarlet letter of American national politics is "C," for Congress. If voters come to associate Congress with the Republicans—or, more accurately, if they come to associate Republicans solely with Congress—it may cause the party long-term branding problems. In fact, it already has: while the public blames the current Washington gridlock on both congressional Republicans and President Obama, a much higher percentage fault the Republicans.[67] If Congress really is the "broken branch" of government, to borrow language from Thomas Mann and Norm Ornstein, being closely associated with it could prove ruinous.

7

RECOVER OR RETRENCH?

Diagnoses of what ails a political party at a given point in its history tend to take three forms. The most common—the ideological critique—defines failure as the consequence of a party moving too far to an ideological extreme, becoming too beholden to its base, and losing its purchase on the vital center. This critique of the Democrats gained prominence in the mid-1980s, around the time the centrist Democratic Leadership Council emerged, and is a popular account of what ails the current Republican Party.

A second critique centers on party strategies and tactics: the ability to master essential functions like candidate recruitment, message development, maintaining and building a coalition, fund-raising, and the identification and targeting of voters. In 2005 and 2006, following Al Gore's and John Kerry's losses in potentially winnable presidential campaigns, Democrats were lambasted for inadequately performing many of these vital functions. Since 2008, this charge has shifted to the Republicans, who were out-strategized and bested tactically by Team Obama's better field operations, more sophisticated social media outreach, and superior small-donor fund-raising efforts.

The third critique involves party leadership and is dependent on the policy performance and ethical-legal problems of party elites, especially presidents and key members of Congress. Prosecuting the Iraq War or passing the Affordable Care Act had major consequences not just for Presidents Bush and Obama, respectively, but also for their respective parties' standing. Parties also suffer brand damage or electoral rebuke when their leaders are implicated in scandals stemming from shady but technically legal activities or outright corruption, from check kiting to Iran-Contra to renting out the Lincoln Bedroom.

In this book I have focused on something else: the mutually reinforcing interplay between institutional power and national party competitiveness. It is no coincidence that as the Republican Party has become Congress-bound and House-heavy, it has also become more conservative. The two trends reinforce each other, at times to the GOP's benefit. The steady transformation of national Republicans since the end of Ronald Reagan's presidency from a strong presidential party into a party that dominates Congress and is dominated by its congressional wing may make intuitive sense. It may even please conservatives who venerate the Constitution as drafted by the founders. But the rise of the congressional Republicans has not been cost- or consequence-free.

Beginning in the mid-1980s, the GOP became path-dependent on a legislative-first strategy and a Congress-centered agenda. Strategic choices by Republican congressional leaders like Newt Gingrich and Trent Lott reinforced the party's standing in Congress, but in ways that limited the ability of the party's presidential nominees to create a salable national brand. Congressional Republicans staked out positions that isolated party officials from major elements of the electorate: unmarried Americans, pro-choice women, nonwhite voters, and people living in urban and inner suburban areas— but these positions were perfectly rational given that rural, white, mostly male, religious, or otherwise conservative primary voters control their electoral fates in highly gerrymandered districts. Once in power, congressional Republicans repeated and in some cases magnified the same Democratic legislative excesses—including sharp increases in earmarks, reelection-minded targeted subsidies, and major entitlements—that the GOP once derided. Party leaders on Capitol Hill and the national campaign committees established cozy relationships with the Washington lobbying community and catered to the demands of the party's wealthier donors.

More specifically, the congressionalization of the Republican Party has become more and more tilted toward the House side of Capitol Hill. In both representational strength and influence, the Republican House Conference has eclipsed its Senate counterpart. The most obvious manifestation of this pattern is that the divided Congress during the first six years of Ronald Reagan's presidency featured a Republican majority in the Senate but not the House, whereas the Congress during most of George W. Bush's first two years in office and all but the first two years of Obama's presidency featured a Republican House but a Democratic Senate. This last arrangement may be the "new normal" for national politics. For

Republicans, this new normal has both good and bad implications. Among the negative consequences is the public's association of Republicans with Congress at a moment when Americans' approval of that body is at near-record lows.[1] Republicans are increasingly associated with congressional dysfunction.

The parties' reversal of fortunes occurred by fits and starts, but the three national elections between 1992 and 1996 proved to be the tipping point after which Republicans emerged as a strong congressional party and Democrats began to dominate presidential politics. Although a party's success in congressional and presidential elections need not be mutually exclusive, the polling data suggest that voters—independent voters especially—may simply prefer divided government. This preference is confirmed by the partisan history of the postwar era: in the sixty years since Dwight Eisenhower's Republicans lost both chambers of Congress back to the Democrats in 1954, the national government has been unified only a third of the time, a total of just twenty years. If the postwar era norm and the public's preference are for divided government, strong congressional parties therefore tend to correspond with weaker presidential parties, and vice versa. If so, Republicans may continue to be more competitive in congressional elections than presidential contests.

There are six possible permutations of divided national government in the United States, and the forty years of divided government during the past sixty years have seen five of them. The most common variant, accounting for twenty-two of the forty years, featured a Republican president with a unified bicameral Democratic Congress (1955–1961, 1969–1977, 1987–1993, and 2007–2009). The inverse case, featuring a Democratic president (Clinton) and a unified Republican Congress, prevailed for six years (1995–2001). Ronald Reagan had a Republican Senate and a Democratic House for six years (1981–1987). And for what were effectively his first two years in the Oval Office, after the early 2001 party switch by Vermont's Jim Jeffords, George W. Bush had a Republican House but a Democratic Senate (2001–2003). There has yet to be, as I write this, a divided government featuring a Democratic president, a Republican Senate, and a Democratic House.

The sixth and current permutation—Democratic president, Democratic Senate, Republican House—is not only new to this era but unprecedented in post–Civil War American history. Republican Speaker John Boehner is treading new ground. Before proceeding to an examination of his political troubles leading the most House-heavy Republican Party in American history, we should consider the conditions that brought him to power.

Fighting the Minority Fight Once More

Unlike the 2012 elections, which bitterly disappointed conservatives and Republican partisans because they rightly believed Barack Obama was beatable, the 2008 election brought a different type of Republican disorientation. Given President Bush's abysmal approval ratings and the GOP's weak field of presidential contenders, Republicans in 2008 expected to have a bad cycle. Republicans were despondent, to be sure. But there was a sense that the party was due for an electoral drubbing.

After Obama's historic victory, which gave Democrats unified control of the government for the first time since 1994, the question for Republicans was how to proceed. National Republicans had to decide if they were going to cooperate with the new president and the Democratic Congress or double down and resist. As told by Robert Draper in *Do Not Ask What Good We Do*, his fascinating account of House Republicans during the Obama era, on the night of

Obama's inauguration top congressional Republicans met for dinner at the swanky Caucus Room in Georgetown to begin strategizing the Republican comeback. The event, organized by consultant Frank Luntz, included some of the party's most powerful Washington figures: House members Eric Cantor, Jeb Hensarling, Pete Hoekstra, Dan Lungren, Kevin McCarthy, Paul Ryan, and Pete Sessions; and Senators Tom Coburn, Bob Corker, Jim DeMint, John Ensign, and Jon Kyl. The only ex-member of Congress to join them was former Speaker Newt Gingrich.

Hoekstra mentioned Gingrich's historic role. In 1993, he pointed out, congressional Republicans had been in the wilderness for almost forty years and Bill Clinton had just been elected president. Just two short years later "it was a whole new world."

What began as a dour wound-licking session turned into a private pep rally. Before the new Democratic president had even spent a night in the White House, these fourteen Republicans settled on a strategy: oppose anything significant the new administration wanted to do, and remain united in opposition no matter what. "If you act like the minority," McCarthy declared, "you're going to stay in the minority. We've got to challenge them on every single bill and challenge them on every single campaign."[2] In Obama's first month, unanimous or nearly unanimous Republicans in the House and overwhelming majorities of Senate Republicans voted against the Lilly Ledbetter Fair Pay Act, the Children's Health Insurance Program Reauthorization Act, and the American Recovery and Reinvestment Act (the "stimulus").

The party's new strategy was immediately evident during negotiations over the Obama stimulus plan. In his book *The New New Deal*, journalist Michael Grunwald chronicles passage of the American Recovery and Reinvestment Act.[3] In opposing the legislation, notes Grunwald, House Republicans voted against tax cuts for 95 percent of Americans, Head Start for kids, Meals on Wheels for senior citizens, and state aid to keep teachers, firefighters, cops, and nurses employed. House Democrats believed the Republicans were committing political suicide. Speaker Nancy Pelosi's office issued a memo the day after the House vote on the stimulus entitled "The Republican Problem"; Pelosi deputy Chris Van Hollen of Maryland predicted that Republicans would suffer the electoral consequences in November 2010. Pelosi compared the GOP's unified opposition to the 1993 vote on Bill Clinton's first budget—a signature moment in Republican politics that came just over a year before the landmark 1994 midterms.

Perhaps Pelosi's and Van Hollen's remarks were political spin. But they sounded a lot like David Broder's prediction in the early 1990s that the electorate would not entrust majority power to House Republicans if they failed to act responsibly while in the minority. A year later, in the 2010 midterms, the GOP recaptured the House, proving Pelosi and Van Hollen wrong.

The irony of this episode, notes Grunwald, is that congressional Republicans had fashioned their own $715 billion alternative stimulus package, which actually included "more traditional infrastructure than the supposedly lavish Democratic bill" initially proposed at around $815 billion. Yet when it came time to vote, every House Republican and all but three Republican senators—Maine's Susan Collins and Olympia Snowe, and eventual party-switcher Arlen Specter of Pennsylvania—voted against the slightly larger Democratic version and denounced it as a socialist giveaway. "Republicans never bothered to explain how $715 billion could be good policy while $815 billion was freedom-crushing socialism," writes Grunwald. "In the minority, they didn't have to."[4]

Therein lies the key point: the politics of "no" may not win every time, but there is an asymmetrical bias that favors the opposition—especially a unified opposition. It made sense for minority Republicans to vote against legislation that might be good for the country as a whole, not to mention GOP states and districts, because there was almost no political upside to giving President Obama and the Democrats a victory when almost all the credit would go to them. Anyone doubting the logic of obstructionism would learn a powerful lesson from the Republican response to Obama's next major initiative: health care reform.

During Obama's first two years, the House was largely ineffective as an instrument of obstruction so long as Speaker Nancy Pelosi kept her majority united. It is easier to obstruct from the Senate when a party is in the minority but easier from the House when it is in the majority. With control of neither chamber of Congress, the task of Republican obstruction during the 111th Congress fell mostly to Senate minority leader Mitch McConnell of Kentucky. With the support of most of his conference, McConnell knew how to slow the legislative process to a halt: use the upper chamber's large toolbox of procedural tricks, most notably the filibuster. The number of filibusters during the 111th Congress reached 137, a new record; more than 400 bills passed by the House died in the Senate, often without even a debate.[5] "Before the health care fight, before the economic stimulus package, before President Obama even took office, Senator Mitch McConnell, the Republican minority leader, had a strategy for his party: use his extensive knowledge of Senate procedure to slow things down, take advantage of the difficulties Democrats would have in governing and deny Democrats any Republican support on big legislation," *New York Times* national political reporters Carl Hulse and Adam Nagourney explained in 2010. McConnell said matter-of-factly that it was important to maintain total unity so that Democrats couldn't point to the support of a few Republicans as evidence of bipartisanship.[6]

Meanwhile, Republican strategists initiated an audacious plan to recapture the House for the near and longer term. In the near term, that meant capitalizing on anti-Obama sentiment and a slow economic recovery in the 2010 cycle. For the longer term, it meant winning as many state legislative and gubernatorial races as they could to maximize influence in the coming round of redistricting. Led by top operatives Ed Gillespie and Karl Rove, the Republican State Leadership Committee launched a well-funded program called the Redistricting Majority Project, or REDMAP, designed to win state legislative seats. "The logic was simple," writes *Rolling Stone* political analyst Tim Dickinson. "If Republicans could seize control of statehouses—and, where necessary, have GOP governors in place to rubber-stamp their redistricting maps—the party could lock in new districts that would favor Republican candidates for a decade." The Republican State Leadership Committee raised three times the amount its counterpart Democratic state legislative committee did, and Republicans captured nine net new state legislatures, empowering them to draw maps for 173 House seats. "Democrats will not soon recover from what happened to them on a state level last night," REDMAP executive director Chris Jankowski told Dickinson the day after the 2010 election.[7]

Republican resistance in the 111th Congress, especially in the House, was often limited to voicing opposition and casting symbolic votes. The GOP controlled few levers of power, and much of the energy generated during Obama's first two years was provided by the nascent tea party movement. But after 2010, the new Republican House majority gave the party the power it needed to leverage the obstructionist agenda devised two years earlier at that fateful inauguration night dinner.

Obstructing Obamanomics

Economic policy battles during the Obama era derive from the fundamentally different views of Democrats and Republicans on issues of taxes and spending, deficits and debts. Although many Republicans claim they doubt the utility of Keynesian economics, most economists don't. Whether a government runs deficits and borrows money to finance them because it spends too much or because it raises too little—often, it does both—the Keynesian principle obtains: fiscal deficits tend to stimulate the economy by increasing aggregate demand. As Michael Grunwald noted, the GOP's 2009 stimulus plan was slightly more tilted toward tax cuts than spending, but Republicans still pushed for a package seven-eighths as big as President Obama's. The Republican plan would have increased the deficit and debt in the interest of spurring the economy—in other words, it was philosophically Keynesian.

Although the national debt increased from $4 trillion to $10 trillion during George W. Bush's two terms, Republican priorities shifted toward fiscal austerity only after Obama took office and their electoral incentives changed. Party leaders advocated austerity as the key to recovery at the very moment most economists believed the government needed to run deficits and loosen credit to jumpstart growth. Debates about how governments can foster economic growth aside, the political question for congressional Republicans was whether they could reframe the national conversation and prosecute an austerity-based agenda from Capitol Hill.

Republicans in the 111th Congress were largely relegated to protesting major Democratic initiatives, but their situation changed in the 112th. Riding the tea party wave, the 2010 midterms put the gavel in Speaker John Boehner's hands and brought Republican freshmen such as Rand Paul and Marco Rubio into the Senate. This changed the calculus of opposition politics. Over the next three years, Americans' fiscal vocabulary would acquire terms like *debt ceiling, sequester,* and *fiscal cliff*—and revive one term familiar to those who followed the partisan fights two decades earlier: *government shutdown.* But the full story of Washington's fiscal fights during the Obama era starts—yet again—with Newt Gingrich.

As we saw in Chapter 2, in the late 1980s and early 1990s the Republican minority's political brief against congressional Democrats consisted largely of procedural complaints rather than policy critiques. When Gingrich took control of the House in 1995, he promptly reversed the so-called Gephardt Rule. Established in 1979 by then–Democratic minority leader Dick Gephardt, the rule automatically raised the debt ceiling whenever the House passed a budget resolution that increased the government's total debt obligation. By reversing it, Gingrich returned the House to the pre-1979 norm of holding a separate vote to raise the debt ceiling. "Gingrich thought the second vote was a good pressure tactic to limit spending," *Bloomberg Businessweek*'s Joshua Green wrote in 2013. "Yet the threat of debt default didn't work because nobody took it seriously. What's different now is that many Republicans seem willing to follow through."[8]

House Republicans indeed followed through—or almost did—in the summer of 2011. Knowing that the previous debt ceiling increase from 2010 would expire that August—that the Congress would need to authorize more borrowing or else the government would default—Republicans demanded significant spending cuts in exchange for a debt ceiling increase. Although revenues as a share of gross domestic product were at sixty-year lows and the Obama White House was willing to pair spending reductions with new taxes, Republicans refused to raise taxes. Many of the new, more aggressive members wanted a balanced-budget guarantee. Meanwhile, Democrats hoped to shield entitlement programs, including Medicare and Social Security, from cuts.

The game of political chicken between Congress and the White House continued until four days before the United States would default—with consequences nobody could predict for certain. A bipartisan deal brokered between Vice President Joe Biden and Mitch McConnell broke the impasse. Both sides accepted a painful automatic and across-the-board sequestration of federal spending that would take effect on January 1, 2013, unless they reached agreement on an alternative package of tax increases and spending cuts. A bipartisan "supercommittee" was authorized to examine various alternatives and propose a budget compromise within three months. Biden and McConnell hoped this temporary solution would at least calm the markets.

The markets reacted anyway, and not well. By tinkering with the full faith and credit of the United States—which the Constitution states must be honored—Republicans had gone too far. "I think some of our members may have thought the default issue was a hostage you might take a chance at shooting," McConnell said. "Most of us didn't think that. What we did learn is this—it's a hostage that's worth ransoming."[9] Even the most devout tax opponent in the country, Grover Norquist—who held signed no-tax-increase pledges from all but 13 of the 288 congressional Republicans[10]—said that threatening default was a "tactical blunder" by Republican backbenchers who "were frustrated because they couldn't use what leverage they had to get more than they were going to get" out of negotiations with the White House.[11]

The consequences for congressional Republicans of holding the debt ceiling hostage became apparent as January 2013 approached and the country headed over a "fiscal cliff"—the simultaneous ending of Bush-era tax cuts, which had been extended through the end of 2012, and the onset of sequestration cuts set to trigger because, of course, the White House and congressional Republicans never made the grand budget agreement the threat of sequestration was supposed to force upon them. Federal Reserve chairman Ben Bernanke warned in summer 2012 that the onset of new taxes and drastic spending cuts all at once could paralyze the economy just as it was gaining momentum. Throughout the autumn, the White House and congressional Republicans negotiated back and forth, with Obama proposing that taxes be raised only on those in the top 2 percent of incomes, while Republicans insisted that the Bush tax cut plan be extended in its entirety. At the last minute—actually, a few hours past midnight on January 1—legislation passed both chambers and was signed the next day by President Obama to delay the sequestration cuts until March 1. Except for ending the temporary payroll tax cut, the tax portion of the cliff was solved with Democrats and the White House getting most of what they wanted—an increase in the top income rate to Clinton-era levels, an increase in the capital gains and estate tax rates, and an extension of unemployment benefits. Markets and American voters could exhale for a few more months.

On January 3, 2013, the day after President Obama signed the American Taxpayer Relief Act to delay the sequester, the new 113th Congress convened. At least one Senate Republican had no plans to trim his political sails: Texas's Ted Cruz, a Cuban American who graduated from Princeton University cum laude and from Harvard Law School and went on to become the nation's youngest solicitor general. Cruz arrived in Washington ready to shake things up, even if that meant shutting things down. He didn't seem to care that early 2013 polls showed that while the public trusted the Republican Party slightly more than Democrats on economic issues, their approval of Republican leaders in Congress lagged significantly behind that of Democratic leaders and President Obama.[12]

Whatever criticisms might be leveled against tea party Republicans, say this much for them: when a massive farm bill was under consideration by Congress in June 2013, sixty-four House Republicans—including tea party–affiliated members Michele Bachmann, Justin Amash, and Steve Stockman—embarrassed Speaker Boehner by voting the bill down because they viewed it as too costly. Failed floor votes are exceedingly rare because House leaders generally never allow legislation to reach the floor unless they have the votes to pass it. Reporters eagerly quoted former Speaker Nancy Pelosi's comment that it was "amateur hour" in the House. "Republicans continue to act as an opposition party and not as a governing party, which is congruent with increasing parliamentary behavior among the electorate and their elected officials," a former Republican lawmaker told the *Washington Post*'s Chris Cillizza. "This is not a path to a majority. House Republicans need to recognize their destinies are intertwined."[13] Tea party Republicans came away looking principled, while Boehner emerged red-faced. Then, proving they were not much better than the members of Congress they had criticized as fiscal sellouts, a month later most of those tea partiers approved an amended farm bill that, while removing the food stamp provisions supported by Democrats, was still larded with corporate subsidies.

Earmarks and farm subsidies were minor undercard fights to the major brawl looming that autumn. By late summer 2013, Cruz and other tea party conservatives were agitating to either deny the next debt ceiling increase or shut down the government entirely on October 1, the first day of the new fiscal year. This time, in exchange for keeping the government open, Republicans demanded that the Affordable Care Act be defunded or delayed. The House passed an appropriations bill for fiscal 2014 that included the Obamacare delays, but Senate majority leader Harry Reid held his caucus together behind a "clean" appropriations bill. Had they known how politically damaging the rollout of Obamacare would be—the state health insurance exchanges were scheduled to open on October 1, when the healthcare.gov website was launched—Republicans might not have shut the government down. But they did, for sixteen days.

Suddenly, Newt Gingrich's name was in the air again, eighteen years after he and his fellow Republicans last led a government shutdown. "[Tea partiers] use the disruption and paralysis they've sown in Washington to persuade Americans government is necessarily dysfunctional, and politics inherently bad," said Clinton-era labor secretary Robert Reich. "Their continuing showdowns and standoffs are, in this sense, part of the plot."[14] In the end, however, Republicans caved in the face of souring public opinion and the clear refusal by either President Obama or Senator Reid to relent. When it was over, an exasperated Boehner allowed that "we went through a very tough period. We fought the fight. We didn't win. We live to fight another day."[15] Soon, the manifold problems with Obamacare's rollout gave the Republicans a more attractive target.

Tea party efforts to shut down or discredit government do not always pan out, and often backfire. At some point, voters reject obstruction for obstruction's sake. Even conservative columnist Charles Krauthammer—no ally of the Obama White House—admits the limitations of the GOP's politics of obstruction, especially when the party's only leverage is the House of Representatives:

The party establishment is coming around to the view that if you try to govern from one house—e.g., force spending cuts with brinksmanship—you lose. You not only don't get the cuts. You get the blame for the rattled markets and economic uncertainty. . . .

The Gingrich Revolution ran aground when it tried to govern from the Congress, losing badly to President Clinton over government shutdowns. Nor did the modern insurgents do any better in the 2011 debt-ceiling and 2012 fiscal-cliff showdowns with Obama. . . . The general rule is: From a single house of Congress you can resist but you cannot impose.[16]

It is a lesson that House Republicans, especially those first elected to Congress in 2010 and 2012, took time to learn. By winter 2014, when House budget guru Paul Ryan had come around to the view that Republicans needed to work across the aisle and with the Senate to craft reasonable bipartisan fiscal agreements, obstructionists had lost some steam. Enough top House Republicans realized that the Democrats' repeated efforts to label them the "Party of No" were working. But "enough" is not the same as "all."

Poor John Boehner

Any House Speaker trying to defend his or her party's national agenda against a White House and Senate controlled by the opposition faces a daunting task. But the ideological orientations of the modern Republican Party mean that Speaker John Boehner faces the additional burden of trying to keep the competing factions within his own caucus from self-destructive infighting.

Those who find it hard to empathize with Boehner should consider the perils of his job. He is the highest-ranking Republican elected official in the United States, but he is hardly the party's most feared or revered politician. The House Republican Conference holds its majority despite a very tenuous electoral mandate—the party actually received less of the national popular vote than the Democrats in 2012—and is often divided against itself. Although the Speaker's Republican allies in the Senate can be used to backchannel into legislation provisions that House Republicans might prefer not to propose directly, Boehner ultimately has to answer to his caucus first.

Media stories describing Boehner's political situation often include words like "beleaguered," "embattled," "hostage," "tight spot," and "in a pickle."[17] (And those are just the terms used to describe Boehner during the 2013 fight over immigration.) Boehner must be having a rough time if even Newt Gingrich openly admits that the Speaker's job is "vastly harder . . . 10 times harder" than it was two decades ago, when Gingrich became the first Republican to lead the House in forty years.[18] During his first two terms, Speaker Boehner has fought some extraordinary political battles, both against Democrats and within his own party: over the Obama stimulus, the so-called sequester, a government shutdown, and two debt ceiling episodes. His experience speaks to the realities of a House-bound party. By early 2014 whispers about secret plans within his own caucus to oust him made national news.

In a piece profiling then-House majority leader Eric Cantor and the battles he, Boehner, and other Republican House leaders are fighting within their caucus, the *New Yorker's* Ryan Lizza explained how politically green the increasingly red Republican House caucus is. Two-thirds of Boehner's 232-member House Republican Conference was elected in 2006 or later, and half were first elected in either 2010 or 2012. To this post–September 11 cohort of freshman and sophomore members, Cantor, first elected in 2000, is a political veteran, and Boehner, first elected in 1990, is a fossil.

Lizza cites the case of Oklahoma's Tom Cole, who served as the executive director of the National Republican Congressional Committee before winning election to the House in 2002. Despite a 92 percent rating from the American Conservative Union, Cole has begun to feel out of place within the House Republican Conference. "This is a very different party than the one I got elected into," Cole told Lizza. "It's much more domestically focused, much more fiscally responsible, much less concerned about America's position in the world or about defending the country. It almost takes for granted the security that we have now. It's not a group shaped by 9/11. Their 9/11 is the fiscal crisis, the long-term deficit."[19] And then in June 2014 came electoral news that shocked Washington: Cantor lost his Republican primary renomination to an underfunded and relatively unknown college professor, and a month later resigned from the House leadership.

Consider the demographics of these new members' districts. When Republicans recaptured the House in 2010, thirty-nine of the sixty-three districts they flipped were older than the country as a whole, forty had more non–college graduates than the national average, and forty-seven—almost three in four—were whiter than the American population nationally. This recurring profile of the Republican electorate—older, whiter, from more rural districts and states, less college-educated—contrasts sharply with the younger, mixed-race urban and inner suburban "ideopolises" that political analysts John Judis and Ruy Teixeira have identified as America's key centers of growth. "Republicans do the best in areas that are typically not growing very fast and don't look like the present, or certainly the future, of the country," said Teixeira in 2010.[20] The Republican House delegation itself remains overwhelmingly white and male despite record numbers of female and nonwhite House members, the vast majority of whom are Democrats. (Thanks to

first-term senators Kelly Ayotte of New Hampshire and Deb
Fischer of Nebraska, plus Florida's Marco Rubio, South Carolina's
Tim Scott, and the newest tea party darling, Ted Cruz of Texas, the
Republicans' Senate delegation is more diverse.)

Boehner's House caucus also includes a handful of members
who practice a roughhouse style of investigatory politics that often
shades into the kind of venomously partisan behavior that independent voters sometimes find off-putting. The new House investigator-
in-chief—a politician who proudly considers himself heir to a
tradition that includes not only his Republican predecessors Tom
Davis and Dan Burton but legendary Democratic watchdog Henry
Waxman too—is Darrell Issa. As chair of the House Oversight and
Government Reform Committee since 2011, Issa takes a political
approach that eerily resembles the Gingrich-era politics of search,
investigate, indict, and destroy. "I'm a salesman," Issa admitted to
National Journal's Susan Davis. And what he sells "is the awareness
of a product" he calls government oversight.[21]

At first, Issa found little success looking into government mal-
feasance in the Obama administration. With an assist from political
stumbles by the Obama White House on controversies surrounding
the September 2012 Benghazi attack and the targeting by the Internal Revenue Service of political groups, Issa regained his footing
and has emerged as the kind of firebrand who excites House Republicans with a taste for tactically aggressive politics. "My team is
more mature this year than last Congress," Issa told reporters early
in his second term as House Oversight Committee chair. "Many of
my members last Congress were freshmen. I was in my first term as
chairman."[22]

There's also the more virulent strain of House Republicans who
have proposed initiating impeachment proceedings against President Obama. On issues including Benghazi and gun policy, of course,

but also the debt ceiling, drone missile use, presidential patronage, and the Defense of Marriage Act, at least thirteen of the twenty-two members of the House Judiciary Committee have implied that Obama's actions may warrant impeachment.[23] Boehner must find ways to appease those who care at least as much about attacking the Obama agenda as about developing the Republicans' own policy priorities. Finally, there are those who have eyes on Boehner's gavel. Catholic University's Matthew Green, an expert on House Speakers, notes that the younger cohort of new, impatient members do not necessarily feel indebted to Boehner. "It is a restless party. It has strong-willed freshmen and strong-willed conservatives," Green said in 2012. "And that leads to . . . rivals for the throne."[24]

Boehner's situation improved by late 2013. After the tea party–led government shutdown ruined Republicans' approval ratings, several outspoken members of his House Republican Conference admitted that the shutdown had backfired and that they no longer wanted to be obstructionists. The Speaker began to push back, gently and at times forcefully, against agitators within the caucus. Without mentioning anyone by name—though he likely had in mind offensive comments made about Latinos that year by Alaska's Don Young and Iowa's Steve King—Boehner told the media that "some of our members just aren't as sensitive as they ought to be."[25] After Virginia's Randy Forbes said the party shouldn't fund gay Republican candidates running for House seats in Massachusetts and California, Boehner immediately rebuked him. The Speaker also lashed out at major conservative advocacy groups for complicating the budget negotiations.[26]

The problem, for Boehner and the Republican establishment, is that these are the kinds of actions that get many members of their caucus elected to Congress. Although some within the party are trying to forge new paths that will avoid the congressional Republicans' self-destructive behavior, the tricky task for Boehner and others is repairing the party's brand.

The (Missing) DLC Analogue

While there is no precedent for the Republicans' current control of the House but neither the Senate nor the presidency, it may be worthwhile to consider the most obvious recent analogue. During the first six years of the Reagan presidency, Democrats, like Republicans today, also controlled only the House. The consensus account of the period, as ably reported in books like Kenneth Baer's *Reinventing Democrats*, is that the Democratic Party, like Republicans today, suffered from a national branding and presidential competitiveness problem.[27] Among the Democrats' problems were the party's capture by high-demand identity groups and its identification with an entrenched, often corrupt congressional wing. These problems are eerily similar to those confronting the national Republican Party today; the party's official diagnostic report, *Growth and Opportunity Project*, admits as much.

What happened next for the Democratic Party was that a new generation of centrist politicians, led by Bill Clinton, Al Gore, and the Democratic Leadership Council, gradually seized control of the party from the failed McGovern-Dukakis liberal wing. Until Clinton's party-rattling speech at the DLC's 1991 Cleveland convention, centrist politicians and DLC financiers expected Gore to lead the party out of the electoral wilderness. But whether the 1992 presidential ticket could have been Gore-Clinton rather than Clinton-Gore is less important than the restoration, led by state governors, of the party's presidential competitiveness.

But the parallels between Democrats then and Republicans today largely end there, and it will be far more difficult for the Republicans to slow their shift to the extreme right. There is little centrist Republican apparatus to counterbalance the party's powerful conservative infrastructure. As I wrote in the *American Prospect* in 2007, the two institutions formed to articulate a moderate Republican agenda—the Republican Main Street Partnership and the Republican Leadership Council—were so debilitated by George W. Bush's second term that conservatives could basically ignore them.[28] The "Gingrich senators" rule the party's caucus in the upper chamber, and the Republican Study Committee dominates the House. As each passing election cycle proves, congressional conservatives' positions on everything from forcible rape to gay marriage, from debt ceiling hostage-holding to cutting unemployment insurance, are more often rewarded rather than repudiated at the polls. Meanwhile, those who have dared to object to the party's marginalization of its shrinking cadre of centrists—Senator Jim Jeffords and Representative Charlie Bass, former governors like Christine Todd Whitman and Charlie Crist—have either left the party, been marginalized and ostracized within it, or been banished from the party altogether. There is simply no serious or significant centrist movement within the Republican Party, and certainly no center-right analogue to the DLC.

Another, more punitive difference for Republicans today compared to the Democrats in the mid-1980s is rooted in an inherent asymmetry between the parties. When Democrats move to the center on nonsocial issues, their moderation generally implies support for lower taxes, business deregulation, expansion of free trade, and other reforms supported by corporate America. The resulting cozier relationship with business interests comes with a price: labor unions and economic liberals concerned about corporate welfare or rising inequality may threaten to defect. But these intraparty consequences are offset by greater corporate money and support. Moving right to reach the center yields a payoff.

For Republicans, moving left to reach the center delivers no such offsetting benefit. Moves by Republicans to the center on issues related to taxes and regulation create serious campaign finance risks—especially in today's climate, in which Republicans once considered reliably conservative find themselves under threat from intraparty challenges and outside-the-party electoral attacks. Republican moderates are outspent by the Koch brothers, Sheldon Adelson, Foster Friess, and an earlier generation of donors going back to Joseph Coors, Richard Mellon Scaife, and the Smith Richardson family. America is in the middle of a heated national argument about the rising influence of corporate money and wealthy interests in politics. But there is no disputing that when corporate money and influence pull both parties rightward, they drag the more liberal party toward the center and the more conservative one toward the extremes.

Meanwhile, what few moderate Republicans are left must bear their own responsibility for the party's failures. "Part of the problem is that moderates are behaving a bit too moderately," wrote Ashley Parker of the *New York Times* during the October 2013 government shutdown. "They have yet to vote with Democrats on procedural maneuvers that could force the hand of the Republican leadership. . . . They are unwilling to defy their leaders to that extent."[29] Following the shutdown, Geoffrey Kabaservice, whose book *Rule and Ruin* chronicles the decline of moderate Republicans, concurs that moderates are partially responsible for the party's rightward shift. Kabaservice explains how conservatives decades ago began their rise as much in reaction to Eisenhower-era Republican centrism as from perceived threats from the left. At many turns, he writes, moderate Republicans surrendered power or failed to push back sufficiently against their conservative colleagues—and they continue to do so in the Obama era. "Why is the body of the Republican Party in thrall to its erratic right foot?" Kabaservice asked in a *New York Times* op-ed. "Maybe the real blame should go to the far more numerous non-Tea Party Republicans, from Speaker John A. Boehner down, who have been unable or unwilling to restrain the radicals." He specifically cited the capitulation of House Republican moderates Peter King of New York and Devin Nunes of California, who in October 2013 voted against a stopgap spending bill that would have ended the government shutdown, as part of the long-term pattern that led to the rise of Newt Gingrich a quarter century ago: "It was Mr. Gingrich who pioneered the political dysfunction we still live with. . . . But here's the catch: Mr. Gingrich, of Georgia, rose to party leadership because he was the preferred candidate of the moderates themselves."[30]

Of course, the definition of a "real" conservative has moved so far to the right in the past decade that politicians once considered rock-ribbed, even in the vanguard, now come under suspicion. Former Reaganites Craig Shirley and Doug Devine publicly mocked Karl Rove as a "big-government conservative," maybe a "compassionate conservative"—but not a true conservative. Former South Carolina senator Jim DeMint may have backed primary opponents of moderate Republicans Arlen Specter and Charlie Crist—but DeMint, now president of the Heritage Foundation, also sided with Rand Paul over chamber leader and archconservative Mitch McConnell's hand-picked successor to fill Kentucky's open seat.[31] It's one thing for Arizona senator and 2008 presidential nominee John McCain to be challenged by conservatives during his path to eventual 2010 renomination: McCain had cosponsored major immigration and campaign finance legislation with über-liberals Ted Kennedy and Russ Feingold, respectively. But Mitch McConnell? And after Utah's three-term Republican incumbent Bob Bennett was ousted by the state party nominating convention for being insufficiently conservative, in 2012 the state's other Republican senator, veteran Orrin Hatch—a fervent and even slightly scary young Reaganite insurgent when he upset an incumbent Democrat to win the seat in 1976—had to fend off the first primary challenge of his career. The list of once certifiably conservative Republicans who have come under attack is growing too long to recount.

Adding to the plight of the party's disappearing moderates are the frustrations of moderate Republican voters. According to a focus group study conducted by Democracy Corps in late 2013, Republican moderates feel caught between the party's two dominant factions: evangelicals and nonevangelical tea partiers. Despite the significant tensions between these two factions, the report's coauthors concluded that moderates feel isolated from both. They are alienated by the social issue stances of the evangelicals as much as by the radicalism of the tea party. On issues like gay marriage, immigration, or climate change, moderates are "very conscious of their discomfort with the other parts of the party base . . . [and] feel isolated within the party."[32] A bottom-up centrist revival led by moderate Republican voters is highly unlikely.

Locked In

Over the past three decades, congressional Republicans evolved in three stages from a noncompetitive party, to a party that boasted solid majorities for a dozen years, to its present incarnation as party anchored to and defined by its congressional wing and its House caucus in particular. In the first stage, described in Chapters 2 and 3, Republicans fought their way out of what looked like permanent minority status through coordinated attacks on congressional procedure and performance; the promotion of new ideas about taxation, the welfare state, and social issues; and the emergence of a new generation of leaders like Dick Armey, Jack Kemp, Trent Lott, and Newt Gingrich. In the second stage—some features of which, such as the 1990 round of redistricting, began simultaneous with the first—Republicans protected and solidified their new congressional majorities, as described in Chapters 4 and 5. Despite railing against fiscal excesses and the growing power of special interests, Republicans helped expand the size of government and built a direct pipeline from Capitol Hill to K Street's lobby networks.

The third and current stage cemented the party's status as a stronger congressional party than presidential party. Partly this happened through conscious choices the Republicans made, but in other respects it happened unwittingly. The result is a lock-in effect from which the party will have difficulty escaping.

For starters, when the Supreme Court's 2010 *Citizens United* campaign finance ruling legalized so-called super PACs, it shifted significant campaign finance power to outside groups. The ruling came less than a decade after passage of the Bipartisan Campaign Reform Act (McCain-Feingold), which limited the parties' ability to raise soft money that they could spend directly or funnel through state parties. Changes in campaign finance law apply to both parties, of course, but the new campaign finance environment presents a much bigger problem for Republicans, and for two reasons.

First, given their stronger connections to corporate interests, politically active millionaires, and a highly motivated conservative organizational universe that includes but is hardly limited to the tea party, any ruling that tips the balance of political power in favor of outside monied interests will disproportionately limit the GOP's ability to centralize control over its political, electoral, ideological, and policy agenda. "When parties are limited and groups are limited, groups *aren't* limited," asserts campaign finance scholar Ray La Raja. "Parties play with one hand tied behind their back compared to outside groups. *Citizens United* will cement this dynamic unless parties get more leeway, and soon."[33] This dynamic also affects the Democrats, but less so, because they have become significantly more reliant on small individual contributions since BRCA was enacted.

The second problem is the timing of these changes. They have come at the very moment the so-called Republican establishment is searching for ways to reassert control over the party. Speaking to conservative pundit Michael Gerson for a column about what he calls the "structural and technological" changes overtaking the Republican Party, Matt Kibbe of FreedomWorks explained the mind-set of outside groups, including his: "You're really seeing a disintermediation in politics. . . . Grass-roots activists have an ability to self-organize, to fund candidates they're more interested in, going right around the Republican National Committee and senatorial committee. That's the new reality. Everything's more democratized and Republicans should come to terms with that. They still want to control things from the top down, and if they do that there will absolutely be a split. But my prediction would be that we take over the Republican Party, and they go the way of the Whigs."[34]

In a story about the rising power of the antitax Club for Growth, *National Journal*'s Josh Kraushaar compared the group's effect on the party to that of the National Rifle Association in the 1990s, when it was "working to defeat its ideological enemies" even if they were within the GOP. "We don't ever look at the measurement of getting things done; it's about getting things right," Club for Growth president Chris Chocola told Kraushaar.[35] These stunning quotes reveal the declining regard with which powerful interest groups hold the Republican Party and its leadership.

The growth in the fund-raising and organizing power of these outside groups contributes significantly to the difficulties confronting Boehner, Senate minority leader Mitch McConnell, and the other congressional Republicans attempting to regain control of their party. As the *Washington Post*'s Dana Milbank observes, Republican-appointed Supreme Court majorities have complicated the Republicans' electoral situation in ways they perhaps did not anticipate. "The unchecked flood of cash goes to fiscal conservatives, social conservatives and even liberal groups, but the bulk goes toward electing candidates devoted to shrinking the federal government," writes Milbank on the effects of *Citizens United*. "Republican lawmakers in Congress know that they'll lose their jobs only if they get beaten in primaries for being insufficiently militant about shrinking government. Hence the fiscal cliff, sequestration, debt-limit showdowns, endless votes to repeal Obamacare and the government shutdown—so much so that business interests, which bankrolled the tea party, are beginning to have buyer's remorse."[36]

During the December 2013 budget negotiations, Speaker Boehner admonished conservative advocacy groups, complaining that "they're using our members and they're using the American people for their own goals. This is ridiculous." Remarking on Boehner's outburst, liberal pundit E. J. Dionne saw the Speaker's tussle with advocacy groups as something different from the fights between so-called establishment Republicans and the party's grassroots. "Boehner denounced [these] conservative fundraising behemoths," Dionne wrote, ". . . because he understands that they now constitute an alternative Republican establishment." This "new establishment is bolstered by conservative talk show hosts who communicate regularly with Republican loyalists and have challenged the party's elected leaders for control over its message."[37] Worse, the protection of the names of super PAC donors means that the identities of these nonparty ac-

tors managing these electoral resources are often unknown. The total amount spent in the 2012 cycle by groups that did not disclose
their donors was more than in the previous six cycles combined.[38]
The party will have a difficult time exorcising electoral ghosts it cannot see.

If the growing assertiveness of conservative outside groups and
their stealth backers is cementing the national political situation,
the systematic rigging of House districts by both parties is accelerating the speed with which the cement hardens. Electoral analyst
Charlie Cook biennially releases his Partisan Voting Index (PVI)
ratings, a measure of the partisan composition of the 435 House
districts based on how each district voted in presidential races. PVI
ratings provide a baseline measure of the partisanship of each House
district that is divorced from local House campaign and candidate
effects. Cook defines "swing" House districts as those with a PVI
ranging between +5 Republican and +5 Democratic—that is, districts where the results are within five points of the two-party voting share from the most recent presidential election.

In 1998, the first year he computed and published this statistics,
there were 164 swing districts. The number of swing districts quickly
dropped to 132 in 2000 and to 111 in 2002, the first cycle after
the 2000 round of redistricting; since then, the total has fallen a
few seats every two years. By 2014 it had declined to ninety seats.[39]
The result is that House election results are more locked in than
ever—good news for the Republicans, insofar as being the party
that controls the House (perhaps only the House) is good news.

Republican Federalism, Redux

Recover or retrench? That remains the Republican Party's fundamental choice. Retrenching has a certain allure: elements within

and outside the party continue to push for voter identification laws and other measures designed to alter the electorate, and gerrymandering will remain an effective way to maximize the number of seats won per votes received. But retrenchment is a political and electoral dead end, and the party's wisest minds and leaders know it.

Taking a page—the first page, as it happens—from the report *Growth and Opportunity Project*, there seems to be an emerging consensus that the party should revive its federalist traditions by drawing inspiration and guidance from the states. In a major *Washington Post* Outlook piece published the Sunday after the government shutdown, former RNC chair Ed Gillespie—who earned his political chops working for the House Republican minority—delivered a powerful message to his colleagues. To "repair the rift" between "establishment conservatives" and tea partiers and improve the party's national standing, Gillespie advised, congressional Republicans need to start listening to state party leaders. "Republican governors and state legislators have figured out how to talk in terms of benefits instead of process, and that positive rhetoric is more appealing than negative," wrote Gillespie. "These state Republicans are enjoying remarkable approval ratings, and they're getting things done. . . . If congressional Republicans talked more about what's happening in the states, they might encourage more minorities, women and new voters to think about voting Republican."[40]

Perhaps taking a cue from Gillespie or merely thinking along parallel lines, a month later two Republican governors echoed this viewpoint. Iowa's Terry Branstad said the party's "leadership is going to come out of the states, not Washington." The same week, controversial Wisconsin governor Scott Walker said that neither Ryan nor any other congressional Republican should run for president. Amazingly, that same month one of Ryan's fellow "young guns," House majority whip Kevin McCarthy of California, said he opposes presidential bids by members of Congress who hadn't served as governors.[41]

As a group, Republican governors also help the party's efforts at diversity. Despite an embarrassingly low number of Republican women and minorities in Congress, the party's governors include two Indian Americans, South Carolina's Nikki Haley and Louisiana's Bobby Jindal; two Latinos, New Mexico's Susana Martínez and Nevada's Brian Sandoval; and four women, including Haley, Martínez, Arizona's Jan Brewer, and Oklahoma's Mary Fallin. The share of Republican governors who are either nonwhite or female is more than twice that of congressional Republicans.

Following the October 2013 government shutdown, which destroyed the party's national approval numbers, neoliberal Republican pundit Josh Barro bemoaned the problems House Republicans were creating for the party. "I think you see at the state and local level a lot of Republican politicians who are not completely nihilistic like the Republican House has become. People like Chris Christie, Brian Sandoval, Susana Martinez, even Jan Brewer," writes Barro. "But what all of those politicians have in common is they've been able to stand up to the Republican base and say no. And they get away with it." A third of the Republican House Conference, says Barro, has "just completely gone bananas," and the remaining two-thirds recognize the party's problems but won't "stand up to these imbeciles" for fear of stirring up a primary threat from the "Ted Cruz wing of the party" that will take them down like they did some of their now-former colleagues.[42] Nominating a Republican governor for president does not guarantee the party's return to the Oval Office. And no matter the background of the party's next presidential nominee, one presidential victory will not solve the party's problems. But it would be a start. Until that happens, however, the rise of the congressional Republicans, especially in the House, continues to paralyze the party and pollute its chances for a full-blown national recovery.

The rise of modern congressional Republicans, which began prior to 1994 but will be forever remembered by that fateful year, transformed the party. In the two decades since, the party has enjoyed many successes. To this day, Newt Gingrich—the politician who, with the benefit of twenty years of hindsight, should rightly be remembered as having a more lasting impact on the party than any other Republican, including Ronald Reagan—continues to brag that it was congressional Republicans, along with Democratic president Bill Clinton, who during the 1990s returned fiscal responsibility to Washington. Republicans helped enact many of the regulatory reforms that Republican presidents before them mostly dreamt about but never quite delivered. The GOP also reorganized Congress and streamlined some of its procedures, and attempted and in some cases succeeded in holding its members to the same legal standards expected from American citizens. In purely political-electoral terms, congressional Republicans shrewdly parlayed their power to fill the party's campaign coffers, take control of the redistricting process, and recruit, train, and elect a new generation of national legislators.

Counterbalancing these policy and political victories are the costs and consequences resulting from the congressional Republicans' rise. Partly because the election or reelection of many Republican senators and most Republican House members relies largely on appeals to white men, the party has made little progress in electing women or minorities at a time when the nation is rapidly diversifying on gender and race. Although some Americans surely support their obstructionist agenda, the "do nothing" and "party of no" posture has tainted the Republican brand among independents seeking at least reasonable, solution-oriented bipartisan progress toward solving the nation's more pressing problems. And, of course, congressional Republicans have moved the party ever rightward, purging its ranks of all but a handful of beleaguered, isolated moderates. The Republican congressional chorus sings with an increasingly unified but politically tone-deaf voice.

And yet, for the most part congressional Republicans have suffered little for these political and policy failures; indeed, just as often they have been rewarded for them. As I have emphasized repeatedly in this book, many of the strategic, tactical, and policy choices advanced by congressional Republicans during the post-Gingrich era made perfect political or electoral sense at the time they were made, and some of these choices still do. Parties and partisans are rational actors, and although they sometimes fail to foresee the pitfalls of a particular decision, most politicians elected to Congress are reliable and shrewd stewards of their best interests. But what's best for congressional Republicans, individually or collectively, has not always been best for the party, and especially its presidential nominees.

Institutional choices have ideological consequences, and the chief consequence of the Republicans' dedication to forging and protecting their congressional stronghold in the post-Gingrich era has been a decline in the party's presidential competitiveness. With its base of older white voters dwindling as a share of the national electorate, the GOP now faces a critical crossroads: What can and should Republicans do to restore themselves to presidential prominence?

The answer to this question is elusive. As tempting as it may seem to try to revive the ideas and iconography of Ronald Reagan, the country has changed too much since the Reagan era. When Reagan was reelected in 1984, he received about 70 percent of the white vote en route to a forty-nine-state landslide; when George W. Bush was reelected in 2004, he received about 70 percent of the white vote but eked out a victory. The party should turn to its governors for new ideas and new blood, as many top party operatives have suggested. But that is only half the solution, for first the party must find a way to release its congressional wing's firm grip on the GOP's national brand. Until that happens, the Republican's congressional stronghold will continue to be a chokehold.

NOTES

Chapter 1. The Path Not Taken

1. Three weeks after the election, Chambers created BarackOFraudo.com, a site dedicated to proving that the Obama campaign stole the election in at least four key states. David Weigel, "From the Maker of Unskewed Polling Comes: The Obama Voter Fraud Map," *Slate*, November 20, 2012, http://www.slate.com/blogs/weigel/2012/11/20/from_the_maker_of_unskewed_polling_comes_the_obama_voter_fraud_map.html.

2. http://mobile.bloomberg.com/news/2013-02-21/obama-rated-at-3-year-high-in-poll-republicans-at-bottom.html; http://www.people-press.org/2013/02/26/gop-seen-as-principled-but-out-of-touch-and-too-extreme/.

3. Sean Trende, "The Case of the Missing White Voters," RealClearPolitics .com, November 8, 2012, http://www.realclearpolitics.com/articles/2012/11/08/the_case_of_the_missing_white_voters_116106-2.html; Sean Trende, "The Case of the Missing White Voters, Revisited," RealClearPolitics.com, June 21, 2013, http://www.realclearpolitics.com/articles/2013/06/21/the_case_of_the_missing_white_voters_revisited_118893.html.

4. Alan I. Abramowitz and Ruy Teixeira, "Is Doubling Down on White Voters a Viable Strategy for the Republican Party?," *Sabato's Crystal Ball*, July 11, 2013, http://www.centerforpolitics.org/crystalball/articles/is-doubling-down-on-white-voters-a-viable-strategy-for-the-republican-party/.

5. Thomas B. Edsall, "The Republican Autopsy Report," Opinionator (blog), *New York Times,* March 20, 2013, http://opinionator.blogs.nytimes.com /2013/03/20/the-republican-autopsy-report/?hp.

6. Matthew Cooper and Rebecca Kaplan, "The Tea Party's Legal Brief," *National Journal,* February 19, 2001, 28–33.

7. Jonathan Rauch, "Group Think," *National Journal,* September 11, 2010, 12–16.

8. Tom Schaller, "New Data on Tea Party Sympathizers," fivethirtyeight .com, April 12, 2010, http://www.fivethirtyeight.com/2010/04/new-data-on -tea-party-sympathizers.html.

9. Pew Research Center for the People and the Press, "Fewer Are Angry at Government, but Discontent Remains High," March 3, 2011, http://www.people -press.org/2011/03/03/section-1-attitudes-about-government/. The rates of anger are "more than double" because, at 43 percent and 47 percent, they were twice that of all respondents, 21 percent and 23 percent, and the latter percentages include and are therefore increased by the inclusion of the tea party self-identifiers.

10. Peter Kelley, "The Tea Party and the Politics of Paranoia," University of Washington press release, May 21, 2013, http://www.washington.edu/news /2013/05/21/the-tea-party-and-the-politics-of-paranoia/.

11. Christopher S. Parker and Matt A. Barreto, *Change They Can't Believe In: The Tea Party and Reactionary Politics in America* (Princeton University Press, 2013), 3.

12. Brian Beutler, "A Pathetic Day for the Republican Party," *Salon,* August 9, 2013, http://www.salon.com/2013/08/09/mitch_mcconnells_too_afraid_of _the_tea_party_to_fire_conservatives_when_theyre_disloyal/.

13. Gary C. Jacobson, "Barack Obama, the Tea Party, and the 2010 Midterm Elections," *Extensions,* Summer 2011, Carl Albert Congressional Research and Studies Center, University of Oklahoma, http://www.ou.edu/ carlalbertcenter/extensions/summer2011/Jacobson.pdf.

14. Jeremy W. Peters, "Bachmann, Facing Inquiries, Will Not Seek Re-election in 2014," *New York Times,* May 29, 2013, http://www.nytimes.com/2013/05/30/us/ politics/michele-bachmann-wont-seek-re-election-next-year.html?_r=0.

15. http://www.nationalreview.com/corner/349899/rove-bachmann-did-noth ing-chair-tea-party-caucus-katrina-trinko.

16. Theda Skocpol and Vanessa Williamson, *The Tea Party and the Remaking of Republican Conservatism* (Oxford University Press, 2012), 170, emphasis in original.

17. Thomas E. Mann and Norman J. Ornstein, *It's Even Worse Than It Looks: How the American Constitutional System Collided with the New Politics of Extremism* (Basic Books, 2012), 57–58.

18. Skocpol and Williamson, *Tea Party and the Remaking of Republican Conservatism*, 160.

19. http://www.washingtonpost.com/politics/border-security-amendment -clears-hurdle-bolstering-chances-for-immigration-bill/2013/06/24/1a26f32a -dcfe-11e2-9218-bc2ac7cd44e2_story.html.

20. The total of fifteen Republican aye votes includes Senator Angus King of Maine, a Republican-leaning independent; http://www.senate.gov/legislative /LIS/roll_call_lists/roll_call_vote_cfm.cfm?congress=113&session=1& vote=00168#position.

21. http://www.cnn.com/2013/02/13/politics/fact-check-immigration.

22. Alexander Burns, "Polls: Huge Support for Immigration Reform," *Politico*, June 13, 2013, http://www.politico.com/story/2013/06/poll-huge-support -for-immigration-reform-92701.html; http://www.people-press.org/2013/02/21 /section-1-opinions-about-major-issues/.

23. Ed O'Keefe, "Border Security Amendment Clears Hurdle, Bolstering Chances for Immigration Bill in Senate," *Washington Post*, June 24, 2013, http:// www.washingtonpost.com/politics/border-security-amendment-clears-hurdle -bolstering-chances-for-immigration-bill/2013/06/24/1a26f32a-dcfe-11e2-9218 -bc2ac7cd44e2_story.html; Chris Cillizza and Sean Sullivan, "The Senate Is Going to Pass Immigration Reform. And the House Doesn't Care," *Washington Post*, June 25, 2013, http://www.washingtonpost.com/blogs/the-fix/wp/2013/06/25/ the-senate-is-going-to-pass-immigration-reform-and-the-house-doesnt-care/; Jonathan Bernstein, "'Regular Order' on Immigration Suffers Another Blow," *Washington Post*, June 18, 2013, http://www.washingtonpost.com/blogs/post -partisan/wp/2013/06/18/regular-order-on-immigration-suffers-another-blow/.

24. http://www.globalpost.com/dispatch/news/afp/130710/white-house -warns-republicans-immigration-reform-0.

25. Janet Hook, "Immigration Bill Faces Uphill Climb in House," *Wall Street Journal*, June 30, 2013, http://online.wsj.com/article/SB10001424127887 324251504578577842451273534.html?mod=rss_US_News.

26. Matt Barreto, "2016 Forecast: Rubio, Bush, Ryan Have Chance to Win Over 40% of Latino Vote," Latino Decisions poll, July 2, 2013, http://www .latinodecisions.com/blog/2013/07/02/2016-forecast-rubio-bush-ryan-have -chance-to-win-over-40-of-latino-vote/.

27. Michael Gerson, "The Republican Party Needs a Reality Check," *Washington Post*, February 21, 2013, http://www.washingtonpost.com/opinions /michael-gerson-republican-party-needs-a-shakeup/2013/02/21/d89d9d82 -7baa-11e2-9a75-dab0201670da_story.html.

28. Geoffrey Kabaservice, *Rule and Ruin: The Downfall of Moderation and the Destruction of the Republican Party, from Eisenhower to the Tea Party* (Oxford

University Press, 2012); Rick Perlstein, *Before the Storm: Barry Goldwater and the Unmaking of the American Consensus* (Hill and Wang, 2001).

29. Thomas F. Schaller, "What Ever Happened to Moderate Republicans?," *American Prospect*, December 2007, 29–34.

30. Frank James, "Political Scientist: Republicans Most Conservative They've Been in 100 Years," NPR.org, April 13, 2012, http://www.npr.org/blogs/itsallpolitics/2012/04/10/150349438/gops-rightward-shift-higher-polarization-fills-political-scientist-with-dread; Ryan Lizza, "The Obama Memos," *New Yorker*, January 30, 2012, 38.

31. *Growth and Opportunity Project*, http://growthopp.gop.com/RNC_Growth_Opportunity_Book_2013.pdf, p. 4.

Chapter 2. Creative Destruction

1. David Corn, "How Close Did Lesley Stahl Come to Reporting Reagan Had Alzheimer's While in Office? Very Close," MotherJones.com, January 20, 2011, http://www.motherjones.com/politics/2011/01/reagan-alzheimers-family-feud-lesley-stahl.

2. Stephen Lowman, "President Reagan Suffered from Alzheimer's While in Office, According to Son," Political Bookworm (blog), Washingtonpost.com, http://voices.washingtonpost.com/political-bookworm/2011/01/president_reagan_suffered_from.html.

3. David John Marley, *Pat Robertson: An American Life* (Rowman and Littlefield, 2007), 112–123.

4. Ibid.

5. See, among many other titles about the rise of Christian conservatives in American politics, David Snowball, *Continuity and Change in the Rhetoric of the Moral Majority* (Praeger, 2001); Clyde Wilcox and Carin Robinson, *Onward Christian Soldiers* (Westview Press, 2010); Sara Diamond, *Roads to Dominion* (Guilford Press, 1995); and William Martin, *With God on Our Side: The Rise of the Religious Right in America* (Broadway Books, 1996).

6. Tony Lee, "Paul Ryan: The Jack Kemp of His Generation," *Human Events*, December 23, 2011, http://www.humanevents.com/2011/12/23/paul-ryan-the-jack-kemp-of-his-generation/.

7. E. J. Dionne Jr., "Dole Wins in Iowa, with Robertson Next," *New York Times*, February 9, 1988.

8. Excerpt from Pat Robertson's Republican National Convention address, August 16, 1988, http://www.patrobertson.com/Speeches/Presidential BidEnded.asp.

9. Tom Wicker, "Bush Makes a Choice," *New York Times*, August 19, 1988.

10. Interview with author by phone, January 13, 2011.

11. Margie Omero, "The Gender Gap in Turnout Likely to Widen," Poll ster.com, December 7, 2007, http://www.huffingtonpost.com/margie-omero /the_gender_gap_in_turnout_like_b_722821.html.

12. Among men, Reagan's approval dropped just six points, from 65 percent to 59 percent, between July 1985 and July 1988, but fell from 60 percent to 43 percent among women during the same three-year period; http://www.cawp .rutgers.edu/fast_facts/voters/documents/GGPrtyID.pdf.

13. Paul Furiga, "Republican Women Fear Gender Gap in Quayle Choice," *Press-Courier* (Oxnard), August 21, 1988, 6.

14. "Women Representatives and Senators by Congress, 1917–Present," http://history.house.gov/Exhibitions-and-Publications/WIC/Historical-Data /Women-Representatives-and-Senators-by-Congress/.

15. "Women in the U.S. Congress, 2014," Center for American Women in Politics, Rutgers University, http://www.cawp.rutgers.edu/fast_facts/levels_of _office/documents/cong.pdf.

16. Lee Edwards, *The Conservative Revolution: The Movement That Remade America* (Free Press, 1999), 276–279.

17. Ibid.

18. Thomas B. Edsall, *Building Red America: The New Conservative Coalition and the Drive for Permanent Power* (Basic Books, 2006), 5.

19. Text of Reagan's 1984 CPAC speech available at http://www.reagan .utexas.edu/archives/speeches/1984/30284g.htm.

20. "The Long March of Newt Gingrich," documentary, *PBS Frontline,* January 16, 1996, http://video.pbs.org/video/2179305565/.

21. *Texas v. Johnson,* 491 U.S. 397 (1989).

22. Don Phillips and Helen Dewar, "Flag Ruling Angers Congress," *Washington Post,* June 23, 1989, A1.

23. Tamar Jacoby, Ann McDaniel, and Peter McKillop, "A Fight for Old Glory," *Newsweek,* July 3, 1989, 18.

24. John Dillin, "Flag Issue Breaks Along Party Lines," *Christian Science Monitor,* July 10, 1989, 8.

25. *Wards Cove Packing Co. v. Atonio,* 490 U.S. 642 (1989).

26. Michael Oreskes, "Elections Strengthen Hand of Democrats in '91 Redistricting," *New York Times,* November 8, 1990.

27. David Lublin, *The Paradox of Representation: Racial Gerrymandering and Minority Interests* (Princeton University Press, 1997), 100.

28. *Thornburg v. Gingles,* 478 U.S. 30 (1986).

29. Roberto Suro, "In Redistricting, New Rules and New Prizes," *New York Times,* May 6, 1990.

30. http://www.census.gov/population/www/documentation/twps0056/tab 01.pdf.

31. Delia Gregg and Jonathan N. Katz, "The Impact of Majority-Minority Districts on Congressional Elections" (paper presented at the Midwest Political Science Association meetings, Chicago, Illinois, April 4, 2005).

32. Interview with author, December 10, 2010.

33. Ibid.

34. Ibid.

35. Wayne King, "The 1990 Election: What Went Wrong? Bradley Says He Sensed Voter Fury but It Was Too Late to Do Anything," *New York Times*, November 8, 1990.

36. Senate results available at the New Jersey Board of Elections website, http://www.njelections.org/election-results/1990-general-election-results-us -senate.pdf.

37. King, "The 1990 Election."

38. Timothy Naftali, *George H. W. Bush* (Times Books, 2007), 61.

39. David S. Broder, "GOP's Anti-tax True Believers Remain Outsiders," *Washington Post*, July 1990, A14.

40. Daniel J. Mitchell, "Bush's Deplorable Flip-Flop on Taxes," Executive Memorandum #271, June 28, 1990, http://www.heritage.org/research/reports /1990/06/bushs-deplorable-flip-flop-on-taxes.

41. Dick Armey, "Down with the Palace Guard," *New York Times*, November 26, 1991, A21.

42. Ann Devroy and John E. Yang, "Beset by Conservatives, Bush Struggles to Keep Peace in Party," *Washington Post*, November 27, 1991, A4.

43. Interview with author by phone, January 13, 2011.

44. Naftali, *George H. W. Bush*, 115–116.

45. George H. W. Bush and Brent Scowcroft, *A World Transformed* (Vintage, 1998), 451.

46. http://www.va.gov/opa/publications/factsheets/fs_americas_wars.pdf.

47. Stephen Graubard, *Mr. Bush's War* (Hill and Wang, 1992), 140–151.

48. Interview on C-SPAN, April 15, 1994, https://www.youtube.com /watch?v=YENbElb5-xY; or see http://en.wikiquote.org/wiki/Dick_Cheney #1990s; Cheney misquotes the fatality rate as 146; it was 148, but see note 46.

49. Mel Steely, *The Gentleman from Georgia: The Biography of Newt Gingrich* (Mercer University Press, 2000), 227.

50. http://www.4president.org/speeches/buchanan1992announcement .htm.

51. Robin Toner, "Buchanan: Urging New Nationalism, Joins '92 Race," *New York Times*, December 11, 1991.

52. J. Jennings Moss, "Buchanan: Balance Books or Shut Down," *Washington Times*, December 10, 1991, A4.

Chapter 3. Reinvention

1. Martin Fletcher, "Right Wing Wants Bush to Seize Initiative with Tax Cut Pledges," *The Times* (London), August 10, 1992; Martin Fletcher, "Bush Pins Hope on Tax Cuts and Saddam," *The Times* (London), August 17, 1992.

2. Buchanan's "Culture War Speech," August 17, 1992, http://voicesofdemocracy.umd.edu/buchanan-culture-war-speech-speech-text/.

3. William Safire, "Bush's Gamble," *New York Times Magazine*, October 18, 1992, 31.

4. Adam Clymer, "Bush Gains from Convention Nearly Evaporate in Latest Poll," *New York Times*, August 26, 1992.

5. Eric Pianin, "Living on the Margin: Cash Bind, Overdrafts Put Edwards on List," *Washington Post*, April 2, 1992, A1; David Zizzo, "Edwards Apologizes at State GOP Meet," *Daily Oklahoman*, April 5, 1992, 1.

6. Clifford Krauss, "Oklahoma Lawmaker Faces 4 Rivals and a Scandal," *New York Times*, August 25, 1992, A19.

7. Clifford Krauss, "Oklahoma Lawmaker Is Defeated," *New York Times*, August 26, 1992.

8. Clifford Krauss, "Gingrich Takes No Prisoners in the House's Sea of Gentility," *New York Times*, March 17, 1992, A18.

9. Ralph Z. Hallow, "Michel's Departure Sure to Leave Aggressive Leader," *Washington Times*, October 5, 1993, A6.

10. Leslie Phillips, "Gingrich Leads Way in Battle for GOP," *USA Today*, June 20, 1994, A13.

11. Richard Fenno, *Home Style: House Members in Their Districts* (Little, Brown, 1978).

12. Michael Kranish, "Emotions Run High in Bush Finale," *Boston Globe*, November 3, 1992. Full quote available at "Remarks on Arrival in Louisville, Kentucky," November 2, 1992, *Public Papers of the Presidents of the United States: George H. W. Bush, 1992* (Government Printing Office, 1992), 2142–2145, http://www.gpo.gov/fdsys/pkg/PPP-1992-book2/pdf/PPP-1992-book2-doc-pg2142.pdf.

13. "Remarks at a Welcome Home Ceremony," November 4, 1992, *Public Papers of the Presidents of the United States: George H. W. Bush, 1992* (Government Printing Office, 1992), 2153–2154, http://www.gpo.gov/fdsys/pkg/PPP-1992-book2/pdf/PPP-1992-book2-doc-pg2153.pdf.

14. Charles Krauthammer, "Bush: Two Great Challenges Met," *Washington Post*, November 10, 1992.

15. Lee Walczak, "George Bush Just Didn't Get It," *Business Week*, November 16, 1992.

16. Interview with author by phone, May 13, 2011.

17. Jacob Weisberg, *The Bush Tragedy* (Random House, 2008), 89.

18. J. Jennings Moss, "Armey, Lewis Vie for GOP Position," *Washington Times*, December 7, 1992, A6; Clifford Kraus, "Staunch Conservative Wins G.O.P. Post in House," *New York Times*, December 8, 1992, B12.

19. Judi Hasson, "Freshmen Arrive to Claim Their 'Mandate,'" *USA Today*, December 2, 1992, A4.

20. As recounted to author during a phone interview with Ed Gillespie, January 13, 2011.

21. Mildred Amer, *Freshmen in the House of Representatives and Senate by Political Party, 1913–2005*, Congressional Research Report, updated June 16, 2005, http://fpc.state.gov/documents/organization/57877.pdf.

22. "Why Congress Doesn't Work," speech by Rep. Christopher Cox to the Heritage Foundation, June 25, 1992, http://policyarchive.org/handle/10207/bitstreams/12765.pdf; "Why Congress Doesn't Work, Part II: Promoting Accountability and Direction," speech by Rep. Jim Nussle to the Heritage Foundation, July 7, 1992, http://policyarchive.org/handle/10207/bitstreams/12769.pdf.

23. See, e.g., Fenno, *Home Style*, as well as David Mayhew, *Congress: The Electoral Connection* (Yale University Press, 1974).

24. Quoted in Kenneth J. Cooper, "Reform Hopes, Party Loyalties Collide in House Class of '92," *Washington Post*, March 21, 1993, A4.

25. "House Republicans Manage to Win One Despite Themselves," editorial, *Washington Times*, January 5, 1993, B2.

26. "Unstereotyping the Class of '92," editorial, *Washington Post*, January 19, 1993, A20.

27. Carolyn Barta, "Will Congress Reform?," *Dallas Morning News*, December 7, 1992, A19.

28. Haynes Johnson and David S. Broder, *The System: The American Way of Politics at the Breaking Point* (Little, Brown, 1996), 39–40.

29. Ibid., 304–305.

30. Michael Ross, "Michel's Plan to Retire Sets Up GOP Leadership Fight in House," *Los Angeles Times*, October 5, 1993.

31. John Dillin, "House Republicans Ready for Aggressive Approach as Longtime Leader Quits," *Christian Science Monitor*, October 6, 1993, 1.

32. Hallow, "Michel's Departure Sure to Leave Aggressive Leader," A6.

33. "The Next GOP Torchbearer," editorial, *Washington Post*, October 10, 1993, C6.

34. Barbara Sinclair, *Party Wars: Polarization and the Politics of National Policy Making* (University of Oklahoma Press, 2006); Nolan McCarty, Keith T. Poole, and Howard Rosenthal, *Polarized America: The Dance of Ideology and Unequal Riches* (MIT Press, 2008); Keith T. Poole and Howard Rosenthal, *Ideology and Congress* (Transaction Publishers, 2011).

35. Ronald B. Rapoport, *Three's a Crowd: The Dynamic of Third Parties, Ross Perot, and Republican Resurgence* (University of Michigan Press, 2007), 163 for quote and figure 8.3 (p. 181) for the data on GOP success rates in House elections; also see all of chapters 7 and 8 for a fuller explanation of what the GOP did between 1992 and 1994 to attract Perot voters in the 1994 midterms.

36. Thomas B. Edsall, *Building Red America: The New Conservative Coalition and the Drive for Permanent Power* (Basic Books, 2006), 135–136.

37. Julian Zelizer, *On Capitol Hill* (Cambridge University Press, 2004), 257.

38. Jerry Gray, "Feuding Goes On as G.O.P. Presents Its Budget Plan," *New York Times*, November 17, 1995, A1.

39. George Stephanopoulos, *All Too Human* (Back Bay Books, 2000).

40. Gray, "Feuding Goes On as G.O.P. Presents Its Budget Plan," A1.

41. Bob Woodward, *The Agenda: Inside the Clinton White House* (Simon and Schuster, 1994).

42. Robert L. Ehrlich Jr., "How the GOP Can Avoid a '96 Repeat," *Washington Post*, February 27, 2011, A19.

43. Newt Gingrich, "Why a Shutdown Beats Standing Down," *Washington Post*, February 27, 2011, A19.

44. Rich Lowry, *Legacy: Paying the Price for the Clinton Years* (Regnery, 2003), 47–48.

45. John F. Harris, *The Survivor: Bill Clinton in the White House* (Random House, 2005), 157.

46. Newt Gingrich, *Lessons Learned the Hard Way* (HarperCollins, 2000), 50.

Chapter 4. Reformulation

1. William Goldschlag, "Pat Has 'Choice' Words for Dole," *Daily News*, March 11, 1996, 13.

2. Ralph Z. Hallow, "Dole Urged to Limit Buchanan's Role," *Washington Times*, March 19, 1996, A1.

3. Interview with author by phone, May 11, 2011.

4. Ibid.

5. "Ford, Bush to Speak; Video to Laud Reagan," *USA Today*, August 12, 1996, 3A.

6. John E. Yang, "House Votes to Curb Gay Marriages; Bitter Debate Precedes Lopsided Outcome; Clinton Would Sign Bill," *Washington Post*, July 13, 1996, A1.

7. http://clerk.house.gov/evs/1996/roll316.xml; http://www.senate.gov/legislative/LIS/roll_call_lists/roll_call_vote_cfm.cfm?congress=104&session=2&vote=00280.

8. Yang, "House Votes to Curb Gay Marriages," A1.

9. http://blogs.mcclatchydc.com/law/2013/03/what-gop-once-said-about-doma.html#sthash.bt87UAFN.dpuf.

10. http://fivethirtyeight.blogs.nytimes.com/2012/05/09/support-for-gay-marriage-outweighs-opposition-in-polls/?_r=0.

11. Sara Fritz, "Dole, Gingrich: A Leadership Odd Couple," *Los Angeles Times*, November 10, 1994.

12. Interview with author by phone, May 13, 2011.

13. Interview with author by phone, May 11, 2011.

14. Ibid.

15. Dan Balz and Ronald Brownstein, *Storming the Gates: Protest Politics and the Republican Revival* (Little, Brown, 1996), 157–158. First emphasis ("below") in original; second emphasis added.

16. Interview with author by phone, May 13, 2011.

17. Interview with author by phone, May 11, 2011.

18. Richard L. Berke, "Trent Lott and His Fierce Freshmen," *New York Times*, February 2, 1997, 40.

19. See, e.g., Ronald Brownstein's "The Blue Wall," *National Journal*, January 17, 2009.

20. "Toeing the Line," *National Journal*, February 26, 2011, 21.

21. Sandy Hume, "Lott Woos House GOP," *The Hill*, June 19, 1996.

22. Sean M. Theriault, *The Gingrich Senators: The Roots of Partisan Warfare in Congress* (Oxford University Press, 2013).

23. Ibid., 49–50.

24. William Kristol and Robert Kagan, "Toward a Neo-Reaganite Foreign Policy," *Foreign Affairs* 74, no. 4 (July–August 1996): 18–32.

25. David P. Schippers, with Alan P. Henry, *Sellout: The Inside Story of President Clinton's Impeachment* (Regnery, 2000), 24.

26. John F. Harris, *The Survivor: Bill Clinton in the White House* (Random House, 2005), 357–358.

27. Peter Baker, *The Breach: Inside the Impeachment and Trial of William Jefferson Clinton* (Scribner, 2000), 98–99.

28. Ibid.

29. The February 1999 special election to fill Gingrich's vacated seat was won by former Georgia state legislator Johnny Isakson, which makes Isakson arguably the third future Republican senator (along with Jim Bunning and John Ensign) eventually born from the fallout of the 1998 election cycle.

30. Baker, *The Breach?*, 160.

31. Schippers, *Sellout*, 56.

32. Ken Gormley, *The Death of American Virtue: Clinton vs. Starr* (Crown, 2010), 589–590, 607.

33. James Carney, with Karen Tumulty, "Attempted Republican Coup: Ready, Aim, Misfire," *Time*, July 28, 1997, http://www.cnn.com/ALLPOLITICS/1997/07/21/time/gingrich.html.

34. David W. Chen, "A Livingston Legacy Revived; Speaker-to-Be Has Rich Bloodlines in North and South," *New York Times*, November 23, 1998.

35. Ceci Connolly and Juliet Eilperin, "Hastert Steps Up to Leading Role," *Washington Post*, January 5, 1999, A1; Jonathan Franzen, "The Listener," *New Yorker*, October 6, 2003.

36. Katharine Q. Seelye, "Impeachment: The Speaker-Elect; After Spotlight, Livingston Exits Center Stage," *New York Times*, December 19, 1998.

37. Melinda Henneberger, "Impeachment: The Politics; Republicans Prevail with a Costly Victory," *New York Times*, December 21, 1998.

38. Lou Dubose and Jan Reid, *The Hammer Comes Down: The Nasty, Brutish and Shortened Political Life of Tom DeLay* (Public Affairs, 2004), 151.

39. Richard A. Posner, *An Affair of State: The Investigation, Impeachment, and Trial of President Clinton* (Harvard University Press, 1999), 121–122.

40. Gormley, *Death of American Virtue*, 620–622.

41. Trent Lott, *Herding Cats: A Life in Politics* (Regan Books, 2005), 174–203.

42. Rich Lowry, *Legacy: Paying the Price for the Clinton Years* (Regnery, 2003), 190–191.

43. Robert G. Kaiser, "Academics Say It's Elementary: Gore Wins," *Washington Post*, August 31, 2000, A12.

44. Dan Balz and David Von Drehle, "For Bush, the Balancing Act Begins," *Washington Post*, June 23, 1999, A1.

45. Ibid.

46. Alison Mitchell, "Governors Carry Bush's Message," *New York Times*, October 23, 2000.

47. Garrison Nelson, "Jim Jeffords's Long Goodbye," *New York Times*, May 25, 2001.

48. "Jeffords Denies Party Switch Was Based on Ambitions," CNN.com, May 25, 2001, http://cgi.cnn.com/2001/ALLPOLITICS/05/25/jeffords.senate.02/.

49. Christopher Graff, "Jeffords Leaves Republican Party," Associated Press, May 24, 2001, http://www.washingtonpost.com/wp-srv/aponline/20010524/aponline101750_000.htm.

50. Ibid.

51. Bruce Shapiro, "Will Trent Lott Pay for Losing the Senate?," Salon.com, May 24, 2001, http://www.salon.com/2001/05/24/jeffords/.

52. http://www.informationclearinghouse.info/article3789.htm.

Chapter 5. Paralysis

1. https://www.govtrack.us/congress/votes/108-2003/h332.

2. Jonathan Allen, "Newt Gingrich Played Key Role in Medicare Drug Benefit," *Politico*, December 12, 2011, http://www.politico.com/news/stories/1211/70332.html.

3. Dick Armey, "Say 'No' to the Medicare Bill," *Wall Street Journal*, November 21, 2003, http://online.wsj.com/news/articles/SB106937758929945900.

4. Charles Babington, "Ethics Panel Rebukes DeLay," *Washington Post*, October 1, 2004, A1.

5. Matthew Yglesias, "The Forgotten Flip-Flop: 2003 Medicare Reform," *Slate*, June 19, 2012, http://www.slate.com/blogs/moneybox/2012/06/19/the_forgotten_flip_flop_2003_medicare_reform.html.

6. Based on 2012 election results and data taken from the Environmental Working Group's farm subsidy database, http://farm.ewg.org/progdetail.php?fips=00000&progcode=total&page=district&regionname=theUnitedStates.

7. http://www.usda.gov/wps/portal/usda/usdahome?contentidonly=true&contentid=2002/02/0052.html.

8. Brian M. Riedl, *How Farm Subsidies Became America's Largest Corporate Welfare Program*, Heritage Foundation Backgrounder #1520 on Federal Budget, February 25, 2002, http://www.heritage.org/research/reports/2002/02/farm-subsidies-are-americas-largest-corporate-welfare-program#pgfId=1009154.

9. Ibid.; House Amendment 346 to H.R. 2646, http://clerk.house.gov/evs/2001/roll365.xml.

10. Chris Edwards and Tad DeHaven, "Republicans Become the Party of Big Government," Cato Institute commentary, February 2, 2004, http://www.cato.org/publications/commentary/republicans-become-party-big-government.

11. http://cagw.org/reporting/pig-book#historical_trends.

12. Scott A. Frisch and Sean Q Kelly, *Cheese Factories on the Moon: Why Earmarks Are Good for American Democracy* (Paradigm, 2011), 139–142.

13. Authors interviewed in Jamelle Bouie, "Getting Over Earmarks," *American Prospect* online, December 16, 2010, http://prospect.org/article/getting-over-earmarks; "Earmarks Emerging from the Shadows," Cheese Factories on the Moon (blog), January 9, 2013, http://cheesefactoriesonthemoon.blogspot.com/2013/01/earmarks-emerging-from-shadows.html.

14. Andrew Taylor, *Elephant's Edge: The Republicans as a Ruling Party* (Praeger, 2005).

15. Frisch and Kelly, *Cheese Factories on the Moon*, 56.

16. Nicholas Confessore, "Welcome to the Machine," *Washington Monthly*, July–August 2003.

17. Ibid.

18. Matthew Continetti, *The K Street Gang: The Rise and Fall of the Republican Machine* (Doubleday, 2006), 16–17.

19. Ibid., 23–42.

20. Michael Crowley, "A Lobbyist in Full," *New York Times Magazine*, May 1, 2005.

21. Thomas E. Mann and Norman J. Ornstein, *The Broken Branch: How Congress Is Failing America and How to Get It Back on Track* (Oxford University Press, 2006), 188–191.

22. Spencer S. Hsu, "Ex-DeLay Aide Is Sentenced to 20 Months," *Washington Post*, February 12, 2011, A2.

23. "Return of the Junket: Lawmakers Trot Globe on Lobbyists' Tab," CNBC, August 19, 2013, http://www.cnbc.com/id/100972702.

24. Gilbert Cruz, "Is Congress's Ethics Reform Serious?," *Time*, July 31, 2007, http://content.time.com/time/politics/article/0,8599,1648556,00.html#ixzz2oobB0siA; Eric Lipton and Eric Lichtblau, "Rules for Congress Curb but Don't End Junkets," *New York Times*, December 6, 2009.

25. http://articles.sun-sentinel.com/2002-12-19/news/0212181086_1_lott-controversy-sen-trent-lott-thurmond.

26. David Frum, "Moments of Truth," *National Review* online, December 9, 2002, http://www.nationalreview.com/frum/diary120902.asp.

27. Kirk Victor, "Frist's Balancing Act," *National Journal*, April 2, 2005, 976–977.

28. Ross K. Baker, "A Half Century of Bicameralism," chap. 3 in *The U.S. Senate: From Deliberation to Dysfunction*, ed. Burdett A. Loomis (CQ Press, 2012), 61.

29. Elana Schor, "Lott Beats Alexander 25–24 for Comeback," *The Hill*, November 16, 2006.

30. Massimo Calabresi, "The Revival of Trent Lott," *Time*, November 19, 2006.

31. Barbara Sinclair, *Party Wars: Polarization and the Politics of National Policy Making* (University of Oklahoma Press, 2006), 239.

32. Jonathan Franzen, "The Listener," *New Yorker*, October 6, 2003, 86.

33. Molly Ball, "Even the Aide Who Coined the Hastert Rule Says the Hastert Rule Isn't Working," *The Atlantic* online, July 21, 2013, http://www.theatlantic.com/politics/archive/2013/07/even-the-aide-who-coined-the-hast ert-rule-says-the-hastert-rule-isnt-working/277961/.

34. Charles Babington, "Hastert Launches a Partisan Policy," *Washington Post*, November 27, 2004, A1, http://www.washingtonpost.com/wp-dyn/arti cles/A15423-2004Nov26.html.

35. Franzen, "The Listener," 85–86.

36. Seth Gitell, "The Democratic Party Suicide Bill," *Atlantic Monthly*, July–August 2003, 106–113.

37. Juliet Eilperin and Helen Dewar, "Campaign Bill Heads for a Vote in House," *Washington Post*, January 25, 2002, A1.

38. Diana Dwyre and Robin Kolodny, "National Political Parties After BCRA," chap. 5 in *Life After Reform: When the Bipartisan Campaign Finance Act Meets Politics*, ed. Michael Malbin (Rowman and Littlefield, 2003).

39. Gitell, "Democratic Party Suicide Bill."

40. Quoted in Tim Fernholz, "What to Expect When You're Expecting a Majority," *American Prospect*, September 19, 2008.

41. *McConnell v. FEC*, 540 U.S. 93 (2003); *Republican National Committee v. FEC* (09-1287); http://politicalticker.blogs.cnn.com/2010/06/29/high-court -affirms-ban-on-soft-money-campaign-donations-2/.

42. Vincent G. Moscardelli and Moshe Haspel, "Campaign Finance Re-form as Institutional Choice: Party Difference in the Vote to Ban Soft Money," *American Politics Research* 35 (January 2007): 79–102.

43. Sam Tanenhaus, "Tom DeLay's Hard Drive," *Vanity Fair*, July 2004, 110.

44. Steve Bickerstaff, *Lines in the Sand: Congressional Redistricting and the Downfall of Tom DeLay* (University of Texas Press, 2007).

45. Ibid., 51.

46. Ibid., 52.

47. Charles Babington, "DeLay Is Letting Others Take Manhattan," *Washington Post*, September 3, 2004, A23.

48. Michael Tomasky, "Texas-Sized Problem," *American Prospect*, April 19, 2005, 21.

49. "Our View: Craig Must Resign," editorial, *Idaho Statesman*, August 30, 2007, http://www.idahostatesman.com/2007/08/30/145494/our-view-craig -must-resign.html#storylink=cpy.

50. http://www.cnn.com/2008/POLITICS/02/13/larry.craig/index.html.

51. Michael D. Shear and Chris L. Jenkins, "Va. Legislator Ends Bid for 3rd Term," *Washington Post*, August 31, 2004, A2.

52. Austin Wright and Jake Sherman, "Rep. Randy Forbes: Deny Money to Gay Candidates," *Politico*, December 4, 2013, http://www.politico.com/story /2013/12/gay-republican-candidates-100686.html#ixzz2me85VVmC.

53. Mary Jacoby, "There Is a House in New Orleans," *Salon*, October 29, 2004, http://www.salon.com/2004/10/29/lousiana_race/.

54. Douglas L. Kriner and Francis X. Shen, "Iraq Casualties and the 2006 Senate Elections," *Legislative Studies Quarterly* 33 (November 2007): 507–530; Christian R. Grose and Bruce I. Oppenheimer, "The Iraq War, Partisanship and Candidate Attributes: Variation in Partisan Swing in the 2006 U.S. House Elections," *Legislative Studies Quarterly* 33 (November 2007): 530–557; "The Electoral Cost of War: Iraq Casualties and the 2004 U.S. Presidential Election," *Journal of Politics* 69 (2007): 633–648.

55. "Iraq Looms Large in Nationalized Election," Pew Research Center for People and the Press, October 5, 2006, http://www.people-press.org/2006/10 /05/iraq-looms-large-in-nationalized-election/.

56. Adam Nagourney and Megan Thee, "With Election Driven by Iraq, Voters Want New Approach," *New York Times*, November 2, 2006, http://www .nytimes.com/2006/11/02/us/politics/02poll.html?pagewanted=all&_r=0.

57. http://content.time.com/time/nation/article/0,8599,1543199,00.htm; "Resign, Mr. Speaker," editorial, *Washington Times*, October 2, 2006.

58. Patrick O'Connor, "House Republicans Learn to Appreciate Their Senate Peers," *Politico*, March 20, 2007, http://www.politico.com/news/stories/0307 /3208.html.

Chapter 6. A Congress-centric Party

1. http://www.foxnews.com/politics/2012/01/03/gop-candidates-await-iowa -verdict/.

2. Rich Lowry, "Newt the Unreliable," *National Review* online, May 17, 2011, http://www.nationalreview.com/articles/267389/newt-unreliable-rich-lowry.

3. Quoted in Mark Halperin and John Heilemann, *Double Down: Game Change 2012* (Penguin, 2013), 255.

4. John Judis and Ruy Teixeira, *The Emerging Democratic Majority* (Scribner, 2004); Thomas F. Schaller, *Whistling Past Dixie* (Simon and Schuster, 2006).

5. Data sources: http://fairmodel.econ.yale.edu/rayfair/pdf/2010C.PDF; http://clerk.house.gov/member_info/electionInfo/2010election.pdf.

6. Martin P. Wattenberg and Craig Leonard Brians, "Partisan Turnout Bias in Midterm Legislative Elections," *Legislative Studies Quarterly* 27, no. 3 (2002): 407–421.

7. Michael P. McDonald, "Voter Turnout in the 2010 Midterm Election," *The Forum* 8, no. 4 (2010), article 8, http://elections.gmu.edu/Classes/GOVT311/Voter%20Turnout%20in%20the%202010%20Midterm%20Election.pdf.

8. Harry J. Enten, "Can the Republicans Expect a Midterm Election Bump in 2014?," *The Guardian* online, June 11, 2013, http://www.theguardian.com/commentisfree/2013/jun/11/democrats-midterm-presidential-elections.

9. Thomas F. Schaller, "Democrats Dread 2014 Drop-Off," *Sabato's Crystal Ball*, January 10, 2013, http://www.centerforpolitics.org/crystalball/articles/democrats-dread-2014-drop-off/.

10. Joshua Green, "The Supreme Court's Voting Rights Decision Is a Poison Chalice for the GOP," *Bloomberg BusinessWeek*, June 25, 2013, http://www.businessweek.com/articles/2013-06-25/the-supreme-courts-voting-rights-decision-is-a-poison-chalice-for-the-gop.

11. David Wasserman, "SCOTUS Ruling: Big Redraw? Not So Fast," *Cook Political Report*, June 25, 2013, http://cookpolitical.com/story/5878?.

12. James Burnham, *Congress and the American Tradition* (Regnery, 1959); Willmoore Kendall, *The Conservative Affirmation* (Regnery, 1963). I wish to offer special thanks to Jeet Heer for pointing me to this subliterature on congressional conservatism.

13. http://www.firstprinciplesjournal.com/articles.aspx?article=710&theme=amexp&loc=b.

14. It's also interesting that both books were imprints of the Henry Regnery Company, the godfather of the conservative book press.

15. "Speaker Newt Gingrich," interview published in *Masters of the House: Congressional Leadership over Two Centuries*, ed. Roger Davidson, Susan Hammond, and Ray Smock (Westview Press, 1998), 323–325.

16. Kendall, *Conservative Affirmation*, chap. 2, but specifically pp. 24–26. Emphases in every case appear in the original.

17. Amanda Terkel, "112th Congress Set to Become Most Unproductive Since 1940s," *Huffington Post*, December 28, 2012, http://www.huffingtonpost.com/2012/12/28/congress-unproductive_n_2371387.html.

18. Stephen Skowronek, *The Politics Presidents Make: Leadership from John Adams to Bill Clinton*, rev. ed. (Belknap Press of Harvard University Press, 1997), 20.

19. Amity Shlaes, *Coolidge* (Harper, 2013).

20. Julian E. Zelizer, *Governing America: The Revival of Political History* (Princeton University Press, 2012), chap. 14.

21. The Supreme Court moves even slower than the two elected branches, and by definition almost always acts in reaction to decisions first taken by the two majoritarian branches.

22. Kenneth Janda, *The Social Bases of Political Parties: Democrats and Republicans, 1952–2012 and 2032*, iTunes book, February 11, 2013, https://itunes .apple.com/us/book/social-bases-political-parties/id602462683?mt=13.

23. Author's notes on Kenneth Janda, "The Social Bases of U.S. Political Parties: 1952 to 2012; Social Support and Political Interests" (paper presented at the Midwest Political Science Association meetings, April 11, 2013, Chicago, Illinois).

24. http://www.prnewswire.com/news-releases/two-in-five-americans -believe-divided-government-good-for-country-110975304.html.

25. http://www.gallup.com/poll/157739/americans-preference-shifts-to- ward-one-party-government.aspx.

26. http://www.gallup.com/poll/139742/Americans-Lack-Consensus-De sirability-Divided-Gov.aspx.

27. Because of party switches like Jeffords's—along with terms unfinished for assorted reasons that in turn led to replacement appointments and/or special elections—the figures sometimes change within any two-year Congress; but Figure 1 reflects the shares immediately following the preceding, regular November election.

28. Jacob S. Hacker and Paul Pierson, *Off Center: The Republican Revolution and the Erosion of American Democracy* (Yale University Press, 2005), 36.

29. See chapter 4 in Frances E. Lee and Bruce I. Oppenheimer, *Sizing Up the Senate: The Unequal Consequences of Equal Representation* (University of Chicago Press, 1999); and Thomas L. Brunell, "Partisan Bias in U.S. Congressional Elections: Why the Senate Is Usually More Republican Than the House of Representatives," *American Politics Quarterly* 27 (1999): 316–327.

30. I say "theoretically," but there is mixed evidence as to whether the small-state advantage has benefited Republicans recently. See, e.g., P. J. Ardoin and B. M. Parsons, "Partisan Bias in the Electoral College: Cheap States and Wasted Votes," *Politics and Policy* 35 (2007): 342–364.

31. Rob Richie and Devin McCarthy, "The House GOP Can't Be Beat: It's Worse Than Gerrymandering," *Salon*, January 13, 2013, http://www.salon.com /2013/01/13/the_house_gop_cant_be_beat_its_worse_than_gerrymandering /?source=newsletter.

32. David Wasserman, "Parallel Universes," *National Journal*, December 15, 2012, 16–20.

33. The ratio is adjusted to reflect the total number of House and Senate seats, which has varied slightly in the House during the past century, as well as for the Senate, which totaled only ninety-six seats prior to the admission of Hawaii and Alaska to the Union.

34. Thomas F. Schaller, "Why the GOP Dominates the House—But Not the Senate," *New Republic*, July 26, 2011, http://www.newrepublic.com/article/politics/92585/house-republicans-senate-john-boehner#.

35. http://www.nbcnews.com/id/43022759/ns/meet_the_press-transcripts/t/meet-press-transcript-may/#.UUM_dzdra6Q.

36. Ryan Lizza, "Fussbudget," *New Yorker*, August 6, 2012, 24–32, http://www.newyorker.com/reporting/2012/08/06/120806fa_fact_lizza#ixzz2M-VU1HEhf.

37. Percentages computed by author. For comparative purposes, the share of Senate Democrats from those same four Congresses who previously served in the House started higher, dipped down, and then rose again: 44.7 percent in the 83rd Congress, 31.9 percent in the 97th Congress, 34.0 percent in the 104th Congress, and 47.9 percent in the 108th Congress.

38. To be exact, all of the senators listed claim Poole/Rosenthal DW-Nominate ideological scores of 0.600 or higher. For full listing of the thirty-three "Gingrich senators" and their ideological scores, see table 1 in Sean W. Theriault and David W. Rhode, "The Gingrich Senators and Party Polarization in the U.S. Senate," working paper, https://webspace.utexas.edu/seanmt/Theriault-Rohde_2011_01_10.pdf.

39. Ronald Brownstein, "Nowhere to Hide," *National Journal*, April 14, 2012, 13–17.

40. Alex Roarty, "How the House Holds the Senate GOP Hostage," *National Journal*, March 3, 2013, http://www.nationaljournal.com//magazine/how-the-house-holds-the-senate-gop-hostage-20130303.

41. http://www.cnn.com/2012/11/14/politics/house-diversity.

42. Jonathan Chait, "Who Needs to Win to Win?," *New York*, February 3, 2013, http://nymag.com/news/features/republican-party-2013-2/.

43. Chris Palko, "The Consistent Vote-Splitting Pattern," *Campaigns and Elections*, January 31, 2013, http://www.campaignsandelections.com/campaign-insider/351122/the-consistent-votesplitting-pattern.thtml.

44. Alan I. Abramowitz, "U.S. Senate Elections in a Polarized Era," chap. 2 in *The U.S. Senate: From Deliberation to Dysfunction*, ed. Burdett A. Loomis (CQ Press, 2012), 30.

45. The amendment failed, 96 to 318 (House Amendment 1183 to H.R. 9, Roll call vote number 370, July 13, 2006).

46. Roll call #370 for H.R. 9, July 13, 2006, http://clerk.house.gov/evs /2006/roll370.xml.

47. Ari Berman, "Conservatives Take Aim at Voting Rights," *The Nation*, February 25, 2013, 11–17; "U.S. Supreme Court Strikes Down Part of the Voting Rights Act," Project on Fair Representation press release, June 25, 2013, http://www.projectonfairrepresentation.org/wp-content/uploads/2008/08 /POFR-Shelby-Co-Press-release-SCOTUS.pdf.

48. The Brennan Center for Justice (http://www.brennancenter.org/analysis/voter-id) has conducted a series of studies about the history and prevalence of voter fraud and the potential implications of voter ID restrictions.

49. Emily Bazelon, "Why No One Should Have to Wait Two Hours to Vote," *Slate*, November 5, 2012, http://www.slate.com/articles/news_and_politics/politics/2012/11/early_voting_republicans_have_tried_to_restrict_access _to_voting_for_partisan.html.

50. http://tpmdc.talkingpointsmemo.com/2010/05/tea-party-call-to-repeal -the-17th-amendment-causing-problems-for-gop-candidates.php; http://www .rollcall.com/news/GOP-Senate-Candidates-Advocate-17th-Amendment-Repeal-216856-1.html; http://www.thenation.com/article/163548/rick-perrys -attack-democracy.

51. Obama would have won initial election in 2008 under nationwide use of the Maine-Nebraska rule because he carried twenty-eight states, 242 House districts, and the District of Columbia for a hypothetical total of 301 electors.

52. http://www.slate.com/blogs/weigel/2013/01/25/michigan_republican _says_that_electoral_vote_rigging_was_only_nixed_in_2012.html.

53. http://www.washingtonpost.com/politics/republicans-in-virginia-other -states-seeking-electoral-college-changes/2013/01/24/430096e6-6654-11e2 -85f5-a8a9228e55e7_story.html.

54. http://tcf.org/blog/detail/graph-why-we-need-filibuster-reform; http:// www.newyorker.com/online/blogs/hendrikhertzberg/2012/11/elections-and -the-filibuster.html.

55. Ezra Klein, "Let's Talk," *New Yorker*, January 28, 2013, 24–29.

56. http://www.whitehouse.gov/blog/2013/03/05/senate-delays-impacting -our-judicial-system.

57. Dan Friedman, "Role Reversal," *National Journal*, July 21, 2012, 19.

58. Interview with author, May 13, 2011.

59. Quoted in Steve Coll, "Gusher," *New Yorker*, April 12, 2012, 30.

60. Linda Killian, *The Freshmen: What Happened to the Republican Revolution?* (Westview, 1998), 238.

61. Lincoln Chafee, *Against the Tide: How a Compliant Congress Empowered a Reckless President* (Thomas Dunne Books, 2008), 54.

62. Thomas E. Mann and Norman J. Ornstein, *The Broken Branch: How Congress Is Failing America and How to Get It Back on Track* (Oxford University Press, 2006), 215.

63. Philip A. Klinkner and Thomas F. Schaller, "A Regional Analysis of the 2006 Midterms," *The Forum* 4, no. 3, (2006), article 9, http://www.degruyter.com/view/j/for.2006.4.3_20120105083451/for.2006.4.3/for.2006.4.3.1143/for.2006.4.3.1143.xml.

64. http://www.nationaljournal.com/daily/anger-with-congress-at-06-10-levels-20111212.

65. http://www.gallup.com/poll/163052/americans-confidence-congress-falls-lowest-record.aspx; http://www.cbsnews.com/8301-503544_162-20125482-503544/congressional-approval-at-all-time-low-of-9-according-to-new-cbs-news-new-york-times-poll/; http://www.rasmussenreports.com/public_content/politics/mood_of_america/congressional_performance.

66. http://www.rasmussenreports.com/public_content/politics/general_politics/october_2013/78_want_to_throw_out_entire_congress_and_start_over.

67. Tal Kopan, "Poll: Blame the Republicans," *Politico*, July 12, 2013, http://www.politico.com/story/2013/07/republicans-president-obama-congress-poll-94078.html.

Chapter 7. Recover or Retrench?

1. http://www.rasmussenreports.com/public_content/politics/mood_of_america/congressional_performance.

2. See prologue to Robert Draper, *Do Not Ask What Good We Do: Inside the House of Representatives* (Free Press, 2012). The book was later republished with the new title *When the Tea Party Came to Town*.

3. Michael Grunwald, *The New New Deal: The Hidden Story of Change in the Obama Era* (Simon and Schuster, 2012).

4. Ibid., 198–202.

5. Garrett Epps, "How the Senate Filibuster Went Out-of-Control—and Who Can Rein It In," *The Atlantic*, December 27, 2012, http://www.theatlantic.com/national/archive/2012/12/how-the-senate-filibuster-went-out-of-control-and-who-can-rein-it-in/266645/.

6. Carl Hulse and Adam Nagourney, "Senate G.O.P. Leader Finds Weapon in Unity," *New York Times*, March 16, 2010.

7. Tim Dickinson, "How Republicans Rig the Game," *Rolling Stone*, November 21, 2013, http://www.rollingstone.com/politics/news/how-republicans-rig-the-game-20131111#ixzz2qxuqNYHt.

8. Joshua Green, "How Congress Wrecked a Smart Debt-Ceiling Fix," Bloomberg BusinessWeek.com, January 17, 2013, http://mobile.businessweek .com/articles/2013-01-17/how-congress-wrecked-a-smart-debt-ceiling-fix ?campaign_id=otbrn.bw.mf.

9. David A. Fahrenthold, Lori Montgomery, and Paul Kane, "In Debt Deal, the Triumph of the Old Washington," *Washington Post*, August 2, 2011.

10. Lori Montgomery, "Among GOP, Anti-tax Orthodoxy Runs Deep," *Washington Post*, June 5, 2011, http://www.washingtonpost.com/business/econ omy/among-gop-an-ironclad-anti-tax-orthodoxy/2011/06/02/AG90SgJH_ story.html?wpisrc=nl_politics.

11. Quoted in John Aloysius Farrell, "Boehner's Last Chance," *National Journal*, May 12, 2012, 19.

12. *Obama Maintains Approval Advantage, but GOP Runs Even on Key Issues*, Pew Research Center for People and the Press report, May 8, 2013, http://www .people-press.org/2013/05/08/obama-maintains-approval-advantage-but-gop -runs-even-on-key-issues/1/.

13. Chris Cillizza, "The Failure of the Farm Bill—and Why House Repub- licans Can't Be Led," *The Fix*, June 20, 2013, http://www.washingtonpost.com /blogs/the-fix/wp/2013/06/20/the-failure-of-the-farm-bill-and-why-house -republicans-cant-be-led/.

14. Robert Reich, "The Sequester and the Tea Party Plot," Nationofchange .org, March 2, 2013, http://www.nationofchange.org/sequester-and-tea-party -plot-1362231367.

15. http://thehill.com/homenews/house/330283-house-gop-says-sequester -is-leverage-in-next-budget-battle#ixzz2rEA9eD8W.

16. Charles Krauthammer, "A New Strategy for the GOP," *Washington Post*, January 18, 2013, A21.

17. "John Boehner Must Act on Immigration Now," editorial, *Washington Post*, November 19, 2013, http://www.washingtonpost.com/opinions/john -boehner-must-act-on-immigration-now/2013/11/19/e8ab56f8-4d80-11e3 -be6b-d3d28122e6d4_story.html; Elise Foley, "Farm Bill Failure Shows John Boehner's Tight Spot on Immigration," HuffingtonPost.com, June 20, 2013, http://www.huffingtonpost.com/2013/06/20/farm-bill-john-boehner_n _3474478.html; Charles Babington, "What Now for Embattled Speaker John Boehner?," *Capitol Hill Blue*, October 17, 2013, http://www.capitolhillblue.com /node/49697; Stephen Moore, "Boehner's Immigration Pickle," *Wall Street Jour- nal*, June 19, 2013, http://online.wsj.com/news/articles/SB10001424127887324 57790457855222774620526.

18. Jennifer Harper, "Newt Gingrich: John Boehner's Job as House Speaker '10 Times' the Challenge He Once Faced," *Washington Times*, October 18,

2013, http://www.washingtontimes.com/blog/watercooler/2013/oct/18/newt
-gingrich-john-boehners-job-house-speaker-10-t/#ixzz2peAnaG73.

19. Ryan Lizza, "The House of Pain," *New Yorker*, March 4, 2013, 39.

20. T. W. Farnam, "GOP's Midterm Gains Concentrated in Blue-Collar Areas," *Washington Post*, November 21, 2010, A4.

21. Susan Davis, "The Overseer," *National Journal,* October 22, 2011, 19.

22. Paul Kane, "With White House on Heels, Watchdog Issa Is Having His Day," *Washington Post*, May 16, 2013.

23. Dana Milbank, "The GOP's Final Option: The I-Word," *Washington Post*, December 4, 2013, A14.

24. Quoted in John Aloysius Farrell, "Boehner's Last Chance," *National Journal*, May 12, 2012, 19.

25. Paul Kane, "For 2014, GOP May Elect to Be Cautious," *Washington Post*, December 6, 2013, A1.

26. Michael O'Brien, "Boehner Lashes Out at Conservative Groups on Budget Deal," NBC News, December 11, 2013, http://nbcpolitics.nbcnews .com/_news/2013/12/11/21863224-boehner-lashes-out-at-conservative-groups -on-budget-deal?lite.

27. Kenneth S. Baer, *Reinventing Democrats: The Politics of Liberalism from Reagan to Clinton* (University Press of Kansas, 2000).

28. Thomas F. Schaller, "What Ever Happened to Moderate Republicans?," *American Prospect*, December 2007, 29–34.

29. Ashley Parker, "A G.O.P. Moderate in the Middle . . . of a Jam," *New York Times*, October 7, 2013, http://www.nytimes.com/2013/10/08/us/politics /a-gop-moderate-in-the-middle-of-a-jam.html?pagewanted=all.

30. Geoffrey Kabaservice, "The Moderates Who Lighted the Fuse," *New York Times*, October 3, 2013.

31. Craig Shirley and Donald Devine, "Trust Us, Karl Rove Is No Conservative," *Washington Post*, April 4, 2010, B5; Jay Newton-Small, "Jim DeMint: Moving the Republican Brand to the Right," *Time*, May 20, 2010.

32. *Inside the GOP: Report on Focus Groups with Evangelical, Tea Party, and Moderate Republicans*, Democracy Corps report published by Stanley Greenberg, James Carville, and Erica Seifert, October 3, 2013, http://www.democracy corps.com/Republican-Party-Project/inside-the-gop-report-on-focus-groups -with-evangelical-tea-party-and-moderate-republicans/#sthash.wBATaa3e .dpuf.

33. E-mail exchange with author, January 11, 2014.

34. Michael Gerson, "Curbing the Tea Party," *Washington Post*, November 5, 2013, A19.

35. John Kraushaar, "Growth Industry," *National Journal*, September 17, 2011, 29.

36. Dana Milbank, "John Roberts, Meet Jacob Marley," *Washington Post*, January 5, 2014, A11.

37. E. J. Dionne Jr., "Republican Crossroads: To Govern or to Fight?," *Washington Post*, December 19, 2013.

38. http://www.opensecrets.org/outsidespending/disclosure.php.

39. David Wasserman, "The Republican Advantage," *Cook Political Report*, April 15, 2013, http://cookpolitical.com/story/5626; fuller explanation and details on computation of PVI available from *Cook Political Report* at http://cookpolitical.com/story/5604.

40. Ed Gillespie, "To Save the GOP, Look to the States," *Washington Post*, October 20, 2013, B5.

41. Paul Kane, "Some Republicans Think Next Nominee Must Be a Governor," *Washington Post*, November 21, 2013, A7.

42. Josh Eidelson, "GOP Is 'Crazy and Awful': The Josh Barro Republicans Are Displeased," *Salon*, October 17, 2013, http://www.salon.com/2013/10/17/gop_is_crazy_and_awful_the_josh_barro_republicans_are_displeased/?source=newsletter.

ACKNOWLEDGMENTS

This book is not the one I set out to write. My original conceit was to discuss the often beneficial but sometimes rocky relationship between the Republican Party and the conservative movement from the start of the first Bush administration to the end of the second Bush administration. The specific plan was to chronicle the tensions between the party and the movement through the recollections of three distinct but authoritative participant-observers of this period: Republican everywhereman (and now U.S. Senate candidate) Ed Gillespie, antitax movement leader Grover Norquist, and centrist former New Jersey governor Christine Todd Whitman.

As I proceeded to interview Gillespie, Norquist, and Whitman, I quickly came to two realizations: first, that I'm neither a reporter nor a historian, but a political scientist more comfortable making arguments than writing chronicles; and, second, that I was proceeding toward an incorrect, or at least incomplete, argument about the party's rightward shift during the post-Reagan era. And then the right argument hit me: The Republican Party's move to the right and its increasing competitiveness in congressional elections created a feedback loop in which the GOP became more comfortable with congressional rule as it became more conservative, and became more conservative because it ruled Congress.

Whether or not any or all three agree with this argument and the related conclusions I draw, my first debt of gratitude goes to Gillespie, Norquist, and Whitman for helping me, even if unwittingly, rethink this project. And thanks, too, to their helpful deputies: Andrea Ueckele and Paul Logan for Gillespie; John Kartch for Norquist; and Heather Grizzle for Whitman.

My second and equally large debt is to my Yale University Press editor, Bill Frucht, for allowing me to shift direction midcourse and for sticking with me as I rewrote huge chunks of the manuscript. He was encouraging yet patient, and never wavered in his support of this project—even in those moments when I did. He offered countless helpful suggestions that shaped the book's new argument and its narrative execution. And although I consider myself an economical writer, Bill is a ruthlessly efficient line editor nonpareil; he pared a too-long first draft of the manuscript down to the word limit without losing any of the book's meaning or argument. That he is also a generous and thoughtful person—and fun to talk politics with—was only a bonus. His team at Yale, including Jaya Chatterjee and Mary Pasti, is superb.

Along the way, I also benefited from comments and contributions generously provided to me by a variety of politically astute academics, analysts, and reporters, including Sean Aday, Matt Barreto, Michael Cohen, Tom Edsall, Froma Harrop, Chris Hayes, Jeet Heer, Kenneth Janda, Ezra Klein, Joe Klein, Robin Kolodny, Kyle Kondik, Alex Koppelman, Steve Kornacki, Ray La Raja, Ryan Lizza, David Lublin, Walter Ludwig, Larry Sabato, Mark Schmitt, Gary

Segura, Walter Shapiro, Nate Silver, Jeff Stanger, Sean Theriault, Greg Veis, Paul Waldman, David Wasserman, and Julian Zelizer.

I was also blessed with support from administrators and colleagues at the University of Maryland, Baltimore County, where I teach. President Freeman Hrabowski, Provost Philip Rous, and Deans John Jeffries (past) and Scott Casper (present) provided resources and encouragement, as did former political science department chair Devin Hagerty and current chair Jeffrey Davis. Department colleagues Laura Hussey and Tyson King-Meadows offered useful ideas and insights for the manuscript. Lisa Akchin, Max Cole, and the rest of UMBC's public relations team were helpful, as ever. I'm also grateful to several UMBC undergraduates who helped with research, data collection, and fact-checking: Max Barnhardt, Brian Frazee, Samirah Hassan, Eliot Johnson, Katrina Smith, Virgil Thomas, and, most especially, Hannah Dier. And I owe a special recognition to Cheryl Miller, a member of our department and recently retired associate dean, who has long served as my mentor and friend. As a teacher, I also want to recognize and thank the teachers who were important influences in my development as a scholar and a person: the late Marge Dinova of Bethlehem Central High School; Ron Davis at SUNY-Plattsburgh; John Kares Smith of SUNY-Oswego; and my dissertation supervisor at the University of North Carolina, Mike Munger (now at Duke University).

Finally, I want to thank Will Lippincott, my indispensable agent for this book and *Whistling Past Dixie*. Will has navigated my publishing career with passion, skill, and grace. He is a fine agent and an even better person. That's two books so far, my friend: I'm up for another if you are.

INDEX

Abortion question, 1996 convention and, 123
Abraham, Spencer, 108, 165
Abramoff, Jack, 186–188
Abramowitz, Alan, 256
Abrams, Elliott, 141
Adelson, Sheldon, 291
Advocacy groups, conservative, 296
An Affair of State (Posner), 154–155
Affirmative action, Bush's reversals on, 50–51
Affordable Care Act (Obamacare, 2010), 4, 9, 11, 236, 282–283
Age differences in voting patterns, 228
The Agenda (Woodward), 112–113
Ailes, Roger, 47
Akin, Todd, 253, 259
Allard, Wayne, 139, 252
Allen, George, 109, 165

Amash, Justin, 282
American Campaign Academy, 49
American Family Association, 35
American Israeli Political Action Committee, 190
American Legislative Exchange Council, 258
American Political Science Association, 159
American Prospect (Schaller), 290
American Recovery and Reinvestment Act (stimulus plan, 2009), 274–275
Americans for a Republican Majority (ARMPAC), 204
Americans for Tax Reform, 58–59
American Taxpayer Relief Act (2013), 281
Angle, Sharron, 14, 253
Anti-gay vitriol, 128–129

Apportionment advantage, in Senate, 243–245

Armey, Dick: on Bush's presidency, 265; Clinton administration, relations with, 104, 148; and Darman, 92; DeLay, views on, 90–91; and Gillespie, 40; Gingrich, coup attempt against, 150; as GOP leader, 294; House Republican Conference, fight for chairmanship of, 89–92; and Livingston-Hastert battle for speakership, 152; no new taxes pledge, 62; and prescription drug benefit, 175–176; president, policy influence on, 250; retirement, 173

ARMPAC (Americans for a Republican Majority), 204

Ashcroft, John, 165

Atwater, Lee, 47, 71, 75, 86

Ayotte, Kelly, 287

Bachman, Michele, 16, 221, 222, 223, 282

Baer, Kenneth, 289

Baker, Howard, 243, 266

Baker, James, 40, 67

Baker, Peter, 146, 147

Baker, Ross, 194

Balanced-budget amendment, 11, 94–95

Ballot access, restrictions on, 258–259

Balz, Dan, 133–134, 161

Banking scandal, House of Representatives, 80–81, 96, 183

BarackOFraudo.com, 303n1

Barbour, Haley, 123, 132–133

Barnes, Fred, 141

Barr, Bob, 129, 157

Barreto, Matt, 12

Barro, Josh, 299

Bass, Charlie, 290

Bayh, Birch, 39

Bazelon, Emily, 258–259

BCRA (Bipartisan Campaign Reform Act, McCain-Feingold, 2002), 200–203, 294

Beck, Glenn, 25

Before the Storm (Perlstein), 27–28

Bennet, Michael, 20–21

Bennett, Bob, 14, 148–149, 293

Benton, Jesse, 14–15

Bentsen, Lloyd, 43

Berke, Richard, 137

Bernanke, Ben, 281

Beutler, Brian, 15

Bicameral party strength ratio, 248–249

Bickerstaff, Steve, 205

Biden, Joe, 280

Big Agriculture, 179

Big-government conservatism, 178

Bin Laden, Osama, 169

Bipartisan Campaign Reform Act (BCRA, McCain-Feingold, 2002), 200–203, 294

Bipartisan supercommittee, 280

Birnbaum, Jeffrey, 183

Bisek, Callista, 147

Black Monday, 60

Blanco, Kathleen Babineaux, 211

Bloomberg polls on Obama's approval ratings, 3

Blunt, Roy, 184, 215

Boehner, John: and congressional page scandal, 215; on conservative advocacy groups, 296; difficulties faced by, 284–289, 296; and election of 2012, 224; on gay candidates, support of, 210; and gerrymandering, 8; Gingrich, coup attempt against, 150; on government shutdown, 283; House-dominant coalition of, 249; as House majority leader, 246, 247–248; as House minority leader, 216, 217; immigration reform bill, position on, 22; on judging Congress, 234; prescription drug benefit, support for, 177; radicals, lack of restraint of, 292; on Republican agenda, 239; Senate companion, lack of, x; tea party movement's impact on, 18–19

Bond, Rich, 124

Border Security, Economic Opportunity, and Immigration Modernization Act (2013), 21

Boschwitz, Rudy, 55

Bosnian conflict, 141

Boxer, Barbara, 65–66

Bradley, Bill, 56–58

Brady, Nicholas, 59–60

Branstad, Terry, 298

The Breach (Baker), 146, 147

Brennan, William, 48

Brennan Center for Justice, 321n48

Brewer, Jan, 299

Brians, Craig Leonard, 227

Broadrick, Juanita, 155

Broder, David, 61, 63, 98–99, 100

Brownback, Sam, 139

Brownstein, Ron, 133–134

Buchanan, Pat, 62, 68–71, 76–77, 123–124, 141

Buck, Ken, 14, 253

Buckley, William F., 55

Budget battles, (1990), 60–61

Budget performance–based merit pay, 94–95

Building Red America (Edsall), 110

Bunning, Jim, 252, 313n29

Burnham, James, 232–233, 236

Burns, Conrad, 55, 188

Burton, Dan, 147, 174, 287

Bush, George Herbert Walker (Bush 41): congressional Republicans, relationship with, 265–266; and Gingrich, 135; and Gulf War, 64–66; intraparty problems under, 87–88; and Jeffords, 163; policy reversals, 47–52; presidential bid (1980), 32–33; presidential nomination acceptance speech, 83; Reagan compared with, 78; Reagan vs. (in 1988), 31–32; reelection campaign, 75–79, 85–87; and Robertson, 33–38; as San Diego convention speaker, 126; tax policies, reversals on, 59–64, 69, 70; vice presidential running mate of, 39–42, 43

Bush, George W. (Bush 43): and congressional Republicans, 122, 195–196, 218, 265–266; and DeLay, 207; election victory, 170–171, 229; father's reelection defeat, responses to, 88–89; and Jeffords, 164; judicial appointees by, 262; and Lott, 193; presidential campaign (2000), 158–164, 168; reelection, 171–172; as San Diego convention chair, 125; seniors, support from, 173; signing statements, use of, 52; TARP program, 10; tea party movement's views on, 13; as Texas governor, 109, 148; and 2006 midterm

Bush, George W. (Bush 43) (cont.)
elections, 212–213, 214; white
vote for, impact of, 301–302
Bush, Jeb, 24, 27, 88, 109, 141
Bush, Laura, 126
Bush, memo to, 75
The Bush Tragedy (Weisberg), 89
Buyer, Steve, 174
Byrd, Robert, 43

Cabinet departments, tea party
movement's views on, 11
Cain, Herman, 221
Campaign finance reform, battle
over, 199–203
Campaigns and Elections (Palko), 255
Campbell, Ben Nighthorse, 165
Cannon, Chris, 146, 157
Cantor, Eric, 177, 274, 285, 286
Cap-and-trade regulation, 11
Capitol Hill. *See* Congress
Carey, George W., 232–233
Carney, Jay, 23, 150–151
Carter, Jimmy, 2, 35
Caucus voters (GOP), conservatism
of, 7
CBN (Christian Broadcast Network),
33–34
Centrists: in GOP, lack of, 290–291;
in Senate, elimination of, 138
Chafee, John, 101
Chafee, Lincoln, 265
Chait, Jonathan, 254–255
Chambers, Dean, 2
Change They Can't Believe In (Parker
and Barreto), 12
Cheese Factories on the Moon (Frisch
and Kelly), 181–182
Cheney, Dick: on Bush 43 presiden-
tial candidacy, 160; on deficits, 63;

and GOP Senate control, 170; and
Gulf War, 64; on Iraq War, 67–68;
and PNAC, 143; and Project for a
New American Century, 141;
responses to election of, 265
Chenoweth, Helen, 147
Children's Health Insurance
Program Reauthorization
Act, 274
Chocola, Chris, 295
Christian Broadcast Network
(CBN), 33–34
Christian conservatives, 35–36
Christie, Chris, 222, 299
Church, Frank, 39
Cillizza, Chris, 282
Citizens Against Government
Waste, 180–181
Citizens for a Sound Economy, 175
Citizens United (2010), 294–295, 296
Climate change, tea party move-
ment's views on, 11
Clinton, Bill: on Bush 41's tax
reversal, 75; control of Democratic
Party by, 289; and DOMA, 128,
130; election of, GOP responses
to, 85–89; foreign policy criticisms
of, 141–142; Gingrich on, 91, 300;
and government shutdown (1995),
111–117; impeachment, 144–149,
154–158, 168; and Iraq Liberation
Act, 142; and Jeffords, 163;
post-Reagan era role, 117;
presidential campaign (1992), 63;
reelection, 130–131; Republicans'
impact on, 122; same-sex
marriage, opposition to, 126
Clinton, Hillary, 77, 98, 100
Club for Growth, 295
Coats, Dan, 100

Coburn, Tom, 129, 252, 274
Codel (congressional delegation)
    trips, 190–191
Coelho, Tony, 53, 185
Cold War, end of, 67
Cole, Tom, 22, 80, 286
Collins, Susan, 165, 275
Commerce Department, tea party
    movement's views on, 11
Concerned Women for America, 35
Condit, Gary, 211
Confessore, Nicholas, 184–185
Conflict-based narratives, 10
Confrontation, Armey on, 90
Congress: congressional delegation
    ("codel") trips, 190–191; and
    congressional rule, conservatism,
    232–242; control of, role of tax
    issues in, 56–58; divided, x, 225;
    dysfunction of, Republican
    association with, 272; end of
    Democratic hegemony in, 74;
    gender changes in, 42; majorities
    in, presidency vs., 132; page
    scandal, 214–215; polarization of,
    168; public opinion on, 267;
    reelection rates, 93–94; Republi-
    can staffers, 44–45; Republican
    stronghold in, as liability, xi;
    structural reforms of, GOP call
    for, 94. See also Congressional
    Republicans; House of Represen-
    tatives; Senate; number of indi-
    vidual session (e.g., 110th Congress)
Congress and the American Political
    Tradition (Burnham), 232
Congress-centered government,
    232–233
Congress-centric party, GOP as,
    219–268; congressionalization,

partisan costs of, 263–268;
    congressional Republicans, rise of,
    224–231; conservatism and
    congressional rule, 232–242;
    House-ification of GOP, 246–251;
    minority-majority Republican
    Senate, 242–245; overview, x–xi,
    8–9, 219–224; partisan institu-
    tionalism, 256–263; Senate,
    House-ification of, 251–256. See
    also Congressional chokehold on
    GOP, recovery from
Congressional Black Caucus, 23, 190
Congressional Budget Office, 25
Congressional chokehold on GOP,
    recovery from, 269–302; Boehner,
    difficulties faced by, 284–289;
    congressional power as locked-in,
    293–297; Democratic Leadership
    Council, lack of analogue for,
    289–293; Obamanomics, obstruc-
    tion of, 278–284; Obama's
    election, responses to, 273–277;
    overview, 269–273; recovery vs.
    retrenchment, 297–302
Congressional elections. See Elections
Congressional Republicans: during
    Bush's presidency, 70–71;
    conservative, x; control of GOP
    by, 72; presidential candidates vs.,
    x, 161–162; retrenchment path to
    party recovery, benefits for, 28;
    rise of, 224–231; tactics under
    Gingrich, 101–105
Connecticut, Democratic Senators
    from, 166–167
Conservatism. See Conservatives and
    conservatism
The Conservative Affirmation
    (Kendall), 232

Conservative Digest on Gingrich, 43–44
Conservative Opportunity Society, 44, 91
Conservative Opportunity Society speech (Gingrich), 44
Conservative Political Action Committee, 45
Conservatives and conservatism: on Bush 41, 71, 86–88; and congressional rule, 232–242; conservatism and congressional rule, 232–242; conservative advocacy groups, Boehner on, 296; conservative agenda, public support for, 172; conservative congressional Republicans, x; conservative opportunities and opportunism, 43–47; conservative talk show hosts, 296; GOP, tipping point of relations with, x, 117–120; on government, 235–236; on immigration reform, 20; modern, Congress's importance to, 232–233; on Obama, 12; on presidency vs. congressional majorities, 132
Constitutional amendment on flag burning, 49
Constitutional originalism, 232
Continetti, Matthew, 185
Contract with America, 105–107, 115
Cook, Charlie, 297
Coolidge, Calvin, 235
Cooper, Matthew, 10
Coors, Joseph, 291
Corker, Bob, 21, 274
Coulter, Ann, 25
Coverdell, Paul, 166
Cox, Christopher, 92–93, 177

Craddick, Tom, 204–205
Craig, Larry, 208–209
Creative destruction (in GOP), 31–72; and Bradley-Whitman contest, 56–59; Buchanan's insurgent presidential campaign, 68–71; Bush 41, policy reversals of, 47–52; Bush 41 and Robertson, 33–38; Bush 41 broken tax promise, 59–64; gender disparity with Democrats, 41–43; and Gingrich, 43–47; Gulf and Iraq Wars, 64–68; overview, 31–33; Quayle as vice presidential candidate, 39–42, 43; race and redistricting, 52–55; Reagan-Bush presidential coalition, end of, 71–72
Crist, Charlie, 14, 26–27, 290, 292
Crowley, Michael, 187
Cruz, Ted, 236, 281–282, 287
C-SPAN, 45–46
Culture-war politics, immigration reform and, 20
Cunningham, Duke, 207
Cuomo, Mario, 109
Currie, Bettie, 144

Dallas GOP national convention (1984), 48
D'Amato, Al, 147
Darman, Richard ("Dick"), 59, 62, 63, 92
Daschle, Tom, 154, 157, 164
Davis, Susan, 287
Davis, Tom, 287
DC Madam scandal, 211
Deal, Nathan, 165
The Death of American Virtue (Gormley), 148–149
Deaver, Michael, 123

Debt ceiling, battle over, 279–280
Defense of Marriage Act (DOMA, 1996), 127–128
Deficits, impact of, 278
DeHaven, Tad, 180
DeLay, Tom: and Abramoff scandal, 189–190; and Bush 43, 161, 266; career of, 173; on CNN, 173; on earmarks, 181; ethics, approach to, 189; Gingrich, coup attempt against, 150; Gradison, battle with, 89–90; "Hot Tub Tom," 173, 174; K Street lobbyists, relations with, 110, 185–186; and Livingston-Hastert battle for speakership, 152, 153–154; as majority leader, 172–173; as majority whip, 109–110, 185; and Medicare Part D, 172–178; political career, end of, 206–207; scandals, involvement in, 203, 206; Texas legislature, battle for control of, 203–207
DeMint, Jim, 252, 274, 292
Democracy Corps, 293
Democratic Congressional Campaign Committee, 202
Democratic Leadership Council (DLC), 56, 78, 289–293
Democratic Party and Democrats: centrist moves by, benefits of, 290–291; GOP critiques of, 93; immigration reform, views on, 19–20; lobbyists, relations with, 185; during Reagan presidency, 289; urban clustering of voters, 247; women in, 42. See also Clinton, Bill; Obama, Barack
Devine, Doug, 292
Dewine, Mike, 108

Dick, Kirby, 209
Dickinson, Tim, 277
Diggs, Charles, 44
Dionne, E. J., 296
DiVall, Linda, 157, 160
Divided Congresses, x, 225
Divided government, 239–241, 272–273
DLC (Democratic Leadership Council), 56, 78, 289–293
Dobson, James, 35
Dole, Bob: foreign policy criticisms of, 141–142; at Iowa presidential caucuses, 33; and Jeffords, 164; as majority leader, 108; as moderate, 138–139; as possible Bush running mate, 40; presidential campaign (1996), 124, 125, 130–136; presidential candidacy, possibilities of, 36–37; resignation as Senate majority leader, 122; Senate career of, 136, 216, 243
Dole, Elizabeth, 126
DOMA (Defense of Marriage Act, 1996), 127–128
Domestic policy issues, 213
Do Not Ask What Good We Do (Draper), 273–274
Do Nothing Eightieth Congress, 234
Do nothing (opposition, resistance, not-going-along, party of no) strategy, 98, 99, 104–105, 274–276, 300–301
Don't ask, don't tell policy, 127
Doolittle, John, 188
Dornan, Bob, 128, 129
Draft Robertson for President Committee, 34
Draper, Robert, 273–274
DREAM Act children, 23

Drudge, Matt, 144
Duberstein, Kenneth, 123
Dubose, Lou, 153–154
Dukakis, Michael, 41, 77, 87, 247
Du Pont, Pete, 46, 130
Durbin, Dick, 21
Dwyre, Diana, 201

Early voting, restrictions on, 258–259
Earmarks (pork barrel spending), 80, 81–82, 180–182
Economic policy battles, during Obama era, 278–284
Edsall, Thomas, 7, 45, 110
Education Department, tea party movement's views on, 11
Edwards, Chris, 180
Edwards, John, 147
Edwards, Lee, 44
Edwards, Mickey, 79–81, 84–85, 182
Ehrlich, Bob, 114
80th Congress, 234
83rd Congress, 224, 245, 251, 252
88 Club, 34
Eisenhower, Dwight, 71, 117, 171
Elections: 1988 and 1990 Senate, 55; 1992 congressional elections, 89, 92–97; 1994 midterms, 105–111; 2000 congressional elections, 165–166; 2006 midterms, 166, 212–215; 2010 midterms, 3, 15–16; congressional, Republican success in, ix–x; GOP share of presidential and congressional, 225–227. See also Gerrymandering; Obama, Barack; Presidential campaigns and elections
Electoral College, 6, 259–260

Electorate, demographic changes to, 257
Elephant's Edge (Taylor), 182
Emerson, Jo Ann, 174
Empower America, 175
The End of Liberalism (Lowi), 183
Energy Department, tea party movement's views on, 11
Engler, John, 124
Ensign, John, 274, 313n29
Entitlement programs, public support for, 112, 113, 117
Environmental Protection Agency, DeLay on, 173
Erickson, Erick, 175
Establishment Republicans, 13, 27
Estes, Todd, 224
Ethics and ethics scandals, 176–177, 188–189, 207–212
Evangelicals, influence in GOP, 35

Faircloth, Lauch, 147
Fallin, Mary, 299
Falwell, Jerry, 35
Farm bills, 179–180
Farmers, support for Republicans, 178–179
Federal government: as a business, 185–186; shutdowns of, 111–117, 282–283, 288, 291; tea party movement's views on role of, 9–10, 12
Federalist Papers, 233
Federalist Society, 87
Feedback loop, ideological, x
Feehery, John, 175, 196
Feeney, John, 188
Feeney, Tom, 176, 216–217
Feingold, Russ, 14, 200, 293
Fenno, Richard, 85

Ferraro, Geraldine, 41
Feulner, Ed, 43, 44
Fierce, Don, 132
Filibusters, 216–217, 233–234, 242, 261–263, 276
Fiscal cliff, 280–281
Fiscal deficits, impact of, 278
Fischer, Deb, 287
Flag burning, 47–50, 51
Flake, Jeff, 21
Fleischer, Ari, 193
Florida: Bush's reelection results, 79; and Electoral College, 260
Florio, Jim, 57
Flynt, Larry, 153
Focus on the Family, 35
Foley, Mark, 214–215
Foley, Tom, 53, 105, 189, 197
Forbes, Randy, 210, 288
Ford, Gerald, 126, 149
Foreign policy, changes to, 141–144
Fourteenth Amendment, tea party movement's views on, 10–11
Frank, Barney, 211
Franking privilege, 80
Franzen, Jonathan, 196, 198–199
Freedom Council, 34
Freedom of Information Act, 180
Freedom Works, 175
Friess, Foster, 291
Frisch, Scott, 181–182
Frist, Bill, 194, 243
Front porch campaigns, 160
Frum, David, 193–194
Fukuyama, Francis, 141
Fund-raising, political. *See* Campaign finance reform

Galen, Rich, 49
Gallup polls, 239–240, 267–268

Gang of Eight, 20–21, 23
Garfield, James, 36, 223
Gay marriage, debate over, 127–130
Gender gap (gender disparity), 41–43, 124–126
The Gentleman from Georgia (Steely), 68
Gephardt, Dick, 33, 279
Gephardt Rule, 279
Gergen, David, 113
Gerrymandering, 8, 23–24, 54–55, 198, 203–206, 247
Gerson, Michael, 27, 295
Gillespie, Ed: on Armey's win over Lewis, 90; on Bush (41), 63; on GOP, rift in, 298; as Quayle, 40; and Redistricting Majority Project, 277; at RNC, 123, 132–133
Gilman, Benjamin, 144
Gingrich, Newt: attempted coup against, 149–151; and Bush 41, 63, 75; and Clinton impeachment, 146–147, 148; and Congress-centered government, xi, 30, 233; DeLay, views on, 90–91; Dole, relationship with, 131–136; domestic agenda, focus on, 68; on earmarks, 181; on Edwards's loss, 81; and ethics, 189; foreign policy criticisms of, 142; Gingrich Revolution, 284; as GOP leader, 74–75, 294; and government shutdown (1995), 111–117; on Hastert, 198–199; and health care reform, 98–101; House career, 83–84, 101–105, 122; Kabaservice on, 292; Kemp, comparison with, 37; legacy of, 300; and midterm elections (1994), 105, 229;

Gingrich, Newt (cont.)
opportunism of, 43–47; and
prescription drug benefit, 175;
president, policy influence on,
250; as presidential challenger to
Romney, 221, 222, 223; proce-
dural changes by, 279; Reagan
administration, influence on, 135;
at Republican strategy dinner,
274; on Ryan's budget plan, 250;
on Speaker's job, difficulty of, 285;
Steely on, 68; strategic choices of,
presidential impact of, 271
Gingrich senators, 139–140, 173,
251–252, 290
The Gingrich Senators (Theriault and
Rhode), 139–140, 251–252
Gitell, Seth, 202
Glickman, Dan, 179
Gohmert, Louie, 22
Goldwater movement, 27
Goldwater-Reagan model, 88
GOP. *See* Republican Party and
Republicans
GOPAC (political action commit-
tee), 46, 91
GOP report (*Growth and Opportunity
Project*, RNC), x, 4–5, 7, 29–30,
289, 298
Gore, Al, 85–89, 158–164, 168, 289
Gormley, Ken, 148–149, 156
Gorton, Slade, 165
Government's End (Rauch), 183
Governorships, 255, 299
Gradison, Bill, 89–90
Graham, Lindsey, 21
Gramm, Phil, 100, 139, 156, 173,
203
Grams, Rod, 165
Grass-roots activists, 295

Graubard, Stephen, 66
Gray, C. Boyden, 93
Green, Joshua, 230, 231, 279
Green, Matthew, 288
Greenberg, Stanley, 107
Greenberg Traurig, 187
Grose, Christian, 213
Grotberg, John, 152
Growth and Opportunity Project (*GOP*
report), x, 4–5, 7, 29–30, 289, 298
Grunwald, Michael, 274–275, 278
Guinier, Lani, 104
Gulf War (Operation Desert Storm),
64–68, 70
Gunderson, Steve, 127–128

Haass, Richard, 64
Haley, Nikki, 299
Hall, Ralph, 205
Hallow, Ralph, 124
Hamilton-Gradison Commission,
97
The Hammer. *See* DeLay, Tom
The Hammer Comes Down (Dubose
and Reid), 153–154
Hard-money donations, 200–201
Harris, John, 116, 145–146
Harris Interactive polls, on divided
government, 239
Haspel, Moshe, 202–203
Hastert, Dennis: Bush 43, influence
on, 266; and congressional page
scandal, 214–215; on earmarks,
181; and House speakership,
151–154, 162, 168, 195–199; on
McCain Feingold, 201; and Medi-
care prescription drug benefit,
174, 176
Hastert Rule, 196–198
Hatch, Orrin, 293

Hawkins, Paula, 42

Hayes, Jimmy, 165

Health care reform, 98–101. *See also* Affordable Care Act

Hensarling, Jeb, 16, 274

Herding Cats (Lott), 157

Heritage Foundation, 43, 44, 92–93

Hoekstra, Pete, 259, 274

Hoeven, John, 21

Homosexuals and homosexuality, 12, 129–130, 288

Honest Leadership and Open Government Act (2007), 191

Hook, Janet, 23

Hostettler, John, 174

Houghton, Amo, 149

House of Representatives: African Americans in, 55; banking scandal, 80–81, 96, 183; Democratic caucus, 28, 254; ethics committee, 176–177, 188–189; freshman classes, size of, 92–93; Judiciary Committee, 146; majority rule in, vs. in Senate, 262–263; party control of, 132; Republican caucus, non-diversity of, 254, 300; as Republican stronghold, x, 231; Tea Party Caucus, 16; 2010 election, 15–16; years of Republican control of, 224–225. *See also* House Republicans

House Republicans and Republican Conference: bad political vs. good electoral arguments for, 23; on Bush's tax plan, 90; conservatism of, 28; demographics of members' districts, 286–287; fight for chairmanship of, 16, 89–92;

Hastert's influence on, 196; inexperience of, 285–286; politics, approach to, 287–288; presidential nominees vs., performance of, 226–227; presidential politics, influence on, 124; strength of, x, 231, 271

Houston GOP national convention (1992), 70, 75–79

Huckabee, Mike, 221

Hulse, Carl, 276

Human Genome Project, 181

Hume, Sandy, 139

Humphrey, Hubert, 228

Hurricane Andrew, 79

Hussein, Saddam, 64, 67, 142

Hutchinson, Kay Bailey, 161, 203

Hutchinson, Tim, 139

Hyde, Henry, 129, 144–145, 147, 148, 157, 196

Hyperpluralism, 183

Idaho Statesman, 208

Identity groups, 77–78

Ideological feedback loop, x

Ideological self-marginalization, x

Immigration reform, 5–6, 11, 19–25

Impeachment. *See* Clinton, Bill; Obama, Barack

Incumbents, 14, 223

Independent voters, support for divided government, 240–241

Indiana, Bayh vs. Quayle in, 39

Inhofe, James, 136, 252

Interest groups (K Street lobbyists), 110, 133, 183–191, 238–239

Internal Revenue Service, targeting scandal, 4

International Paper Company, 163

Iowa presidential caucuses, 33, 37, 221, 223
Iowa straw poll (1987), 34
Iraq and Iraq War, 67, 142, 212–215, 217
Isakson, Johnny, 313n29
Issa, Darrell, 287
Istook, Ernest "James," 80–81, 84, 90, 97, 182

Jacobson, Gary, 15
James, Fob, 109
Janda, Kenneth, 237–238
Jankowski, Chris, 277
Jeffords, James, 163, 243, 290
Jindal, Bobby, 299
Johnson, Gregory Lee, 48
Johnson, Haynes, 98–99, 100
Johnson, Lyndon, 69, 228
Johnson, Ron, 14
Jones, Paula, 144, 148–149
Jordan, Vernon, 144
Judiciary Committee, House of Representatives, 146
Judis, John, 224, 286
Junkets, domestic and foreign, 190–191

Kabaservice, Geoffrey, 27–28, 291–292
Kagan, Robert, 141–142
Kaplan, Rebecca, 10
Kassebaum, Nancy Landon, 42, 126
Kaye, Michael, 55
Keating, Frank, 109
Keene, David, 102
Kelly, Megyn, 2
Kelly, Sean, 181–182
Kemp, Jack: Bush 41, memo to, on taxes, 75; as GOP leader, 294;

House Republicans' letter on, 62–63; as possible Bush 41 running mate, 40; as possible presidential candidate, 36–37, 130; president, policy influence on, 250; Reagan administration, influence on, 135; as rising star, 33
Kendall, Willmoore, 232–234, 236, 242
Kennedy, John, 223
Kennedy, Ted, 50, 66, 108–109, 156, 211, 292–293
Kerry, John, 100, 214
Keynesian economics, 278
Kibbe, Matt, 295
Killian, Linda, 264
King, Peter, 292
King, Steve, 23, 177, 288
Kissinger, Henry, 141
Klein, Ezra, 261
Klinkner, Phil, 224, 266
Koch, David and Charles, 11, 291
Kolbe, Jim, 129
Kolodny, Robin, 201
Kraushaar, Josh, 295
Krauthammer, Charles, 86, 141, 283–284
Kriner, Douglas, 213
Kristol, Bill, 25, 99, 141–142
K Street lobbyists (interest groups), 110, 133, 183–191, 238–239
Kunstler, William, 48
Kuwait, 64, 65
Kyl, Jon, 137, 194, 252, 274

Labor movement, views on immigration reform, 20
LaHaye, Beverly, 35
Landrieu, Mary, 167
La Raja, Ray, 295

Latinos, 20, 23
Laughlin, Greg, 165
Leahy, Patrick, 163
Lee, Mike, 14, 259
Legacy (Lowry), 115
Legitimate rape, 253
Lessons Learned the Hard Way
   (Gingrich), 117
Lewinsky, Monica, 111, 121, 144
Lewis, Jerry, 89–92
Lieberman, Joe, 55, 167
Lilly Ledbetter Fair Pay Act, 274
Limbaugh, Rush, 87
Lincoln, Blanche, 167
Line-item veto, 94–95
Lines in the Sand (Bickerstaff), 205
Litmus tests, 50
Livingston, Robert Linlithgow, IV,
   145, 148, 151–154, 210
Lizza, Ryan, 250, 285–286
Lott, Trent: and Clinton impeach-
   ment, 154–158; congressional
   career, 55, 56, 108, 136–140,
   168, 170, 193, 194, 243; Dole on,
   131; and Gingrich, 44; as GOP
   leader, 294; and health care
   reform, 100; on majority leader-
   ship, 262; political arc of,
   191–195; strategic choices of,
   presidential impact of, 271;
   and 2000 election cycle, 166
Lowi, Theodore, 183
Lowry, Rich, 25, 115, 159, 222
Lublin, David, 53
Lugar, Dick, 42, 144
Lungren, Dan, 274
Luntz, Frank, 274

Mack, Connie, 165
Madigan, Edward, 90, 196

Magaziner, Ira, 98
Maine: Electoral College elector
   assignment method, 6, 259;
   Senators from, 167
Majority-minority districts, 53–54,
   93, 96, 230–231
Majority of the majority standard
   (for House legislation), 196–198
Malapportionment, 233–234, 256
Mann, Thomas, 17, 188, 265, 268
Mapmaking, race-based, 55
Martínez, Susana, 299
Mason, David, 102
Massachusetts, Democratic Senators
   from, 166–167
McCain, John: and Abramoff
   scandal, 188; bipartisanship of, 21;
   and Bush 43 presidential candi-
   dacy, 161; campaign finance
   reform, sponsorship of, 200;
   conservatives on, 29, 292–293;
   House candidates vs., 227; as
   moderate Republican, 218;
   presidential election defeat, 143
McCain-Feingold (Bipartisan
   Campaign Reform Act BCRA,
   2002), 200–203, 294
McCarthy, Devin, 246–247
McCarthy, Eugene, 69
McCarthy, Kevin, 274, 298–299
McConnell, Mitch: debt ceiling, deal
   over, 280; difficulties faced by,
   296; filibuster, use of, 261; and
   losses to tea party-backed candidates, 14–15; obstructionism of,
   276–277; as Senate minority leader,
   216; and 2000 election cycle, 166
McCurry, Michael, 128
McDonald, Michael, 227
McGovern, George, 39, 131

Medicare and Medicare Part D, 13, 133–134, 172–178, 265
Meehan, Marty, 200
Melcher, John, 55
Menendez, Bob, 21
Michel, Robert: and Bush 41, 52; Gingrich as deputy to, 83; as House Republican leader, 196; as minority leader, 91, 95–96, 101; retirement, 84, 101
Michigan: Electoral College elector assignment method, 260; Republican state party convention (1986), 34
Midterm elections: 1994, 105–111; 1998, 147, 151; 2002, 171, 195; 2006, 212–215; 2010, 3, 15–16, 278–279; and divided governments, 241; partisan bias in, 227–228
Mikulski, Barbara, 42
Milbank, Dana, 296
Miller, Joe, 259
Miller, Zell, 166
Minard, Dick, 34
Minority-majority Republican Senate, 242–245
Minority parties, policy decisions and, 100
Minority voters, increase in (2008–2012), 5
Mitchell, Alison, 162
Mitchell, Daniel J., 61
Mitchell, George, 43
Mochary, Mary V., 57
Moderate politicians, 103, 291–293
Molinari, Susan, 126
Mondale, Walter, 41, 131
Moral Majority, 35
Morris, Dick, 130

Moscardelli, Vincent, 202–203
Mourdock, Richard, 253, 259
Mr. Bush's War (Graubard), 66
Mr. Smith Goes to Washington (movie), 261
Muravchik, Joshua, 141
Murkowski, Lisa, 14
Murray, Alan, 183

NAFTA (North American Free Trade Act), 197
Naftali, Tim, 63, 64
Nagourney, Adam, 276
National Conservative Political Action Committee, 44
National debt, during Bush 43 administration, 278
National Economic Commission (NEC), 60
National Journal, on Senate centrists, 138
National Republican Campaign Committee (NRCC), 54, 80, 198
National Review, on Lott, 193
National Security Administration, domestic spying scandal, 3–4
Nebraska, Electoral College elector assignment method, 6, 259–260
NEC (National Economic Commission), 60
Nelson, Bill, 165, 167
Nelson, Gaylord, 39
Neo-conservative foreign policy, 141–144
"Neville Chamberlain of the Republican Party." *See* Darman, Richard
New conservatives, paleoconservatives on, 77
New Deal coalition, 228

New England, decline of Republican competitiveness in, 166–167

New Hampshire: contact with Republican presidential candidates, 223; Democratic Senators from, 166–167

New Jersey, Senate elections (1990), 56–58

The New New Deal (Grunwald), 274–275

Newsweek polls, on flag burning, 48

New Yorker, Hastert profile in, 196

New York Times, on Gingrich, 81

New York Times/CBS poll, on Iraq War, 213

Ney, Bob, 188, 207, 265

Nickles, Don, 156

97th Congress, 251, 252

98th Congress, 248

Nixon, Richard, 44, 71, 132, 228–229

No new taxes pledge, 59–64

Norquist, Grover, 44, 88, 132, 263, 280

North American Free Trade Act (NAFTA), 197

North Dakota, marriage amendment, 126

Northern Republicans, disappearance of, 137, 266

Norwood, Charlie, 258

Not-going-along (resistance, opposition, do nothing, party of no) strategy, 98, 99, 104–105, 274–276, 300–301

NRCC (National Republican Campaign Committee), 54, 80, 198

Nuclear option (on Senate rules), 217, 262

Nunes, Devin, 292

Nussle, Jim, 92–93, 177

Obama, Barack: conservative/Republican views on, 1–2; election of, 172, 223, 235, 273–277; electoral victory as incumbent senator, 223; filibusters against, 261–262; first-time Iowa caucus-goers, mobilization of, 37; on gay marriage, 130; immigration reform, promise on, 20; impeachment threats against, 287–288; Obamanomics, 278–284; reelection, 1–9, 220; scandals in early second term, 3–4; tea party movement's views on, 12

Obamacare (Affordable Care Act, 2010), 4, 9, 11, 236, 282–283

Obey, David, 153

O'Connor, Patrick, 216

O'Donnell, Christine, 14, 253

Ohio, Electoral College elector assignment method, 260

Olson, Mancur, 183

104th Congress, 251, 252, 264

107th Congress, 225

108th Congress, 251, 252

110th Congress, legislative strategy for, 216–217

111th Congress, 276–277

112th Congress, 234, 263, 278–279

113th Congress, 236, 254, 281

O'Neill, Tip, 46, 102, 265–266

Operation Desert Storm (Gulf War), 64–68, 70

Oppenheimer, Bruce, 213

Opportunism, Gingrich's, 46

Opportunity society, 45

Opposition (resistance, not-going-along, do nothing, party of no) strategy, 98, 99, 104–105, 274–276, 300–301
Organizations, in tea party movement, 10
Ornstein, Norman, 17, 188, 265, 268
Otter, Butch, 174
Outrage (documentary), 209

Paleoconservatives, 77
Palfrey, Deborah Jeane, 211
Palko, Chris, 255
Paralysis. *See* Partisan polarization
Parker, Ashley, 291
Parker, Chris, 12
Parker, Frank, 54
Parker, Michael, 165
Partisan dealignment, 228–229
Partisan institutionalism, 186, 256–263
Partisan polarization, 170–218; campaign finance reform, battle over, 199–203; conclusions on, 217–218; earmarks, spending on, 180–182; farm bill (2002), battle over, 178–180; Hastert as House speaker, 195–199; Lott, political arc of, 191–195; Medicare Part D, DeLay and, 172–178; mid-term elections (2006), 212–215; 110th Congress, legislative strategy for, 216–217; overview, 170–172; sexual scandals, 207–212; special interest groups, rising influence of, 183–191; Texas legislature, battle for control of, 203–207
Partisan resistance, as GOP strategy, 98, 99
Partisan Voting Index (PVI), 297

Party-line votes, 103
Party of no (do nothing, opposition, resistance, not-going-along) strategy, 98, 99, 104–105, 274–276, 300–301
Party-switchers, 164–165
Pataki, George, 109
Path dependency, 26
Path not taken. *See* Recovery vs. retrenchment path to regaining political power
Paul, Rand, 14, 252, 278, 292
Paul, Ron, 173, 220, 221–222, 223
Paulson, Henry, 13
Paxon, Bill, 150
Peacetime, legislative bias during, 233
Pelosi, Nancy, 18, 212, 275, 282
Pence, Mike, 174
Pennsylvania, Electoral College elector assignment method, 260
People's Republic of Vermont, 164
Perle, Richard, 141
Perlstein, Rick, 27–28
Perot, Ross, 85, 93, 106–107, 131, 225
Perry, Rick, 203, 205, 221, 259
Pew Research: memo on GOP approval rating (2013), 3; survey on tea party identifiers (2010), 12; voter survey (September 2006), 213
Plebiscitary political systems, 233, 265
PNAC (Project for a New American Century), 68, 141–144
Podhoretz, John, 141
Polarization: of Congress, 168; of the Senate, 140. *See also* Partisan polarization

Political fund-raising. *See* Campaign finance reform

Political media, conflict-based narratives, desire for, 10

Political parties: diagnoses of illnesses of, 269–270; social attraction and social concentration of, 237–238. *See also* Democratic Party and Democrats; Republican Party (GOP) and Republicans

The Politics Presidents Make (Skowronek), 235

Pork-barrel spending (earmarks), 80, 81–82, 180–182

Porter, John, 181

Posner, Richard, 154–155

Powell, Colin, 65, 124, 126, 193

Powell Doctrine, 65, 67

Predator drones, funding for, 181

Presidency: congressional majorities vs., 132; and political order, 235; presidential obsolescence, congressional Republicans and, x, 9; Skowronek's typology of presidents, 235. See also *names of individual presidents*

Presidential campaigns and elections: Buchanan's insurgent presidential campaign (1992), 68–71; Bush 41 reelection campaign (1992), 75–79, 85–87; Bush 43 (2000), 158–164, 168; Clinton (1992), 63; Clinton-Gore, GOP responses to, 85–89; consecutive victories by single party, 159, 231; and divided governments, 241; Dole (1996), 124, 125, 130–136; Gore-Bush (2000), 158–164, 168; House-inspired platform for,

134–135; lack of GOP candidates for (1996), 130–131; Obama reelection (2012), 2, 220; taxes as political issue in, 56. *See also* Obama, Barack

Preston Gates Ellis & Rouvelas Meeds, 186–187

Priebus, Reince, x, 4, 7, 260

Project for a New American Century (PNAC), 68, 141–144

Project on Fair Representation, 258

Pryce, Deborah, 94

Pryor, Mark, 167

Public opinion on immigration reform, 22

Quayle, James Danforth, 39–42, 43, 143

Quinn, Jack, 146

Race: racial hiring quotas, 50–52; and redistricting, 52–55; Republicans' use of, 192–193; tea party movement's views on racial minorities, 12

Rapoport, Ronald, 106–107

Rational actors, parties and politicians as, 301

Rauch, Jonathan, 11, 183

Read my lips—no new taxes promise (Bush 41), 59, 69

Reagan, Michael, 32

Reagan, Nancy, 126

Reagan, Ron, 32

Reagan, Ronald: and Alzheimer's, 31–32; approval ratings, gender gap in, 41, 307n12; Bush 41 vs., 31–32; congressional Republicans, relationship with, 265–266; on Democratic Party, 26; election of,

Reagan, Ronald (cont.)
229, 235; and Gingrich, 117;
Houston national convention,
speech at, 82–83; immigration
bill, signing of, 19; on opportunity
society, 45; party-switching by,
164–165; patriotism of, 49; white
vote for, impact of, 301
Reagan-Bush presidential coalition,
end of, 71–72
Reagan Democrats, 71
RealClearPolitics, 5
Real conservatives, rightward
movement of, 292–293
Reapportionment, prior to 1992
election, 92–93. *See also* Gerrymandering
Recovery and Reinvestment Act, 9
Recovery vs. retrenchment path to
regaining political power, 1–30;
challenges for, xi; conclusions on,
297–302; and GOP rightward
lurch, 26–28; and immigration
reform, 19–25; Obama's reelection, Republican responses to,
1–9; overview, 5–9, 297–302;
recursivity of GOP's conservatism
and congressionalization, 28–30;
and tea party movement rise,
9–19, 25–26. *See also* Congressional
chokehold on GOP, recovery
from
Rector, Robert, 25
Redistricting, 52–55, 205–206, 277.
See also Gerrymandering
Redistricting Majority Project
(REDMAP), 277
Reelection rates, 93–94
Reformulation of GOP, 121–169;
Clinton impeachment, 144–149;

conclusions on, 167–169; Dole's
presidential campaign, 130–136;
foreign policy, changes to,
141–144; gay marriage, debate
over, 127–130; Gingrich, attempted coup against, 149–151;
Gore-Bush presidential campaign,
158–164; Livingston-Hastert
battle for speakership, 151–154;
Lott as Senate majority leader,
136–140; Lott's role in Clinton
impeachment, 154–158; overview,
121–122; Rockefeller Republicans,
twilight of, 164–167; San Diego
national convention, 123–126
Regional over-representation,
266–267
Regula, Ralph, 181
Reich, Robert, 283
Reid, Harry, 14, 167, 212, 262, 283
Reid, Jan, 153–154
Reinventing Democrats (Baer), 289
Reinvention of GOP, 73–120;
Clinton-Gore election, responses
to, 85–89; congressional tactics,
under Gingrich, 101–105; and
government shutdown, 111–117;
House Republican Conference,
fight over chairmanship of, 89–92;
House Republicans, divisions
within, 79–81; House Republicans, rhetorical strategy adopted
by, 81–85; Houston Republican
National Convention, 75–79;
midterm elections (1994),
105–111; national health care
reform, battle over, 98–101; 1992
election, importance of, 92–97;
overview, 73–75; tipping point for,
118–120

Religious right, 35–36
Republican Party (GOP) and Republicans: changes in, since Reagan, 301–302; Congress-centeredness, x–xi, 29–30, 122, 135–136, 219–268; congressional chokehold on, recovery from, 269–302; congressionalization of, 28, 74, 263–268; conservative movement, tipping point of relations with, 117–120, 270; conventional wisdom on problems of, ix; creative destruction in, 31–72; diminishing voter base, maximization of power derived from, xi, 5; diversification needed, 126; divisions in, 79–85; domestic agenda, need for, 68; electorate, demographics of, 286–287; establishment Republicans, 13, 27; evolutionary stages of, 293–294; governors, diversity of, 299; House-ification of, 246–251; immigration reform, views on, 20; intraparty problems under Bush, 87–88; locked-in congressional power of, 293–297; national, death spiral of, 267; national security advantage, end of, 172; northern Republicans, disappearance of, 137; outside funding of, problems of, 294–296; and partisan polarization, 170–218; presidential victories vs. Congressional victories, 226–227; presidential wing, end of dominance of, 71–72, 224; recovery vs. retrenchment path to regaining political power, xi, 1–30; reformulation, period of, 121–169; reinvention of, 73–120;

Republican Leadership Council, 28, 290; Republican Main Street Partnership, 28, 290; Republican National Committee, x, 7, 132–133, 204, 295; Republican National Conventions, 48, 70, 75–79, 123–126, 162; Republican National State Elections Commit-tee, 204; Republican Senatorial Campaign Committee, 57; Republicans in Name Only (RINOs), 14, 163; Republican State Leadership Committee, 277; Republican Study Committee (RSC), 17, 290; as socially concentrated, 238–239; Southern captivity of, 230; state successes of, basis for, 298; tea party movement's position on, 12–13; veteran policy leadership, lack of, 250–251; women in, 41, 42. *See also* Bush, George Herbert Walker; Bush, George W.; Congressional Republicans; DeLay, Tom; Dole, Bob; Gin-grich, Newt; House of Represen-tatives; Lott, Trent; Reagan, Ronald; Senate; Tea party movement; *names of other indi-vidual Republicans*
Republican Revolution (1994), 17, 119
Resistance (not-going-along, opposition, do nothing, party of no) strategy, 98, 99, 104–105, 274–276, 300–301
Retrenchment. *See* Recovery vs. retrenchment path to regaining political power
Revolutionary Communist Youth Brigade, 48

Reynolds, Tom, 176
Reynolds v. Sims (1964), 234
Rhode, David, 252
Richards, Ann, 109
Richardson, Smith, family of, 291
Richie, Rob, 246–247
Richmond v. Croson (1989), 50
Ridge, Tom, 109
Riedl, Brian, 179
Rightward lurch, 17, 26–28
The Rise and Decline of Nations
   (Olson), 183
Roarty, Alex, 253
Robb, Chuck, 165
Roberts, Pat, 139
Robertson, Pat, 33–38, 70, 87
Rockefeller Republicans, twilight of,
   164–167
Roe v. Wade (1973), 35
Rogers, Mike, 209
Rohrabacher, Dana, 102
Romer v. Evans (1996), 127
Romney, Mitt, 27, 29, 135, 219–223,
   227, 249–250
Roosevelt, Franklin, 171
Roosevelt, Teddy, 142
Rostenkowski, Dan, 105
Roth, Bill, 165
Rove, Karl: on Bachmann, 16; and
   Bush 43 presidential candidacy,
   160; on Bush 43's lack of popular
   vote majority, 5; characterizations
   of, 292; on long-term Republican
   realignment, 171; and midterm
   elections (1998), 148; and Redis-
   tricting Majority Project, 277;
   Texas, influence on, 47–48, 109,
   203; and 2012 election results, 2
Rubio, Marco, 14, 21, 24–25, 252,
   278, 287

Rule and Ruin (Kabaservice), 27–28,
   291–292
Rumsfeld, Donald, 141, 143
Ryan, Paul: on bipartisanship, 284;
   on Bush 43's presidency, congressional Republicans' response to,
   265; fiscal policy, prominence
   on, 250–251; and immigration
   reform, 24; prescription drug
   benefit, support for, 177; prominence, 246; rape, views on, 253; at
   Republican strategy dinner, 274;
   as Romney running mate,
   249–250

Safire, Bill, 77
Same-sex marriage, debate over,
   127–130
Sanders, Bernie, 127, 167
San Diego GOP national convention
   (1996), 123–126
Sandoval, Brian, 299
Santelli, Rick, 9
Santorum, Rick: and Clinton
   impeachment, 156, 157; election
   of, 108, 137; ethics, approach to,
   189; lobbyists, meetings with, 184;
   as presidential challenger, 221,
   223
Scaife, Richard Mellon, 291
Scalia, Antonin, 48
Scanlon, Michael, 187–188, 189
Schaller, Thomas F., 224, 266,
   290
Schieffer, Bob, 234
Schippers, David, 144–145, 148
Schrock, Ed, 209
Schumer, Charles ("Chuck"), 21,
   147
Scowcroft, Brent, 64

Scully, Thomas, 174

Sellout (Schippers), 144–145

Senate: cloture rules, 216–217; Committee on Indian Affairs, 187; and elections, of 1988 and 1990, 55; filibusters in, 216–217, 261–263; former House Republicans in, 137, 139, 156, 251, 252; House-ification of, 136–137, 156, 251–256; Lott as majority leader of, 137–140; majority rule in, vs. in House, 262–263; minority-majority Republican, 242–251; nuclear option, 217, 262; polarization of, 140, 251–252; popular election of senators, call for end to, 7, 236, 259; Republicans' diversity, 287; split state delegations to, 137–138, 256; women in, 42; years of Republican control of, 225

Senate Republican Conference, House-ification of, 251–256

September 11, 2001, terrorist attacks, 171

Sequestration, 281

Sessions, Pete, 274

The 700 Club (TV program), 34

Seventeenth Amendment, tea party movement's views on, 11

Sexual scandals, 207–212

Shays, Chris, 166, 167, 200

Shelby, Richard, 165

Shelby County v. Holder (2013), 230, 231

Shen, Francis, 213

Shirley, Craig, 292

Shlaes, Amity, 235

Showdown at Gucci Gulch (Birnbaum and Murray), 183

Shutdowns, of federal government, 111–117, 282–283, 288, 291

Signing statements, 52

Silver, Nate, 2, 159

Simpson, Alan, 194

Sinclair, Barbara, 195–196

Sitting vice presidents, election as president, 159

Sixteenth Amendment, tea party movement's views on, 11

Skocpol, Theda, 17–18

Skowronek, Stephen, 235

Small-state advantage, in Senate elections, 242–245, 255

Smith, Brad, 176

Smith, Nick, 176, 179–180

Smith, Peter Plympton, 163

Snowe, Olympia, 126, 165, 275

Social attraction, of political parties, 237–238

The Social Bases of Political Parties (Janda), 237–238

Soft money donations, 199, 200–201, 202

Souter, David, 70

Southern captivity (of GOP), 230

Southern Democrats, disappearance of, 137, 266

Southern GOP delegations, growth in power of, 91

Soviet Union, declining influence of, 67

Special interest groups. *See* Interest groups

Specter, Arlen, 13, 165, 181, 275, 292

Stafford, Robert, 163

Stahl, Lesley, 31

Starr Report, 144, 154–155

State of the Union address (Bush, 1990), 60

States: ability to overturn federal laws, tea party movement's views on, 11; one-party vs. multi-party control of, 53. See also *individual states*

Steely, Mel, 68

Stennis, John C., 55

Stephanopoulos, George, 112

Stevenson, Adlai, 131

Stimulus plan (American Recovery and Reinvestment Act, 2009), 274–275

Stockman, Steve, 282

Storming the Gates (Balz and Brownstein), 133–134

Sununu, John, 62, 63, 93

Supercommittee, bipartisan, 280

Super PACs, 294, 296–297

Supply-side economics, 36

Supreme court (Hawaii), 126

Supreme Court (U.S.): on BCRA's soft money ban, 202; *Citizens United*, 269, 294–295; on DOMA, 130; reactiveness of, 319n21; *Reynolds v. Sims* (1964), 234; *Richmond v. Croson* (1989), 50; *Roe v. Wade* (1973), 35; *Romer v. Evans* (1996), 127; *Shelby County v. Holder* (2013), 230, 258; *Texas v. Johnson* (1989), 47–50; *Thornburg v. Gingles* (1986), 54; *Wards Cove v. Atonio* (1989), 50–51; *Wesberry v. Sanders* (1964), 234

The Survivor (Harris), 116

Swing districts, 18, 297

The System (Johnson and Broder), 98–99, 100

Talk show hosts, conservative, 296

Talmadge, Herman, 39

Tauzin, Billy, 165

Tax policies, 18, 57–59, 69, 70

Taylor, Andrew, 182

The Tea Party and the Remaking of Republican Conservatism (Skocpol and Williamson), 17–18

Tea party movement, 9–19; and Bachmann, 16; central structure of, 11; emergence of, 9–10; farm bill, actions on, 282; GOP's Senate problems, impact on, 252–253; and government shutdown, 282–283; House Republican caucus, impact on, 17–18; House Tea Party Caucus, 16; incumbents, primary challenges to, 14; movement agenda, 10–11; organizations in, 10; revanchist views of, 12–13; and 2010 House elections, 15–16

Teixeira, Ruy, 224, 286

Temporal symmetry of Republican victories, 229–230, 231

Term limits, GOP calls for, 94–95

Texans for a Republican Majority (TRMPAC), 204–205

Texas: legislature, battle for control of, 203–207; Rove's influence on, 47–48

Texas v. Johnson (1989), 47–50

Theriault, Sean, 139–140, 251–252

Third way policies of triangulation, 130

34th and 36th Congresses, 247

This Week with David Brinkley (ABC news show), 70

Thompson, Tommy, 124

Thornburg v. Gingles (1986), 54

Three's a Crowd (Rapoport), 106–107

Thurmond, Strom, 165, 192–193

Tomasky, Michael, 207
Toomey, Pat, 13
"Toward a Neo-Reaganite Foreign
  Policy" (Kristol and Kagan),
  141–142
Trende, Sean, 5–6
Triangulation, third way policies of,
  130
Tribal casinos, Abramoff and,
  187–188
Tripp, Linda, 144
TRMPAC (Texans for a Republican
  Majority), 204–205
Troubled Assets Relief Program
  (TARP), 10
Truman, Harry, 234
Tutwiler, Margaret, 123
Two majorities thesis, 232
Two-party share of presidential and
  congressional votes, 225–227

Undocumented residents, problem
  of, 19–20, 24
"United We Stand, America" (Perot
  platform), 107
University of Oklahoma, 182
UnSkewedPolls.com, 2
USA PATRIOT Act, 265
Use-of-force doctrine, 65
Utah, marriage amendment, 126

Van Buren, Martin, 159
Vander Jagt, Guy, 46
Van Hollen, Chris, 275
Velde, Harold, 101
Veneman, Ann, 179
Vermont: liberalization of, 163–164;
  Republican decline in, 166–167
Vice presidents, sitting, election as
  president, 159

Viguerie, Richard, 43
Virginia, Electoral College elector
  assignment method, 260
Vitter, David, 210, 252
Vitter, Wendy, 211
Von Drehle, David, 161
Voter and voting restrictions, 6,
  257–259
Voter turnout, at midterm elections,
  227–228
Voting Rights Act (VRA, 1965),
  53–54, 230, 257, 258

Walker, Robert, 44, 45, 110
Walker, Scott, 298
Wall Street bailout, 13
Wall Street Journal, Armey op-ed
  piece for, 175–176
Wamp, Zach, 153
Wanniski, Jude, 36
Wards Cove v. Atonio (1989), 50–51
War in Iraq, 212–213, 214, 215, 217
Washington Monthly, on Republicans'
  K Street connections, 184–185
Washington Post: on DeLay, 206;
  Ehrlich in, 114; on Gingrich, 102–
  103; Gingrich in, 115, 116; on
  Hastert Rule, 197–198; on
  intraparty revolt against Bush,
  62–63; on 1992 congressional
  freshmen, 96–97; on 2002 election
  results, 171
Washington Times: on congressional
  page scandal, 215; on freshmen
  GOP members, 95–96
Wasserman, David, 230–231, 247
Wattenberg, Martin P., 227
Watts, J. C., 126
Waxman, Henry, 287
Wead, Doug, 33–34

Webb, Jim, 167
Weber, Vin, 44, 75, 87, 143
Weicker, Lowell P., 55, 56, 138
Weisberg, Jacob, 89
Wellstone, Paul, 55, 56
Wesberry v. Sanders (1964), 234
Weyrich, Paul, 17, 43, 44
White House staff, problems under
    Clinton, 113
White voters, disappearing, 5–6
Whitman, Christine Todd, 56–58,
    109, 124–126, 133, 290
"Why Congress Doesn't Work"
    (Nussle and Cox), 92–93
Wicker, Tom, 39
Wildmon, Donald, 35

Will, George, 70
Willey, Kathleen, 155
Williamson, Vanessa, 17–18
Wilson, Pete, 109
Wolff, Brian, 202
Wolfowitz, Paul, 141
Women voters, 41, 76
Woodward, Bob, 112–113
Wright, Jim, 43, 46, 102, 183, 189

Yglesias, Matt, 177
Young, Don, 288
Young boy's network, 39–43

Zelizer, Julian, 110, 236
Zorinsky, Edward, 138